AF660291

KRIYA YOGA

THE SCIENTIFIC PROCESS OF
SOUL CULTURE AND THE ESSENCE OF ALL RELIGIONS

The real meaning of Tantra has always been misunderstood. From a highly evolved spiritual science, Tantra got demeaned as a tool for magic or occult power or an enhancer of sensual enjoyment. Tantra is none of these and it is an ancient discipline that provides a deep understanding of life, and a methodology to attain self-realisation.

Interpreting deep philosophic thoughts, Prajnanandaji manages to reveal the hidden truths contained in the complex passage of Jnana Sankalini Tantra texts.

– Bhavan's Journal, February, 2007

KRIYA YOGA

THE SCIENTIFIC PROCESS OF
SOUL CULTURE AND THE ESSENCE OF ALL RELIGIONS

PARAMAHAMSA HARIHARANANDA

MOTILAL BANARSIDASS
PUBLISHING HOUSE • DELHI
Email: mlbd@mlbd.in • Website: www.mlbd.in

3rd Reprint : Delhi, 2022
First Indian Edition : Delhi, 2006
Fifth Edition : 1988
Earlier published by Prajna Publication Diefenbachgasse 38/6, A-1150 Vienna in 1977,

© MOTILAL BANARSIDASS PUBLISHING HOUSE
All Rights Reserved.

No part of this book may be reprinted or reproduced or utilised in any form or by any electronic, mechanical, or other means, now known or hereafter invented, including photocopying and recording, or in any information storage or retrieval system, without permission in writing from the publishers.

ISBN: 978-93-94201-05-7 (Hardcover)
ISBN: 978-93-94201-13-2 (Paperback)

Printed & Published by
Rajendra P Jain *for*
Motilal Banarsidass Publishing House
A-44, Naraina Industrial Area, Phase I,
New Delhi–110 028 (INDIA)
Email: mlbd@mlbd.in
Website: www.mlbd.in

EASY WAY TO SALVATION

One need not renounce the mundane world and live the life of an ascetic to become a yogi. Neither is it a must for one to continue in one's practice of yoga to attain the Ultimate Reality, God. For, according to Hariharanandaji, anyone, male or female above the age of 13 leading a normal family life, can aspire to mingle with the Divine being in his or her lifetime, if he/she practices Kriya Yoga.

Kriya Yoga as expounded by him is a combination of three yogas: Karma, Jñana, and Bhakti. Its scientific technique closely follows the method of Patañjali. The technique involves six stages. Hariharanandaji describes not only these stages in detail, but also the feeling the *kriyavan* (the practitioner) is supposed to experience in each of the successive stages. Side by side he also discusses how during each stage the *kriyavan's* bodily functions are toned up.

Another merit of Hariharanandaji's preaching is that it is remarkably free from any religious dogma or sectarian belief. His non-sectarian outlook is reflected in his scientific approach to the subject.

AMRITA BAZAR PATRIKA, November 24, 1985

CONTENTS

LIST OF DIAGRAMS

FOREWORD

The life and teaching of great souls are real treasures for humankind. They have not only dedicated their lives to perfection and higher consciousness, but also their every moment is dedicated to all of creation to quicken spiritual evolution. Sage Narada in his beautiful work, Bhakti Sutra: Aphorisms on Divine Love, beautifully described that a realized one has not only reached the goal overcoming the veiling play of *maya*, but also helps others to cross this ocean of illusion. The life of the realized one is like a burning flame; it illumines itself, illuminates others, and also kindles fire in other lamps.

We have very clearly seen in the life of our beloved Gurudev Paramahamsa Hariharananda the beauty of his spiritual wisdom, intuitive insight, burning flame of love, and selfless service for humanity in general. His long span of divine life, which includes sixty-four years of renunciation and more than fifty years of tirelessly teaching Kriya Yoga, was spent moment to moment for the betterment of all. His daily life started from the early hours of dawn and brought joy and love in the life of many seekers in various ways. He used every moment of his time for all, continually reminding us that time wasted is life wasted. He pointed out repeatedly, "Waste time with none but God, then time will not be wasted."

Gurudev shaped the lives of many as a true lover of God. He wrote countless inspiring letters to his disciples all over the world. As an author, he presented us with many beautiful spiritual books. Proficient in many languages, he wrote books primarily in English, Odia, and Bengali. He wrote a few books related to Kriya Yoga in Odisha. Some of his books are not yet translated into English. His most popular book is, *Kriya Yoga: The Scientific Process of Soul-Culture and the Essence of All Religions*. This book has been a source of inspiration and spiritual handbook for people worldwide.

It is with great pleasure that we bring forth the sixth edition of this inspiring book. It has been more than twenty-five years since the first edition was published and it continues to be accepted and appreciated by spiritual seekers. Due to requests from people worldwide this book has been translated into many languages. We want to bring it in the hands of all seekers of Truth.

Gurudev's light and love through his words of wisdom will continue to inspire us for all time.

—The Publishers

INTRODUCTION

Restlessness and calmness are always together. Restlessness comes from the mundane body. Submerge your soul in the Infinite before, during, and after every act — then you will get calmness.

We are born for Self-realization — the God consciousness in us. Think of God constantly, no matter what you are doing. Practice makes man perfect. An ounce of practice is worth a ton of theories. Theory will take a devotee outside, while practice will take him inside. Theory will make an individual restless and selfish. Practice will give him inner peace and liberation from ego. Practice, practice, and practice in order to feel the presence of God in every breath, in every sound you hear, in everything you see, in every thought that comes to your mind, and even in the breathless state. Feel the presence of God as much in your enemy as in your friend. Remain firmly anchored in the Divine Omnipresent, the Divine Omniscient, the Divine Omnipotent — even when you are occupied in worldly activities.

— Paramahamsa Hariharananda

PARAMAHANSA YOGANANDA
empowers Swamijee to initiate people into Kriyayoga.

SELF-REALIZATION FELLOWSHIP
3880 San Rafael Avenue,
Los Angeles 65, Calif.
U.S.A.

Telephone:
Capitol 0212

Cable:
"SELFREAL"

October 6, 1951

Brahmachari Robynarayan
Yogoda Ashram
Puri, India

Sananda will soon finish the bldgs at Puri

Dear Robinarayan:

I have received your many letters and am sorry I have been unable to answer them sooner. My life is one whirl-wind of activity and struggle for the work. One thing I must ask of you all is that you please do not write letters to me in Bengali because none of my secretaries can read -- I read them carefully when they come, but have not the time to re-read again when dictating. I am at this moment dictating the following to you at 1 a.m. I love to read the letters written in Bengali, but for the above-stated reason, I ask that you tell all writing to me to write in English.

I received a letter from a man who has gone to the Ashram at Puri to stay, leaving his family. If his whole soul is tied to the work and he will follow it 100%, then it is alright for him to remain. I am glad he has come but he must follow all the rules of Brahmacharya.
I am very pleased with the work you are doing at Puri. Keep on with it with great diligence and at the same time remain faithful to your meditation. Every minute of your existence hold to the thought of Divine Mother -- no matter what work you are performing.

What is the name of the student initiated by me here -- you wrote that he stopped there with his family and you discussed Kriya Yoga. Give his address too.

Partly due to your recommendation I have already sanctioned the buying of the Bhuboneswar property and sometime I will make a small ashram.

I give you permission to give the Kriya Yoga to those who are truly in earnest -- but only after they have received all the other preliminary techniques -- the tension exercises, concentration exercise (Hang-sau) and meditation (listening to Om sound. Contact Prokas about the technique -- I will instruct office to also send you the form to follow. Let me hear from you further

Why don't you train some workers who can carry on the work there? It requires two years of training to bring anyone here and then on my recommendation. I have written to Sananda to begin work in Puri and he will do so. One thing I must ask of each of you, and that is that you all work harmoniously together for the common cause. Do not seek to find faults in others for then your whole lives become tied to negativeness. Every person has some faults and needs love and understanding. Be humble and loving toward others. Keep your minds engrossed with the Divine and you won't have time to think of these lesser things. My love and blessings are with you always.

Very sincerely yours,

P Yogananda

[illegible]

PY:vw

FOLD SIDES OVER AND THEN FOLD BOTTOM UP AND SEAL.
NO OTHER ENVELOPE SHOULD BE USED.

The author on his Birthday, 27th May 2002.

ABOUT THE AUTHOR

Paramahamsa Hariharananda (1907–2002), one of the greatest realized masters in Kriya Yoga, is a legend among the spiritual seekers. He attained *nirvikalpa samadhi*, the state of no pulse and no breath, the state of cessation of all activities of the body, mind, thought, intellect, and ego, merged and absorbed in God. *Nirvikalpa samadhi* is the long-cherished goal of all aspirants in the spiritual path. In the Kriya Yoga tradition, he is placed in the lineage of the realized masters: Babaji Maharaj, Shri Lahiri Mahashaya, Swami Shriyukteshwarji, and others.

He was born on the 27th of May, 1907, in the hamlet of Habibpur, on the bank of the sacred river Ganga, in the district of Nadia, West Bengal, India. A few kilometers from the birthplace of Shri Chaitanya Mahaprabhu, a God-intoxicated divine incarnation of the fifteenth century, this village of Habibpur was sanctified by the birth of this holy child, whose childhood name was Rabindranath. His father, Haripada Bhattacharjee, was a disciplined, dedicated, devout, and determined *brahmin*, well-versed in all Hindu scriptures. So also was his mother, Nabinkali Debi, a pious, generous, and loving lady *par excellence*.

Endowed with uncommon and marvelous brainpower, this divine child memorized all the intricate mantras, hymns, and prayers in Sanskrit, astounding all. At the age of eleven, in 1918, he took the vow of *brahmacharya* (i.e., the *upanayana* ceremony of the *brahmins*). His desire for spiritual upliftment continued to grow, so he went to his family's preceptor, or spiritual guide, Shri Bijoy Krishna Chattopadhyaya, a realized householder master living in Howrah to the west of Kolkata, and took initiation into the path of Jñana Yoga at the age of twelve. He excelled in sacred and secular education and after completing his schooling was well placed in the society as a technocrat.

His thirst for spiritual enlightenment could not be quenched by material achievement. He was inspired by Shri Bijoy Krishna to meet Shriyukteshwarji, the most befitting disciple of the great master of Kriya Yoga, Lahiri Mahashaya. As advised, he called on Shriyukteshwarji at his Serampore Ashram in 1932 and at last received initiation into Kriya Yoga, the sacred and scientific meditation technique.

Under the holy guidance of Shriyukteshwarji, he learned much more of astrology, astronomy, and palmistry, as well as strict spiritual discipline and meditation. Three years later, when Paramahamsa Yogananda returned to India from the United States in 1935, on the advice of Shriyukteshwarji, Rabindranath was blessed to witness his state of *samadhi* and was initiated into the second Kriya by Paramahamsa Yogananda.

Shriyukteshwarji wished that this young celibate Rabindranath should renounce the material life and take charge of his ashram in Puri. However, by God's will, it took several years for the fulfillment of his noble wish. In 1938, Rabindranath moved to the land of Lord Jagannath, the seaside city of Puri in Eastern India. Later he resided at Karar Ashram and accepted asceticism with the new name of Brahmachari Rabinarayan.

He started a strict spiritual practice of sincere meditation, observing silence for several years. Within a short time, he attained perfection in three yogic *mudras*: *khechari*, *bhramari*, and *shambhavi*. After this attainment, a supernatural divine light (i.e., aura) emanated from his body, which was observed by many.

In the early 1940s, the then-head of Karar Ashram of Shriyukteshwarji, Shrimat Swami Satyananda Giri initiated him into the third Kriya. Subsequently, he learned all the other higher Kriyas from Shrimat Bhupendranath Sanyal Deva Sharman, a householder and realized yogi, the youngest disciple of the great guru Yogiraj Lahiri Mahashaya.

In the mid-1940s, the most secret technique of *samadhi* was revealed to him by a young, anonymous, and mysterious yogi, who appeared in Karar Ashram. During this period, he attained six stages of *samadhi*. Finally in 1948, he was blessed to achieve the highest spiritual attainment, the state of *nirvikalpa samadhi* (breathless state with no pulse) and Paramahamsa stage.

During this period of spiritual practice and attainment of perfection, Baba (as he had come to be known) not only engaged himself fully in meditation and God communion, but also looked after the construction and beautification of the holy Karar Ashram, including the *samadhi* temple of Shriyukteshwarji.

In the late 1940s, the divine master, the great-incarnate Mahavatar Babaji, miraculously appeared in his closed living room and again in his personal meditation room in the premises of Karar Ashram, blessed him, and expressed satisfaction on his spiritual practice and attainment. Babaji also foretold making Baba his divine instrument to propagate Kriya Yoga in the East and West. In the 1960s Baba visited Ranikhet in the Himalayas and meditated in the holy cave, where Babaji initiated Lahiri Mahashaya, and heard the divine voice of Babaji, "This time you cannot see me. Go and spread my work everywhere."

As a symbol of divine love and service, in spite of his busy schedule, Baba housed many helpless orphan children in the ashram, who, with his loving care and guidance in the course of time, became well educated and were well placed in society.

In 1951, Paramahamsa Yoganandaji requested and authorized Baba to initiate sincere seekers into Kriya Yoga. From that time, he began initiating and teaching the divine technique of Kriya

Yoga to thousands of people, and leading them along the spiritual path. (Such authorization is printed herein, page 16.)

Baba made his life as the symbol of synthesis of karma (action), *jñana* (knowledge), *bhakti* (devotion), and, above all, an ideal symbol of Kriya Yoga practice. Most of the time, he would meditate throughout the night before his presiding deity Mother Kali, a form of formless Divine Mother. On September 27, 1958, the Divine Mother appeared before him with Her divine effulgence, graced him with blessings, and directed him to spread the divine mission for the spiritual upliftment of the world.

In the Indian tradition, a *brahmachari* ultimately becomes swami, a monk. With some rites and rituals, the then-Shankaracharya of Puri, Gobardhan Pith, Jagadguru, Shrimat Swami Bharati Krishna Teerthajee Maharaj initiated Baba into the life of *sannyasa* (i.e., complete renunciation). Whiteclad Brahmachari Rabinarayan became saffron clothed Swami Hariharananda Giri. Hariharananda means the divine bliss coming from the Absolute formless God. It happened, incidentally, on his birthday, May 27, 1959.

During his stay in Puri, he was loved by almost all monks living in Puri. Many came to him for some discussion or explanation of the scriptures or clarification of their doubts.

He was blessed by many God-intoxicated divine masters like Anandamoyee Ma and Nanga Baba Digambara Paramahamsa, a naked and realized master living in Puri near Lokenath Temple.

From then, he dedicated most of his time to teaching and preaching Kriya Yoga. People of all castes, creeds, and social strata gathered to hear his sweet divine interpretation of the scriptures in a new metaphorical way. He travelled to different parts of India and widened the Kriya Yoga network throughout the country.

In the early 1970s, a conference of religions of the world

was held under the auspices of the Divine Life Society, a leading spiritual organization, at Cuttack Barabati Stadium. Several thousand spiritual people from different parts of the world packed the venue. Baba delivered two talks in English, *The Essence of All Religions* and *The Message of Spiritual Life*. All monks and renowned intellectuals were amazed by his brilliant, highly convincing, and influential talk. Afterwards, many spiritual organizations invited him to their ashrams and conferences to bless and grace the devotees with his divine messages.

The smell of the flower cannot be hidden; likewise, the divine qualities of Baba became known. Hundreds of people from different parts of the world gathered in Puri Ashram of Shriyukteshwarji and accepted him as their divine guide, their master. Baba's message spread in the Western world through those who came in his company. They sincerely requested Swamiji to come to the West to make the extrovert and restless minds of Western people introvert and tranquil, and make them spiritually advanced by perceiving inner calmness through breath control.

By 1974, he had no choice ultimately, but to accept their requests and invitations to go to the West and to carry out the divine will of Babaji, Lahiri Mahashaya, and Shriyukteshwarji: to give people the taste of original Ḳriya practice. He first went to Switzerland and then later to Germany, France, Holland, Belgium, England, and many other European countries. In 1975, Baba went to the United States, Canada, South America, and many other countries. Thousands of people in the West were transformed by his holy touch, which enabled the student to perceive triple divine perceptions: visualization of divine light, hearing the divine sound, and a divine sensation in the whole body. Since that time, until his *mahasamadhi* in 2002, he carried out the divine work.

Baba was well versed in the Vedas, the Upanishads, the

Bhagavad Gita, the Brahmasutra, the Smruti Shastras, the Karmakanda, other holy Indian scriptures, along with thorough knowledge of the Torah, the Bible, the Quran, the Buddhist scriptures, and the ethical and metaphysical teachings of all the religions of the world. Master of different systems of yoga, Paramahamsa Hariharanandaji was a unique spiritual preceptor, who, through his simple lifestyle and with love, taught the scientific technique of Kriya Yoga in theory and practice.

Saffron clad, blessed with a body of unique divine aura, with a red vermilion mark on the forehead like a rising sun, beard and long hair, his divine physical appearance drew the mind to the divine state. Until he left his body at the age of ninety-five, despite health difficulties, he marched forward, with God in himself, to spend every moment and breath for the betterment and spiritual upliftment of humankind.

Paramahamsaji mastered many languages, and his sweet divine voice, like a singing bird, touched the hearts of the disciples. His simple smile was enough to perceive divine bliss. He was a child to the children, young to the youth, and old to the aged. He was so loving, caring, and affectionate, that everyone who came in his divine company remembers the sweet memory. He did not believe in an outward show of spiritual power. He was an incarnation of love, compassion, and service. His life was an ideal of sacrifice and God consciousness. He taught at every moment in different ways how to progress along in the spiritual path.

Baba authored many books, with a scientific approach to yogic and metaphorical interpretation. His works have been translated into many Indian and Western languages. He spent much time in writing and sending his message to different parts of the world. Due to his proficiency in many languages, his teachings are widely acceptable and easily accessible to even an illiterate person. That is why sincere seekers around the world gathered around him to realize their own Self.

Paramahamsa Hariharanandaji, lovingly addressed as Baba, the divine Father, the unique world teacher, free from religious dogma and sectarian belief, was a God-like personality. He may be described as having the love of Jesus, head of Shankara, devotion of Shri Chaitanya, and the heart of Buddha. Many came to him and realized his spiritual stature and love. In this book, you will sit face to face with this God-intoxicated and God-realized master, and hear his lilting sweet voice declaring, in a nutshell, the key of the authentic Kriya Yoga:

"Breath control is self-control.
Breath mastery is self-mastery.
Breathlessness stage is deathlessness stage."

At 6:48 p.m. Eastern Standard Time on December 3, 2002, Paramahamsa Hariharananda peacefully left his mortal body after one final breath. Baba exited the body land to immerse himself once more in the supreme almighty Lord. Traditional Vedic last rites were performed the next morning. Hariharanandaji's mortal body remained in his Homestead, Florida, USA ashram for one week so his disciples could have a final *darshan* with the breathless master.

On the 10th of December, 2002, the mortal body of Paramahamsa Hariharananda left the Florida ashram, homeward bound for the distant shores of Mother India to be laid to rest with his forefathers.

At Bhubaneswar, Odisha, on the 14th of December, Baba received the State Guard of Honour, an honour never before bestowed on a monk. On that day, thousands waited to pay tribute to Baba in Hariharananda Gurukulam, Balighai, his final resting place. The *mahasamadhi* ceremony commenced at 12:30 p.m. on the 15th of December, 2002, with many distinguished monks, guests, state officials, and devotees present. Baba's body was buried with traditional Vedic monastic burial rites. To complete the ceremony, a *Shiva lingam* named Harihareshwara was installed in the *samadhi* shrine, a symbol of Baba's union with the Divine.

On the day of the full moon, the 18th of December, more than 200 monks and *sadhus* from many traditions gathered to offer prayers. Realized masters are eternally present through their teachings. Anyone who prays or meditates can feel the masters' presence all along their spiritual journey. Paramahamsa Hariharanandaji has promised to help sincere seekers at the time of their need.

EDITORS' NOTES

Second Edition

The blessings of our reverend Gurudev have enabled us to bring out the second edition of *Kriya Yoga: The Scientific Process of Soul-Culture and the Essence of All Religions*. The first edition was published on the 22nd of March, 1977, by the Kriyavan Sammelan, of Karar Ashram, Puri. The first edition, along with a modified edition of the book published in Germany, was widely acclaimed in Western countries. Its wide popularity and demand inspired the second edition of the book. This edition is an improvement over the first, in that subheadings have been incorporated in each chapter with additions and alterations wherever necessary and two new chapters and new explanatory notes to unfamiliar terms have been added.

We feel fortunate and blessed to bring to light the teachings, speeches, and message of a great Indian yogi. The book is the quintessence of the philosophy of his life and a guide to Self-realization, which is the craving of each human soul. The significance of such material, which bears the stamp of personal and direct experience of a realized yogi in days of chaos and confusion, can be realized by true seekers of divinity and bliss.

We pray for the blessings of Gurudev for all those in India and abroad who have been associated and have helped in some way or other in bringing out this edition.

— Editors, India, 1981

Corrigendum

Publication of third (1986) and fourth (1989) editions of this book was accomplished without incorporating conventional editor's notes.

Fifth Edition

Nothing is possible without the grace of God and Guru. After a long wait, the fifth edition of the most loving book, *Kriya Yoga*, by our beloved master has come into the hands of spiritual seekers. Its previous edition has been translated into many Indian and European languages, which shows its appreciation among the lovers of Truth.

Our beloved Gurudev is a Self-realized yogi and master of Kriya Yoga in the line of Babaji Maharaj, Lahiri Mahashaya, and Shriyukteshwarji. His life and teachings are ideal models for all humankind in general and true aspirants in particular, which is reflected in this book.

This present edition is a thoroughly revised and enlarged one, with improvements in different aspects: new chapters and a few more diagrams are included, along with other additions, alterations, and corrections. A few chapters were excluded. The editors humbly apologize for mistakes, if any, unwillingly committed in bringing out this coveted edition. We always remember the words of our revered master, "Mistake is not for mistake. It is always for correction."

May the blessing of God and Gurudev be upon those who helped and participated actively to bring out this edition.

— Editors, India, 1998

Sixth Edition

It is with greatest honor and blessings that the sixth edition of Gurudev's writing on Kriya Yoga is once again printed, giving spiritual seekers the opportunity to benefit from the wisdom and teachings of this great master. To maintain the integrity of Gurudev's teaching, this edition incorporates only some minor grammatical corrections, a more detailed glossary, additional photos, and information about Gurudev's activities as well as his *mahasamadhi*.

— Editors, 2004

I

SELF-REALIZATION

God is one, absolute, and non-dual. Before creation, God existed as Absolute Brahman or Impersonal Soul. God wished to be manifested in various forms of existence. Thus, from Absolute Brahman, He transformed into relative existence and became the manifest universe. Therefore, whatever we perceive and recognize and whatever exists as matter or life is God's manifestation. According to the Katha Upanishad, the indwelling Self in all creatures is this one Brahman manifesting itself in different forms. This transformation into the ever-changing manifest universe is the conception of Jagannatha, the Lord of the world. The word *jagannatha* is composed of two words — *jagat*, the ever-changing world, and *natha*, the Lord. Hindus worship this conception of God in the Jagannath Temple in Puri, Odisha, India.

Of all creatures, only human beings are rational and have the faculty of discrimination. Therefore, only human beings can realize God, Who exists as the all-pervading spirit in the human body, as well as in all existence. Man can realize that he is the living God and that the whole cosmos is but a manifestation of God. In practice, however, we do not have such a realization as part of our direct experience. But still, nothing exists anywhere except the presence of God.

Why do we not experience this truth? According to the will of God, man is acted upon by two powerful forces — one centripetal, the other centrifugal. The centrifugal force is extrovert by nature and, therefore, draws man towards the external world, thus dissipating all of his energy and engrossing him in illusion, delusion, and error. But this centrifugal force is merely a different manifestation of the centripetal force, the *atma* (Self). It is a misconception to think that the centrifugal force is a separate entity. The indwelling Self in the body is the ruler of the person. The Self is ever pure, full of bliss, eternal, and immutable, as it is nothing other than Brahman.

God and Self

The Self is like a mirror that reflects the entire universe. Although a mirror reflects the images of thousands of objects, it does not retain any of them; in fact, it remains detached and indifferent to the objects it reflects. Similarly, although man is absorbed in love, lust, anger, pride, arrogance, avarice, and illusion, the Self remains detached, pure, luminous, untarnished, and incorruptible. Among all beings, man alone can avert the power of the centrifugal force by meditation. Through sincere efforts, he can realize that the whole of existence — including himself — is God.

As the whole universe is the manifestation of God, the ultimate goal of life is the realization of the Self in body, mind, and spirit. Due to illusion, delusion, and attachment to external objects, we are unable to realize that God exists in us as the Self and that every person is a living God. God exists in the body as the Self, whereas the Self, in its all-pervading, omnipotent nature, is God. God rules the gross human body by means of the seven cerebro-spinal centers (Diagram 1; page 58) and the blood vessels, all of which act as defensive forces to preserve and sustain it. Though the Self is invisible and impersonal, it provides a taste of divine bliss by its innumerable manifestations. But people are so bound up in passion, anger, illusion, and sensory stimulants that they ignore that bliss.

The Rig Veda declares that Truth is one, though the wise call it by different names. That Truth is the Supreme Being, the *purusha* whom we perceive through past, present, and future as the all-pervading existence. The Yajur Veda says that He is the Soul of the universe and it is through this knowledge alone that man attains immortality. He is Brahman, the Supreme One, independent, imperishable, indivisible, self-luminous, self-sustained, and the indescribable. He is the basis of all names and forms, the support of all creation. He pervades all creation and yet transcends it. All creation is in Him, but He is detached from it.

He is the silent witness of the three states of waking, dreaming, and deep sleep. The *atma* is the immortal part of a person and is beyond body and mind — beyond time, space, and causation. It is without beginning, without end, and without cause. It is Knowledge Absolute, Existence Absolute, and Bliss Absolute. The realization of this spiritual knowledge, or *brahma jñana*, frees one from the cycle of births and deaths.

Behind this world, behind all physical phenomena, behind all names and forms, behind feeling, thought, emotions, and sentiments, lies the Truth. How can that which has no permanent existence be true? The Truth is eternal; only illusion makes the unreal appear real. That Truth is the Self, the silent witness and ruler, which is the only thing that will provide bliss and make a person absolutely free. Self-realization is not for the weak or cowardly; it is for the strong and courageous who can face all storms and sacrifice their ego on the altar of Truth.

The Bhagavad Gita also teaches that the Self is indestructible, eternal, unseen, undecaying, all-pervading, ancient, unmanifest, and incomprehensible. Not being subject to birth and death, It does not cling to the body. Just as a person discards worn-out garments and puts on new ones, the embodied soul discards a worn-out body and enters a new one. The Infinite underlies and animates all finite existence; the Self, being essentially one with It, is not affected by birth and death, growth and decay, limitation and change — though the body returns to the dust from whence it is taken. God is all-pervading. He has hands, feet, eyes, face, and head everywhere. Though devoid of all senses, He recognizes all senses and sense objects. Unattached and without attributes, He is yet the sustainer and enjoyer of all. He constitutes both animate and inanimate creation. Being subtle, He is incomprehensible. He is very near and very far. He is the Light of all lights. He is knowledge itself, as well as the object of knowledge. He is the *atma* dwelling in the body and is transcendental. As such, He is the witness, guide, sustainer, the experiencer, and the Supreme Lord.

God's Dream

There is a famous saying that states the entire system of *advaita-vedanta* can be summarized in half a verse: *brahma satyaṃ jagan mithyā jīva brahma iva nāparam*. It means that Brahman is the only Reality. The world is ultimately illusory and the individual soul is not different from Brahman. Brahman and *atma* are identical and the world is the creation of *maya*. The embodied soul (because of its inherent *avidya*, or ignorance) imagines itself to be different from Brahman and thus lives in a world of plurality, imagining itself to be a separate entity. The truth is that everything is Brahman and it is only illusion that makes Brahman appear to be non-Brahman, just as the rope is mistaken to be a snake due to illusion. *Avidya* vanishes with the dawn of knowledge — the oneness with Brahman leading to liberation.

The illusory nature of the world, *maya*, is perceived after a stage of realization. This was given great importance by Shri Shankara, as the experience was very vivid to him. This *maya* is His cosmic play, or *lila*. According to Shri Aurobindo, the word *lila* includes the idea of *maya* and exceeds it. God is one, but this oneness does not limit Him. He appears to be many because He so wills. Outside manifestation, He transcends definition and cannot be defined either as one or as many. This is the teaching of the Upanishads, which further say He is the limited and limitless, one without a second, and whatever is perceived is He. The manifest world is the play of His consciousness in its infinite aspect and is thus real. Everything is God.

God is everywhere and each embodied soul with its seemingly separate individuality is He. God is the first being and He united with *para-prakriti*, symbolically called *radha*. Whereas human beings are slaves of *prakriti* or *maya*, God is its master and can withdraw it into Himself and project it out of Himself whenever He so wills. According to one school of thought, *maya* and He are identical; according to another school, both are separate and *maya* always exists, whether latent or manifest. Only by realizing God can all doubts be cleared.

Brahman cannot be expressed by speech or cognized by the mind. It cannot be described, as it is beyond description. It can be expressed only by the term *sat-chit-ananda* (that is, existence, consciousness, and bliss). It is both personal and impersonal.

Being the immanent inner ruler, He is called *antaryami*, the Soul of souls — also the Soul of *prakriti*. Being transcendental, He transcends the universe. He is the creator, sustainer, and destroyer of this universe, symbolically represented by Brahma, Vishnu, and Shiva respectively. He is the origin of all and the end of all. He is the object of devotion and inspirer of morality. He is, in short, all in all.

Brahman, or *atma*, is the only reality, the unqualified Absolute. There is no duality, no diversity. Even doubt about the Self rests on the Self, as all means of cognition are founded upon It. For the knower, there is no change. Eternal existence is His very nature. He who knows Brahman becomes Brahman, for It is unknowable by finite intellect. Only by the removal of *avidya* (ignorance) can the non-separation from Brahman be perceived.

The invisible Self, abiding within each of us, is the presiding deity of a person — guiding, sustaining, and preserving us. Hindus worship this invisible Self in the form of several deities, like Shiva, Kali, Durga, Krishna, Ganesh, and Surya. This is not image or idol worship, but the worship of the Self in the form of images. Moreover, as God is all-pervading, we do not have to establish divinity in the images. It is already present. The ego of a person and the Self are contradictory in appearance, but the basis of the existence of the ego is the Self. Without the Self, nothing exists.

Immortality of the Self

When we transcend the world of relativity and attain the realm of the Absolute, we find two apparently different beings that are immortal: the Self and God. In reality, however, both are identical. This immortality of the Self is the theme of the Upanishads, Vedanta, and the Bhagavad Gita. It can be safely said that immortality is the chief concern of all world religions — in fact, the ultimate goal of our existence.

The Bhagavad Gita teaches that both matter and spirit are without beginning and without end. All modifications and qualities belong to nature. It is matter that has produced the gross body, the physical form, while the spirit within is the cause of the experience of pleasure and pain. The spirit inherent in matter is the enjoyer of all objects of nature composed of the three *gunas* or qualities of nature — *sattva* (purity), *rajas* (activity), and *tamas* (inertia). The cause of birth in good or evil environments is the attachment to these qualities. The Self, even when dwelling in a body, is transcendent, beyond the triple qualities of nature. To realize the Self, one must go beyond these three qualities.

These qualities of nature are subject to modification and are, therefore, unreal. As the Gita (2:16) teaches, the unreal has no existence, while the Real never ceases to be. Eternal existence is beyond nature and its three qualities, and is the only Truth. This immortality beyond nature is called *sat*, one of the definitions of Brahman. Mere existence is vegetation; therefore, knowledge of this existence is essential. Knowledge beyond intelligence is *chit*. A miserable existence is meaningless. Hence, realization of one's immortality brings infinite bliss, which is beyond pleasure or happiness. This bliss is called *ananda*. Brahman is definitely *sat-chit-ananda*.

The world is simply the play of His being. Matter itself is not real, but only a form of consciousness. Matter, life, mind, and everything beyond are all merely modifications of Brahman playing in the world as *sat-chit-ananda*. When we attain this realization, we realize the truth of the teachings of the Upanishads: whoever possesses the bliss of Brahman has no fear of anything in the world thereafter. The vision changes: the whole world appears as an ocean of beauty, light, and bliss. Once this realization is attained, one perceives God in everything, everywhere.

The Upanishads proclaim the highest philosophy of the identity of the Self and Brahman, and thus destroy all barriers standing between man and God. This is not just a theory but the experience of the seers of the Upanishads. It is not the monopoly of one, but the property of all mankind.

We are, in reality, not the individual wave of consciousness separated from the sea of cosmic consciousness, but the ocean of consciousness itself, only considered to be individual waves of human life owing to *avidya* (ignorance). The spirit of God has become man and he is the ocean of cosmic consciousness, God Himself. The real nature of man is this omniscient Self, the unchanging witness of the changing body, mind, and external world. This Self is the only constant factor in man, integrating all physical and psychic factors into a coherent whole and coordinating the diverse functions of the body, mind, and other organs. It maintains the identity of man, despite all changes in the external and internal worlds. Man is essentially spirit, luminous, and self-sustaining. The Kena Upanishad (1:2) says, "He is the Life of the life."

This real Self makes a person aware of his individuality and of the plurality of the world. This awareness distinguishes all sentient beings from insentient things. It is self-evident. It requires no proof. The immortality of the Self, *atma*, is described in detail in the Gita. The knowledge of the immortality of the Self banishes all fear of death, which is merely clinging to the ego with consequent anxiety, fear, and misery. It is the desire for worldly pleasures that leads to the reincarnation of the Self. Desire can be overcome by knowledge and the death of desire leads to immortality. This immortality of the Self can be realized in meditation by the scientific technique of Kriya Yoga. This is the heaven within.

Story of Two Birds

Due to nescience (ignorance), a person adopts a subjective consciousness (I-ness) in connection with the body and its environmental relationship. This "I-ness" is called ego. On the other hand, the Self is essentially spirit — ever-existing, ever-conscious, ever-new bliss. The Gita teaches that just as the rising sun dispels darkness, the knowledge of the Self ends all delusion.

This fact is brought out in the Mundaka Upanishad (3:1:1) by the imagery of two birds. Two beautiful birds live on the same tree — one on a branch near the top, the other on a lower branch. The bird on the lower branch busies itself with tasting the fruits of the tree whereas the one on the top merely looks on, remaining calm and majestic, absorbed in its own glory. As the first bird occasionally tastes bitter fruits, it hops to a higher branch and notes the detachment of the other bird, who cares neither for the sweet nor the bitter fruits. It is satisfied in itself, seeking nothing beyond. The first bird seeks to get near the second, but, as it hops onto a higher branch, it again starts tasting the fruits on that branch out of habit. Again it tastes a bitter fruit and looks up, observing the self-satisfaction of the other. It again hops to a higher branch and due to force of habit, again starts tasting the fruits on that branch. In this way, it hops higher and higher until it comes close to the second bird. The light from its plumage is reflected on the first bird and the latter's own plumage starts melting away. When the first bird finally reaches the branch on which the second is sitting, the whole vision changes. It finds that all along it had been the second bird. The apparent duality existed only because it had deserted its true Self for the fruits of the tree. Its former Self was only a distorted reflection of its true Self.

Such is the nature of man. He pursues sense enjoyments, the many varied pleasures of the world. Like the first bird, he lives for the sweet fruits of the world, the sense pleasures. When, however, he occasionally tastes bitter fruit, in the shape of blows from the sense world, he begins a process of Self-examination and catches a glimpse of the majestic one, his real Self. But, since old habits die hard, people again lose themselves in the sense world. Repeated blows make him turn to his inner world for happiness. Finally, he discovers the Self, which is present in everything and is the essence of all things. God is revealed and he is merged in the ocean of bliss, free from all bondage.

The Self is not seen by the eye, not recognized by the mind, nor by other senses. It cannot be realized by penance or good work. It is not revealed by the study of the Vedas or by intellect or learning. Neither can it be realized by one who is devoid of moral strength or is afraid of sacrifice. Only when a person's nature has become purified by the light of knowledge is the Self revealed in all its glory in meditation. He becomes merged in the consciousness of Brahman and established in the Self.

This is absolute union (yoga), which is the same as absolute freedom (*kaivalya*). The person knows that all his faculties have attained fruition and that he has attained perfect knowledge. He experiences the state where nothing remains to be done, no desire remains to be fulfilled. The Gita also describes this state, which when attained, all the universe seems negligible. When a person has the inner vision of the Self with direct perception and experience of the Absolute, he feels an ineffable joy pervading his whole system. A sense of expansion and fullness is observed in every dimension of his being. Contact with the Absolute makes one saturated and perfect. This direct experience is the only criterion of attainment of real knowledge.

The Bhagavad Gita teaches that Brahman is perfect harmony. The sense of bondage arises due to the ignorance of the real nature of the Self, but by discriminate knowledge, the Self can be realized. When our eyes, which are blinded by the idea of matter, are opened to the supreme light of knowledge, we will find that nothing is inanimate. Everything is a manifestation of Brahman, which is *prana* (life), *manas* (mind), *vijñana* (knowledge), *ananda* (bliss), *chit* (divine force), and *sat* (being). The entire world and every object have been created as an abode of the Lord. Realization means the ability to see Him in all incidents, actions, thoughts, in one's own Self, and in others throughout creation. This is because God is manifested everywhere. He can be compared to a circle whose center is everywhere with circumference nowhere.

The Mystery of Life and Death

From the very beginning, humanity has been faced with the problem of death and has, therefore, pondered the mystery of life and death. We are born to work out our karma. As we sow, so do we reap. The chain that binds us to the wheel of life and death is the law of karma. Karma binds us, but it can also set us free. Karma is bondage, as long as we cling to the transient world of the senses. Once we turn to the eternal, karma sets us free.

When we observe the world around us, we find that some are born rich, healthy, and intelligent while others are born poor, diseased, and ignorant. The thoughtful naturally ponder over this apparent injustice and are wont to question the existence of an all-merciful benevolent providence. However, it is absurd to blame God for our miseries and unhappiness, which are self-wrought. How many of us follow the teachings of the scriptures in thought, word, and deed?

We ourselves become the cause of miseries when we violate the laws of God. God merely looks on, letting His laws mete out justice. Krishna says in the Gita (9:29), "As the Lord, I am equally present in all beings; there is none hateful nor dear to Me." God remains detached in all beings as the *atma*. Having given human beings free will, He lets us write our own destiny. We do so and become bound by the chain of karma, which we slowly and painfully work out from birth to birth. If there was no prior birth and if every effect has a cause behind it, then what is the cause behind the person who is born an invalid or a moron? It is the past actions of our prior birth that makes us what we are and what we do.

Biologists propound the theory of heredity and claim that it satisfactorily explains human beings. If heredity were all, how can one account for the fact that the offspring of the same parents exhibit such a marked difference in temperament, character, intelligence, and so forth? Similarly, the children of the same parents brought up in the same environment do not possess identical personalities. Julian Huxley attributes the birth of a genius or moron to chance or "accident of birth." But there is no such thing as chance in the universe. Everything is well regulated and follows laws. Nothing is accidental in this world; rather all is only incidental. We see this all around us. Is it just chance that makes the apple fall to the ground? Ignorance of a fact does not mean that it does not exist. Only the law of karma explains why each individual is what he is. Nothing happens without a cause. Effect and cause correspond to each other. Neither heredity nor environment, nor even their interaction, can explain these facts of life. A physical process can produce only a physical effect, nothing more. Only the body and mind of a person can be attributed to heredity and environment. We have to seek elsewhere for an explanation for the personality of an individual. Only when we accept the doctrine of reincarnation do we get an explanation for all that goes to make a person what he is. Only when a person understands what he is and why he is, can he change his life and destiny. By knowing his karma, he can master karma.

Karma means action, both physical and mental. Every action leaves its impression in the subconscious mind and has either a good or a bad effect on the life of a person. The impressions of the actions of past lives are stored in the superconsciousness and germinate under suitable environments. These constitute the inner environment, which, along with the outer environment, govern a person's actions. Karma is divided into three categories — *sanchita*, *prarabdha*, and *kriyamana*. *Sanchita* is the karma of our past lives, stored in the midbrain. These have not yet fructified. *Prarabdha* are those karmas of our past lives that have determined the present life. *Kriyamana* is the karma we are accumulating in this life and that will fructify in future lives.

Once a person loses his ego and ceases to identify with actions, they cease to bind. The solution is not inertia but detachment. This will nullify the law of karma and make one free. The life of a Kriya yogi is not guided by past actions, but by the direction of his inner Self. The aspirant rapidly reaches the goal, avoiding the path of haphazard evolution based on karma, becoming free from life and death.

The problem of death is not really a mystery. The truth is that there is no difference between life and death. Nothing is actually dead. Just as atoms in inanimate matter, like metals, are in continuous motion and rapid vibration, similarly, the atoms in the flesh of a corpse are in continuous motion and rapid vibration. Different forms of matter are the manifestation of the same life force, just as ice, water, snow, and steam are different manifestations of the same substance. All matter, including inanimate and dead bodies, is the manifestation of life. As Gurudev Paramahamsa Yoganandaji says, "Life sleeps in the crude earth, dreams beauty in the flowers, wakes with power in animals, and in man has consciousness of infinite possibilities."

At birth, something enters the world, while at death something departs. This something is the theme of all religions and they have attempted to probe it and have come up with certain answers. People are immensely interested in this "something." The actions of prior births produce the character of individuals, leading to new actions that, in turn, help further evolution. This process ends in liberation, the destiny of all living beings. A person is born in accordance with his karma. When the planetary positions are in conformity with his karma, the subtle body enters the womb of the mother and proceeds to manufacture the gross body. At the appropriate time, the baby is born.

The individual passes through the various stages of life and gathers the experiences and impressions of its actions in the subconscious. As soon as the *prarabdha karma* that had caused the birth is exhausted, the astral body is separated from the gross body. This phenomenon is called death. In reality, however, it is only the separation of the two bodies.

The indications of life and death are the presence or absence of the *prana* (the vital air, commonly called breath). The absence of the *prana* stops the functioning of the heart. Thus, when the breath and heartbeat stop, the person dies. However, a realized yogi can consciously control these two and remain in a state of absolute tranquillity or *samadhi*, having gained control over life and death, which is the means to enlightenment. When the yogi is no longer dependent upon the breath and the heart for existence, the highest knowledge dawns upon him. He no longer fears death, as death means freedom from bondage, liberation.

At death, the embodied Self moves from one place to another. Death itself is either painful or peaceful according to the karma of the individual. If the individual has attained the state of conscious separation of the Self from the body during his lifetime, death holds no pains for him. He will have foreknowledge of the time when his *prarabdha karma* is to be exhausted. When the time comes, he consciously leaves the world. This, however, can be achieved only by the regular and faithful practice of meditation.

Death is not the end of an individual, just as birth is not the beginning. What then is death? Death means that the Self (along with the subtle body, which is comprised of the mind with all its impressions) leaves the gross body. These impressions become the seeds of future birth. It is mostly the last thought of an individual that decides future birth. The last thoughts are molded by the predominant desires of life. Therefore, desires are the root of birth and death. By destroying desire, one strikes at the root of karma and escapes from the cycle of birth and death. This, however, is possible only by sincere meditation. The Bhagavad Gita (2:71) clearly says, "He who gives up all desires and moves free from all attachment, egoism and thirst for enjoyment attains peace." Such is the state of a God-realized soul. Having reached this state, he has overcome delusion;

remaining established in this state, even at the last moment, he attains the bliss of Brahman. When an individual realizes the immortality of the Self, liberation is attained. The cycle of birth and death stops for that particular individual. Therefore, it is the responsibility of each individual to attain liberation with the grace of God and liberated ones.

As God is infinite, the embodied souls (*jivas*), according to the Hindu scriptures, are also infinite. A *jiva* passes through 8,400,000 wombs before attaining liberation. Out of this, 400,000 births are from human wombs. When one has attained human birth, he should act sensibly, using discrimination, to know the will of God. Then, by the practice of meditation, one can develop intuition and quicken his evolution in one birth.

The Goal of Life

The goal of human life is to reach the shore of immortality, using the human body as the boat. By this boat, one has to cross the ocean of life and death and become immortal. This can be achieved only by the perception of the Self. We cannot easily perceive it, since we are enmeshed in the jungle of matter — the body and mind. To the ignorant person, the body is Self; whereas to the learned, the ego appears to be the Self. Needless to say, both are deluded.

The different waves that arise in the *chitta* (memory) cover the Self. A slight reflection of the Self is perceived in these waves that cover the Self. These waves are the *samskara* (the sum total of the impressions of our actions). The real nature of the Self cannot be realized so long as a single wave exists in the lake of the *chitta*. As soon as all the waves subside, the meditator attains *nirvikalpa samadhi* or the seedless state. The seedless state is attained when actions no longer form impressions in the subconscious and, therefore, cease to bind. In this state, all veils are lifted and the Self is perceived, shining in its own glory. Then we will know that the Self is not a compound. It is the eternally existing ground of being. As such, it cannot be born, nor can it die. It is immortal and indestructible, the everlasting essence of intelligence.

Life on Earth is characterized by incessant change. The Bhagavad Gita (9:33) refers to the world as full of unhappiness, the abode of miseries, and transient. The sages of yore declared from direct experience that "Truth is one." And the goal of human life is the realization of this Truth. The Mahabharata declares that contact with this universe is as temporary as the contact of a log of wood with a flowing river. Therefore, the message of the ancient sages to humanity is, "Ye children of immortality, know thyself as the Infinite. Become the All. That is the Supreme Blessing" (Shvetashvatara Upanishad 2:5).

Life is precious, yet short. The time of death is uncertain. Self-exertion means *purushartha*, which can lead us to the highest goal. The kingdom of peace is beyond speech, beyond thought. It is a positive state of spiritual attainment. It is our center, our ideal, and goal. It is the perfect awareness of the Self. The goal of life is the attainment of Self-realization. The feeling of saturation and eternal satisfaction can only be obtained by the realization of the Self. Life on this Earth, in this body, is merely a preparation, a step towards the higher life. Life is divine worship. We live because God exists; we exist in God's being; we breathe and move in Him. Once a person understands the significance of this spiritual truth and makes the essence of this realization part and parcel of daily awareness, he becomes God on Earth.

Moksha, or liberation, is the *summum bonum* (the be-all and end-all) of life. It is the fulfillment of life's purpose. The bondage of life and death on Earth, as well as on other planets, no longer exists for him who has attained *moksha*. The real object of life is the realization of this freedom. Realization of the identity of the individual soul with that of the universal soul is liberation. By annihilating the individual ego, we reach true universality. We attain life eternal, a fuller life.

Each person is the master of his own destiny. He can do anything and everything. *Prarabdha karma* is under his control. By utilizing free will, he can attain the highest realization. In fact, there is nothing impossible under the sun for him to accomplish. He has incapacitated himself, because he has forgotten the power of his real Self.

The goal of life for all beings is happiness, peace, satisfaction, security, knowledge, and immortality. This desire for perfection springs from the Self, the image of God within us. The perfect image of God within us is seeking to express itself through each individual. The only way to realize this fullest expression is to unite our isolated consciousness with the ocean of cosmic consciousness — God. Gurudev Paramahamsa Yoganandaji says, "An individual wave rising out of the ocean is bound by the laws of change. It is born, it exists, and it dies. But when the wave realizes that it is but a manifested form of the sea, when it knows that the sea has become that wave and all other waves, when the wave knows that it is the sea, then it knows that although its form may change, it is never lost or annihilated."

Similarly, our individual existence can become immortal only by acquiring the immortality of God. Our consciousness can become unceasing only when dissolved in the cosmic consciousness of God. Our joy will be unending, ever-existent joy only when united with ever-new joy of God. Self-realization means knowledge of one's own Self and its identity with Brahman or God. Then one goes beyond time, space, and causation. This state is, in reality, the regaining of the original status of humanity and not a new acquisition. Karma is the cause of bondage, or imperfection. Desires produce karma and mind produces desires.

Only by merging the mind in the cosmic or universal mind, are desires destroyed. Becoming desireless, a person's actions do not bind him. He becomes free.

The essence of religion lies in the personal experience of the Divine. By *sadhana,* this becomes possible. *Sadhana* means any spiritual practice that enables the aspirant to realize God. It is the means by which one can attain the goal of life. *Sadhana* is merely a means to an end. It presupposes some discipline for that specific end. In religion, *sadhana* includes all the religious practices and ceremonies that lead to the realization of spiritual truths. *Sadhana* is religion in practice.

To love God we must know Him in our own consciousness, not through books or philosophy. Only then can there be genuine love. Spiritual practice is the means to that knowledge. From action comes knowledge and from knowledge, love. Without direct knowledge, there can be no real love, only sentimentality. The surest way to know God is that which was discovered and practiced by the great masters and yogis. By mere prayers we cannot and will not discover spiritual truth. Like the scientists, we have to concentrate and systematize our activities and experiments. The difference is that, while scientists apply themselves to the laws of nature, we must go within and apply ourselves to the laws of spirit. Kriya Yoga is the scientific method that guides true seekers of God to their goal.

Religion belongs to the deepest consciousness of humanity. Psychological and physical training are necessary, as spiritual realization is the unfolding of the spirit encased in the human form. The finite gradually unfolds the Infinite. But as the Infinite has assumed a finite form, the unfoldment of the former is linked to the growth and development of the body. All-around development of the physical, mental, intellectual, moral, and intuitional aspects of a person is essential for spiritual realization. The body is the instrument for the expression of the life force.

The disciplining of the body and mind is essential for the person who seeks realization. Moreover, it is a priceless asset that helps one in all situations of life. Therefore, religion must educate and develop the whole person: the head, heart, and hands. Then only can there be perfection. There should be simultaneous development of body, mind, and soul.

The Role of Guru

A guru, or preceptor, is indispensable for any spiritual practice. The scriptures say that the guru is Brahma, the creator; Vishnu, the preserver; and Shiva, the destroyer. The guru creates new *samskaras*, the longing for *moksha* (liberation). The guru preserves the physical, mental, and spiritual well-being of the disciple, and destroys the effects of bad karma and base desires and leads the disciple towards light. The guru is God in His manifest and personal aspect. *Gu* means the Invisible (i.e., God), while *ru* means the visible. The Invisible uses the visible as its instrument. The relationship between the guru and the disciple is eternal. He is responsible for his disciples until they attain *moksha* (liberation).

Indian culture puts special emphasis on the guru-disciple relationship. The would-be disciple seeks access to the guru through humility, love, and service. The real guru is one who has attained Self-realization, which means complete mastery over the pulseless and breathless state (i.e., *samadhi*). Only then will one be fit for the role of a guru, not because one speaks eloquently or has a large following. If a person sincerely seeks enlightenment, God sees that he gets a true guru. Most people fail to find the Truth because they become lost in the forest of theology and travel from one thicket of theory to another. True religious principles are found in good books, but their full meaning cannot be grasped until their manifestation is seen in the life of a guru. Such an enlightened person can help his disciples, provided the latter are attuned to him. After that, the physical presence of the master is not necessary for guidance. The real guru is God Himself. The human guru is only His instrument or agent.

The aspirant who seeks to know God must first rise above the consciousness of the body and material existence. By the practice of the great yogic method discovered by the sages of India, we can easily rise above the limited consciousness of the body. We can then feel our identity with God. We can feel that our own existence is spirit. We are the beginning and end of all. We can feel that we work through all hands and think through all minds, that our hearts throb through all hearts. We will feel our presence in everything and perceive that the stars are but the ornaments of our vast body. We are spreading over the stars, twinkling through their luminosity and creation is floating on the ocean of eternal existence.

Body and mind are but two forms of spirit. Spirit manifested as matter is still spirit. The spiritual tradition of India teaches how to realize that this spirit is living within us. The divine memory of the soul has to be awakened, as it has forgotten its real nature due to the bondage of body and matter. Then we will find that we are God, everything is God, and nothing exists but God. This is the treasure of India that can be acquired by the technique of Kriya Yoga. The profound and ultimate truth will be realized.

All true gurus are alive, regardless of whether they have retained their physical forms or not. In the beginning of the spiritual search, we may have many teachers, but there can be only one guru. They are "disciples" who come to the guru for an eternal relationship. The guru is the living embodiment of spiritual truth. When the devotee's heart has been purified, God sends the guru; it is easier to follow a living embodiment of Truth than to live on abstractions. No book, however noble, can substitute for the guru. The question is, how to know who is fit for the role of guru in the path of Self-realization. Shri Shankara says, "A real teacher is he who is well versed in the Vedas, sinless, unsmitten by desire, and the best among the knowers of Brahman, who has withdrawn himself into Brahman, is calm like fire that has consumed its fuel, who is a boundless reservoir of mercy (i.e., ineffable and a friend of all good people that prostrate themselves before him)" (Viveka Chudamani 33).

The Bhagavad Gita (2:56) says that the person whose mind remains unperturbed in sorrow, whose thirst for pleasure has altogether disappeared and who is free from passion, fear, and anger is of stable mind. A liberated sage is free from desire, selfishness, egoism, "I-ness," attachment, greed, and hatred. He is full of pure love, compassion, and mercy, and is a powerhouse of spiritual energy. It is a rare fortune indeed to come in contact with such a sage or *sadguru*. God always sends His representatives to those who earnestly seek Him. Only a few have attained *nirvikalpa samadhi*. But one must seek a true guru, if there is genuine desire for spiritual progress. Of course, a yogi advanced in spiritual practice can also guide an aspirant, but only a realized master can lead him to the goal.

A *sadguru* (or realized master) can purify the body of the disciple at the time of initiation by infusing spiritual power into the disciple. By purifying the spine at the six spiritual centers, the untapped spiritual energy, the cosmic force latent in the human body is awakened. As a result of this, the disciple gets the triple divine qualities: light, sound, and vibration. These six spinal centers keep man attached to the material world in accordance with his karma and do not allow him to transcend animality and rationality. If a disciple, under the guidance of the guru, can control the six spinal centers through the technique of Kriya Yoga and establish God consciousness there, he will overcome all vices and evolve into a divine being. Then ignorance disappears and the light of wisdom shines upon him. (Diagram 1; page 58)

A Sanskrit maxim says, "Worship God after becoming God." Unless a person raises the latent spiritual force present in the coccygeal center to the brain, after passing it through the different centers of the spine, he cannot become spiritual. Prayers, worship, and rituals are of no avail. They produce no change either in his consciousness or in his heart. Only a realized master can rouse the latent cosmic power, the *kundalini*. Direct association with a guru is, therefore, essential.

Shri Shankara says, "There are three things that are rare indeed and they are attained only by the grace of God. These are: a human birth, desire for liberation, and the protecting care of a perfect sage" (Viveka Chudamani 3). Anyone and everyone cannot be a guru. In every age, God incarnates Himself as the guru to teach humanity. *Sat-chit-ananda* alone is the guru. The guru is only one, but *upagurus* may be many. An *upaguru* is one from whom anything is learned. The great Avadhuta, a monk mentioned in the Bhagavatam, had twenty-four *upagurus*. God sends the *sadguru* or realized master only to the earnest disciples.

Paramahamsa Yoganandaji says that spiritualism cannot be bought in the market. The father and mother give the physical birth. But it is the guru who gives the spiritual birth and leads the disciples to the shore of Self-realization. The disciple has to follow the instructions of the guru faithfully and sincerely, and practice meditation regularly to gain full benefit from the contact with the guru. Words cannot do justice to the soul-revealing power of Kriya Yoga. It is not necessary to be familiar with the theory of Kriya Yoga in order to progress in it. Only concentration and sincerity are required. A true guru is a nominee of God, through whom God teaches the devotees so that they may realize their real Self.

The Attributes of Guru

Guru, the preceptor, the master of the spiritual path is the friend, philosopher, and guide of the aspirant and constantly leads to the divine goal. The master himself is realized. The medical professor makes the students qualified in medical education, both in theory and practice. Similarly, the spiritual preceptor trains the disciple to be ready and fit in every aspect to reach the ultimate reality. The guru dispels the darkness of ignorance from the life of the disciple and helps the disciple to walk in the path of light (i.e., wisdom). One who walks in the light never stumbles.

The scriptures of different religions repeatedly emphasize to be very careful, selective, and scrutinising in accepting the master; because there are many false prophets (i.e., masters in pretension, from outward show) so that the disciple may not be cheated.

The scriptures emphasize the quality of the master, which may be carefully noted. The master is one who has realized the Truth (i.e., God) and teaches others to reach that goal with all efforts. The guru or master is one who is the master of the body, senses, and mind, not a slave of them. The master is the master of the lower self and is merged in the supreme Self. The master himself is the spiritual path, it is not obtained as a degree from a school, university, religious institution, or a family; rather, it is a state of spiritual attainment.

The master is the mouthpiece of supreme knowledge (*paravidya*) and the master of special skill. The master is the living temple of spirituality and wisdom. Spiritual wisdom cannot be collected from books or from lectures, discussions, or conversations, but from apprenticeship to a competent master.

The guru is the burning lamp who enlightens the lamp of spiritual life of the disciples, dispelling darkness from the mind and heart, so that they will not walk any more on the path of darkness leading to misery and suffering.

It is written in the Guru Gita (4:111):

"O my disciple Parvati, there are many who claim and talk proud of themselves by proclaiming themselves to be guru, but their eyes are constantly on the prosperity of their disciples, how to exploit and extract material objects, but on the other hand the real realized guru is very rare who is constantly trying to take away the dangers, difficulties, disturbances, delusion, and ignorance of the disciple."

In the Mundaka Upanishad (1:2:8), it is declared:

"Remaining in the stronghold of ignorance, and thinking of himself, 'I am wise and learned,' the fools with boastful nature ramble about like the blind led by the blind. The result is evident."

In the Tantra Sara, an ancient spiritual text in India, the quality of the master is explained scrutinisingly. The guru, the preceptor, must be:

1. *shanta* — With thorough control over the mind and other internal instruments: the *buddhi* (intellect), *ahamkara* (ego), *chitta* (mindstuff).
2. *danta* — With thorough control over the senses (organs of knowledge and organs of actions), self-restraint.
3. *kulina* — Normally hails from a spiritual family; the family endowed with purity, nobility, generosity, and divine love.
4. *vinita* — Full of humility.
5. *shuddhaveshavan* — Putting on a pure and clean dress. Symbolically, the ochre-colored dress

	that monks put on represents the fire color, burning all the negatives, including body consciousness.
6. *shuddhachara*	Humble, polite, embodiment of noble nature, and divine behavior.
7. *supratishtha*	Well established in Truth, constantly God conscious.
8. *suchi*	Purity; one who is always aware of the indwelling Self as ever pure.
9. *daksha*	Able, competent, efficient, and expert to remove the doubts of the disciples and to discipline them to be realized.
10. *subuddhiman*	Endowed with divine intelligence, not material or mundane intelligence.
11. *ashrami*	Living in an ashram, fulfilling the requirements of ashram life.
12. *dhyananishtha*	Always in meditative and contemplative attitude, always God conscious.
13. *tantra visharada*	Knower of the spiritual technique necessary for Self-realization.
14. *mantra visharada*	Well versed in the secret of spirituality, scriptural and practical knowledge.
15. *nigrahe kshama*	Having the power to discipline others.
16. *anugrahe kshama*	Able to forgive and lead the disciple in the divine path with love and compassion.

Anyone endowed with the above qualities is, no doubt, a burning example of purity, spirituality, and Self-realization.

The Spiritual Legacy of India

The evolution of spiritual concepts has been very slow. Even now in the world, there are people who adore departed souls as their gods and guides. Practically, we can say that this concept has been the basis of spiritual progress. The idea of duality came from this concept, that man is separate from God, the Creator. This idea persists in most religions. Hinduism declares that all people are living Gods, everything is God, and there exists nothing except God. Some religions preach dualism and pantheism. They teach that God is a separate being, sitting somewhere in the heavens and ruling the universe like a dictator. Yet they define God as all-pervading and omnipresent. If God exists, He exists equally in all beings. It is easier to seek God within one's own Self than elsewhere. Again, some religions preach that human beings are separate from God, having individual souls. This only highlights the confusion of the logicians.

A person's inner being — the Self — and God are one. If not, a person could not become divine. Human beings are God, but we must learn to manifest our divinity. It is spiritual cowardice that frightens people from acceptance of this fact and provides them shelter in the comforting thought that they are only ordinary people and, as such, are condemned to a life of sin.

Hinduism not only boldly asserts this spiritual truth, but it also offers various methods to realize this truth. This has made India, from time immemorial, a land of spiritual guides with an ancient and highly developed civilization. India was advanced in every field. The degeneration of India began when it abandoned spiritualism for materialism and forgot its noble heritage and culture. As a natural corollary, Hinduism also degenerated into dogmatism, fanaticism, and rituals. But there are undercurrents in India at present and, when they come to the surface, India will once again find its rightful place in the world. The day is not far off.

The spiritual truths propounded by Hinduism are not the products of speculation, but are the result of centuries of patient investigation. The date of the origin of Hinduism cannot be fixed. The Ultimate cannot be discovered in a few thousand years. Hinduism has discovered the Ultimate and worships It through symbols. As such, there is no idolatry in Hinduism. A particular idol only represents a particular aspect of the Divine. The idol can be destroyed, but the ideal cannot. These ideals combine the manifold aspects of the ultimate truth that can only be realized through spiritual practice.

Endeavour for Self-realization is the tradition and speciality of India. From time immemorial, India has specialized in soul culture. It is the land of pilgrimage for all those who seek soul culture and Self-realization through yoga. Only by the practice of yoga can one attain peace, happiness, bliss, and Self-realization. The physical sciences have failed to provide happiness. Material progress has left a feeling of emptiness and lack of purpose. This is evident everywhere. Advancement in materialism has eroded culture and has dealt a hard blow to moral and social values. Only by complete withdrawal from the external world and the exploration of the internal world can one be at peace within and attain bliss. Yoga shows the way.

The word "yoga" raises a lot of confusion in people unfamiliar with it. This confusion is further compounded when they come across self-styled yogis professing to teach "the real yoga." They are bewildered and ultimately feel disgust for the science of yoga when they see so-called yogis performing physical exercises. Their inherent spiritual tendencies make them revolt at the sight. These yogis are not only doing a disservice to yoga, but they are also misleading a large number of people. The word "yoga" means union and denotes the union of a person with

God. This union is always present and has merely to be realized. The Bhagavad Gita (2:48) says, "Equanimity is yoga," and further states that perfect severance from all personal desires and hatred is yoga. Detachment is yoga. This detachment cannot be achieved by reasoning or intellectual conviction, but only by a technique such as Kriya Yoga. Once perfect detachment is achieved, a person gains knowledge of hidden things.

Kriya Yoga is the panacea for all the ills of humanity — physical, mental, and spiritual. It is the answer to all suffering on these planes and produces all-around development and peace. It transforms a person and leads him to his goal. It can transform societies and nations, ushering in an era of peace, prosperity, and happiness in the world.

II

THE QUICKENING OF HUMAN EVOLUTION

The world is no longer the huge place it was once thought to be. Distance has been incredibly reduced by rapid means of transport and communication. Great scientific inventions have liberated us from servitude to nature and have quickened world evolution. Science has relieved us of grinding poverty and physical pain.

On the other hand, humanity today faces the challenge of destiny. We are in the midst of the greatest crisis of history. The human predicament is due to the lack of adjustment of the human spirit to the startling developments in science and technology. Science has increasingly put more and more power in the hands of human beings and with that power it has already turned the world into a house full of explosives. So man lives a scorched life, frantically searching for meaning and security. The solution lies in a moral and spiritual revolution embracing the whole world.

Kriya Yoga is the most effective medium to bring about this change. It is a practical philosophy suitable for every person of the modern world. It offers guidance and help to a generation that is perplexed at its failure to find satisfaction and is groping for light. The general evolution has been quickened through scientific method. This can similarly be applied to all other spheres of life, including the inner life.

In his classic book, *The Origin of Species*, Charles Darwin demonstrates that life on this planet has evolved by a gradual process. Evolution is a continuous process from the earliest forms of living organisms to the latest product: human beings.

The Seven Spiritual Centers in Human Body

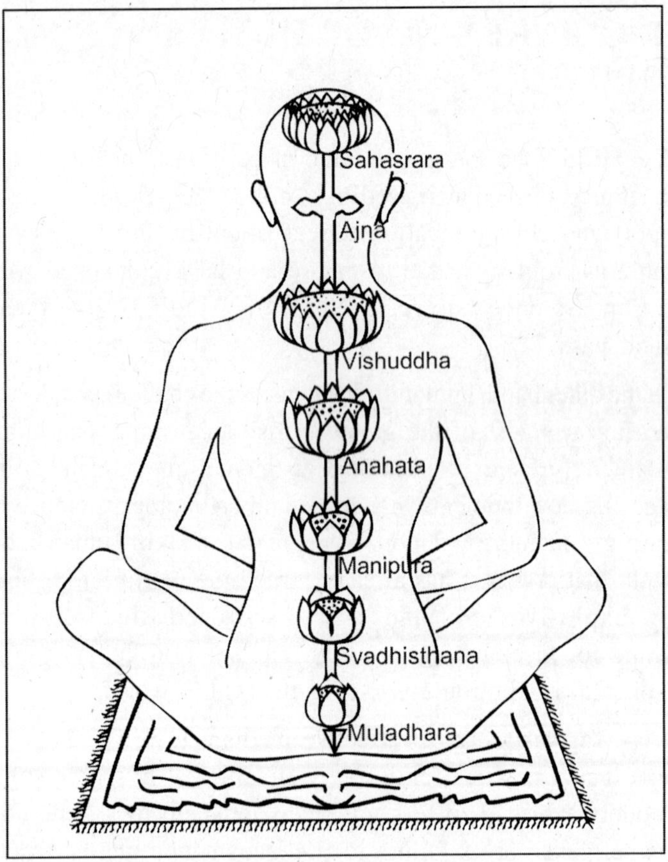

DIAGRAM 1 - The seven spiritual centers shown in the diagram of the human body (from lower to upper): four petal lotus in money center (muladhara); six petalled lotus in the family center (svadhisthana); ten petal lotus in the food center (manipura); twelve petalled lotus in the heart center (anahata); sixteen petalled lotus in the education center (vishuddha); two petalled lotus in the soul center (ajna); thousand petalled lotus in the cosmic body center (sahasrara).

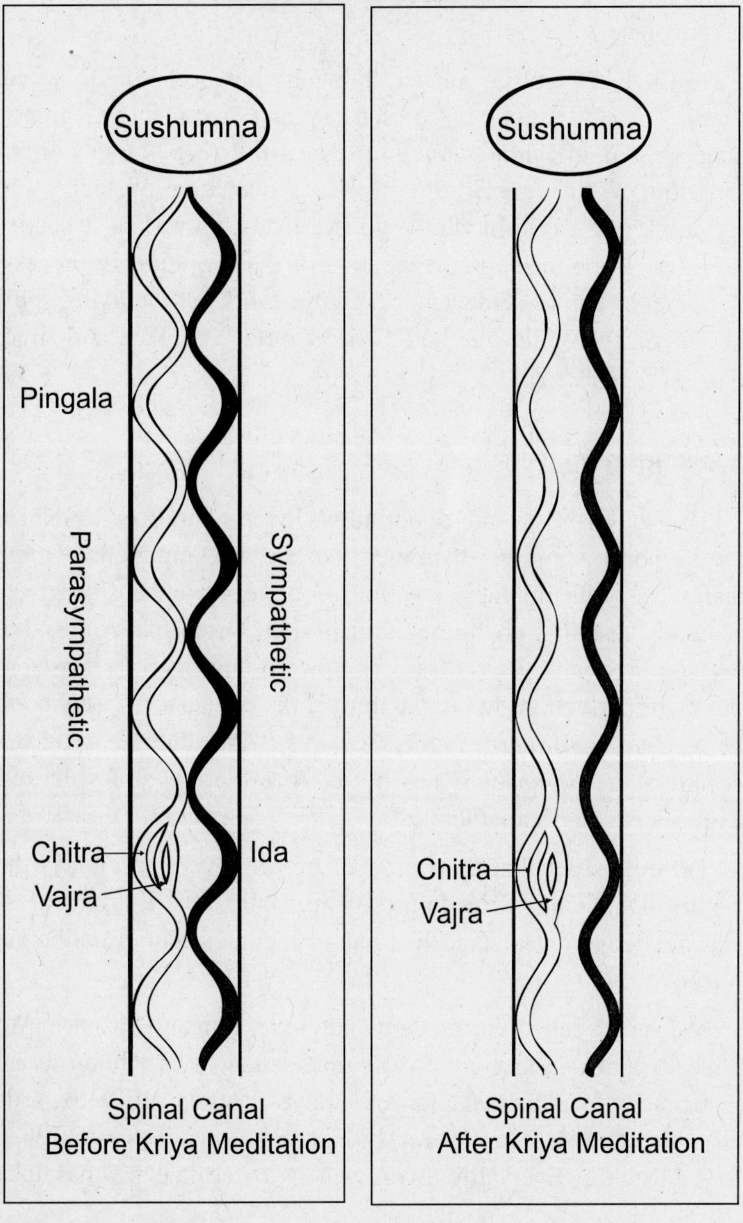

Diagram 2 - Sushumna

Biologists accept the idea of Darwinian evolution as a broadly satisfactory account of the mode of change that has actually taken place.

In the history of our planet, humanity has been able to attain, thanks to the development of sensory and emotional machinery, a degree of efficiency unequalled in the rest of the animal kingdom. We have used this power to overcome obstacles and to modify the world in which we live in such a way as to justify the claim to be the supreme creation of the evolutionary process. All great scientific achievements are the works of the living spirit of humanity. While our bodies are limited in space and time, our spirit is eternal.

The Opportunity

Human birth is a rare opportunity. It can be utilized to realize the immortal spirit and thereby transcend the limitations of time and space. Life implies evolution — a steady onward progress, a steady ascent into higher and higher states of progressive perfection. Therefore, it means an upward movement, a ceaseless quest for perfection. Julian Huxley, in the conclusion of his book *Evolution: A Modern Synthesis*, says, "True human progress consists of increase of aesthetic, intellectual and spiritual experiences and satisfaction."

He points out that the future of progressive evolution is the future of humanity. The future of humanity, if it is to progress and not remain at a standstill, must be guided with a deliberate purpose.

We must realize the precious nature of human existence. We have to realize the wonderful significance of this body as an instrument for spiritual practice and as a great guide towards the ultimate goal. Man grows through countless lives into divine Self-existence. Every life, every act, is a step that we may take either backward or forward. One's thought, will, and action determine what one is likely to be. Dr. Radhakrishnan says, "Our feet are set on the path of higher life, though they wander uncertainly and the path is not seen clearly."

Freedom from birth and realization of the divine state is the dream of all religions. It is the *moksha* of the Hindu, the *nirvana* of the Buddhist, and the Kingdom of Heaven of the Christian. Realization of cosmic consciousness is the goal of life. In the language of religion, Spirit is God, the ultimate reality which is one and all-comprehensive. Cosmic consciousness, Spirit, God, the Absolute, and the Self all are one and the same. The realization of the Self is the only *summum bonum* (the be-all and end-all) of life and in this alone does life find its fulfillment.

We are all living sparks of Divinity. The one who dives deepest into his Self not only realizes his identity with the Cosmic Spirit, but tastes the sweetness of infinite joy. In the rush and clamor of our conscious life, we do not pay attention to the mystery of our being.

The Self is the source of all joy. It is the dearest thing to humanity. Life is dear because there is joy in living it. One loves another person or thing because he identifies his own Self with that person or thing. To feel oneness with the Self is to become one with the Infinite God. To strive toward that end is our birthright. Kriya Yoga can lead us to that end.

Soul is the microcosmic image of Spirit. As such, the soul first manifests the vibrations of superconsciousness, which turn into life energy. This life energy, in turn, vibrates through the gross human body. Mind exists, matter exists. Both are vibrations of spirit. Invisible mind vibrating as life energy is converted into gross matter. Matter does not exist as it appears to us. It is merely the vibration of energy, which is the vibration of consciousness. Cosmic energy is finer than electrons and other vibratory forces existing in nature and it is conscious. It is the missing link between consciousness and matter. The modern philosopher, Herbert Spencer, derives his philosophy from Darwin's observations. He seems to account for the rise of the living from the non-living and the mental from the non-mental, while Darwin only breaks down the lines between lower and higher forms of life but assumes that life always came from life.

Indian sages have observed that there is a law of metempsychosis. It is written in the Hindu scriptures that there are 8,400,000 categories of wombs that are divided into different types. It is understood that 900,000 of these are water-born; 1,100,000 comprise the worm category; 1,000,000 belong to the birds; 2,000,000 to animals; 3,000,000 to plants; 400,000 to human beings. As part of the evolutionary process, it is believed that the soul is to travel through all these wombs before it reaches the human form. But since in lower forms of life there is no sense of discrimination, this evolution takes place automatically through divine will and action. It is astonishing to see that the observations of science and biology come very near to the aforesaid numbers, even though science and biology clearly admit their inability to arrive at definite conclusions regarding the number of species. After the attainment of a human body, a person should act sensibly and discerningly. His intellect and power of judgement makes him superior to all other species.

When we realize the true nature of the Self and understand we are all manifestations of that cosmic consciousness, we shall love the whole world. There is no such thing as inanimate matter. There is life in everything. Matter is vibrant with life. This has been conclusively proven by modern science. This remarkable evolution from stone to God goes on through millions of years, through eons of time. But in the individual life, this process takes place more rapidly and quickly with all the forces of its past behind it. These forces that manifest and unveil themselves in evolution are cumulative in their power.

Embodied in stone in the mineral world, life forces grow and put out a little more strength and begin the process of unfolding. Then they become too strong for the mineral world and pass on into the vegetable world. There they unfold more and more of their divinity, until they become too strong for the vegetable and become animal. Expanding within and gaining experiences from animal life, they again overflow the limits of the animal and appear as human. In the human being they still grow and accumulate with ever increasing force and exert greater pressure against their barriers and then out of the human they pass into the superhuman. The last process of evolution is called yoga. This process of evolution can be quickened by conscious effort through scientific means.

From the animalistic plane of life we have to move to the rationalistic plane, from the rationalistic plane to the intuitional or superconscious plane, from the superconscious plane we can merge ourselves in cosmic consciousness and then in wisdom (i.e., *nirvikalpa samadhi*, the highest state of realization). At this stage — besides the consciousness of perception and action of the animal world and self-consciousness with intelligence and will of the human plane — one has spiritual experience through which new aspects of reality reveal themselves. Evolution is quickened if one attains this stage and remains enshrined in the divine or superconscious stage and develops the supra-rational organ in the body. Everything depends upon the receptivity of our mind, brain cells, and spinal column.

Saints have found that if it were possible to live in health, without disease or decrepitude, then by solar and chemical energy in one million years humans could develop a brain capable of expressing cosmic consciousness and absorbing the entire knowledge of the universe. The saints also learned that by some special method this evolutionary process can be accelerated by changing the brain cells through magnetization.

This can be accomplished by the use of the Kriya technique, which allows the attainment of cosmic consciousness in one lifetime. The Kriya Yoga system is one of the simplest and quickest means of achieving the state of Self-realization. It is truly an integral yoga, which brings about the higher evolution of human beings in nature through the simultaneous development of body, mind, intellect, and soul.

Emergent Evolution

In his *Emergent Evolution*, Morgan says that evolution is the name we give to the comprehensive sequence in all natural events. Bergson, the French thinker, suggests that the evolution of the world can be satisfactorily explained by admitting a common living force that is striving constantly for balance and harmony. This force he calls the vital impetus, the *élan vital*. It is identical with the basic reality or force underlying all manifestations.

It is observed that the vital impetus struggles to manifest itself in the living world in different kinds of material environments. As a result, evolution of life takes place along three chief paths — plants, lower animals, and human beings. Consciousness is still in a state of sleep or torpor in plants, whereas in animals it is partially liberated from the overpowering influence of the material body and environment, as is indicated by the power of sensation and movement. In human beings consciousness supersedes matter, especially in intelligent action preceded by deliberate choice and free movement. The three main tendencies that help distinguish the three chief paths along which life evolved are the vegetative torpor, animal instinct, and human intelligence.

To produce a new individual, two living germ cells — the sperm from the father and the ovum or egg from the mother —

Mahavatar Babaji Maharaj

Lahiri Mahasaya

Swami Shriyukteshwar

Bhupendranath Sanyal Mahasaya

Paramahamsa Yogananda

Swami Satyananda

Paramahamsa Hariharananda

Paramahamsa Prajnanananda

unite when conception takes place. Both the egg and the sperm contain tiny threadlike structures called chromosomes, the threads of life. Life is not a byproduct of matter, because the quality that is life vitalizes and pervades matter, determining the degree of complexity required for emergence of biological activity. Mind emerges in a living organism of a higher degree of complexity. Though life is manifesting in any material body, the constitution of the living body shows new types of relationships and characteristics when sufficiently evolved to possess the power of thought.

Matter viewed externally and superficially appears to be unconscious, just as human bodies and plants may appear to be unconscious based only on our external observation. However, plants and even metals exhibit symptoms of sensitivity when measured on fine scientific instruments. According to Shri Aurobindo, matter is the Self-expression of the Absolute that has playfully plunged itself into apparent sleep in order to enjoy the delight of Self-discovery by ascending back to itself through the successive stages of evolution. Matter is essentially creative; matter is activity. The creative activity observed in inorganic matter is more evident in the behavior of living matter.

With the emergence of consciousness in the organism, a new quality is generated that cannot be completely reduced either to matter or to life. Self consciousness indicates a higher degree of consciousness and it is a new level of emergence. The human being is a microcosm of the universe. The first three manifestations of reality — matter, life, and mind — are embodied in human beings. In addition, the human being has an inner and abiding psychic entity called the soul around which the body, life, and mind are organized into an individual entity that stores up the individual's experiences and that persists through the changes of body, life, and mind.

According to the Upanishads, matter (*anna*), life (*prana*), and perceptual consciousness (*manas*) are the truer expressions of the spirit. The spirit in human beings is the reality underlying all existence. The Self, God, and the Absolute are all names of the one universal spirit in its different aspects. The Self is the manifestation of the spirit in the human form through the body and mind. The human self, like matter, life, and other expressions of spirit is an organized whole. It is the latest and highest product of the creative process of emergent evolution.

Conscious realization of humanity's unity with the spirit is the goal of life and, consciously or unconsciously, every person tries to advance towards that end. The spirit of a person is always shining in him. When he realizes his unity with the universal Self — his own spiritual existence — a person becomes one with the universe. Meditation is the way to Self-discovery. To know truth we have to go deeper. There is only one method to acquire knowledge. From the ordinary person to the highest yogi — all must use the same method and that method is concentration. This is the knock that opens the gates of nature and lets out floods of light. Concentration is the only key to the treasure of knowledge. The power of the human mind is unlimited. The secret of the world is ours, if we know how to knock, how to give the necessary blow. The strength and force of the blow come through concentration.

There are three sorts of instruments of knowledge. The first is instinct, which is most highly developed in animals. This is the lowest instrument of knowledge. In human beings, it is developed into reason. Yet reason is still insufficient. To acquire perfection, further evolution is essential. Through the practice of Kriya Yoga during one year, one gets the results of many years of evolution. (Diagram 3; page 92) The great scientific method is to magnetize and send the current around the brain and spinal column and, thereby, secure one year's evolution in every inhalation and exhalation, which is equal to one Kriya. When by the purifying effect of Kriya, the brain cells are purified, divine magnetism touches them. Every cell becomes vibrant with divine energy, attaining the state of cosmic consciousness. All the knowledge of the world is grasped very easily.

The Process to Quicken Evolution

The spinal cord and brain are wonderful structures. They are comprised of highly specialized nerve cells and nerve fibers, surrounded by cerebro-spinal fluid and a thick and intertwined network of blood vessels. The length of the vertebral column is 70 cms. and the spinal cord is 45 cms. The spinal cord (*sushumna*) starting at the base of the skull, ends in the lumbar region behind the umbilicus in a cone. From there, a delicate threadlike bluish-white structure — the *filum terminale* — extends down to and is anchored at the coccyx. The vertebral column starts at the base of the skull and ends at the top of the coccyx. A central canal traverses the whole length of the spinal cord and up to half or three-fourths of the *filum terminale*. A thick bundle of nerves descends down the terminal cone of the spinal cord, surrounding the *filum* and occupying the sacral region. This bundle is the *cauda equina.* (Diagram 2; page 59)

A yogic exercise in Kriya Yoga, known as *mahamudra*, is a simple but effective method to straighten the spine and encourage the right distribution of *prana* (life currents) along the spine. Correct practice of *mahamudra* equalizes the flow of life energy to all parts of the body. Because of the effectiveness of *mahamudra* in magnetizing and adjusting the spine, this technique may be practiced whenever the body requires adjustment. By magnetizing the spine, the life force can be transmuted into radiant, all-accomplishing spiritual force that, in turn, can hasten physical and mental regeneration and rejuvenation.

The great yogis, the masterminds of India, have taught a method of revolving certain currents around the spine and brain. The spine is the only ladder by which one can ascend to cosmic consciousness. Physical and mental rejuvenation through Kriya Yoga effects the awakening of latent super-sensory powers and perceptions. In meditation our consciousness and energy have to be consciously withdrawn from the senses and muscles to the spine. The practice of Kriya magnetizes the spine by circulating life current lengthwise around it, thereby withdrawing life current from the senses and involuntary organs and concentrating it in the spine.

During the practice of Kriya, the entire spine is converted into a magnet that draws bodily currents away from the senses and nerves. The pituitary, the center of the will, becomes the positive pole and the coccygeal plexus becomes the negative pole. The current created by continuous inhalation and exhalation becomes a magnet of energy that draws into the spine more energy from the nervous system and from the cosmic source. The Kriya technique transfers our attention from sensations of sight, smell, sound, taste, and touch to the subtler perceptions in the spine and brain. A devotee then becomes automatically introverted and experiences the divine sensation of sound, vibration, touch of heaviness above the forehead, vision of glow of light in the mid-brain, and becomes absorbed in meditation. Therefore, the Kriya technique is the foundation of Self-realization. It makes the brain clear and calm, because the entire consciousness is centralized in the spine. There is nothing to be compared with the soothing sensation of joy felt in the spine. By revolving the life force once around the spine, as the Kriya yogi is wont to do, one can effect a change in the brain and body that is ordinarily possible in one year of diseaseless existence, careful eating, and absorption of solar energy. The passing of this current around the spine once corresponds to the effect of sunlight during 365 days.

Cosmic consciousness is spread all over the universe and pervades everything. Human consciousness is limited to the human body and its environment. To attain cosmic consciousness, it is necessary to expand the consciousness that resides in every living cell of the body and brain. Kriya practice clears and stimulates the brain and strengthens the medulla. It also greatly magnetizes the body, saturating and feeding all its physical cells with undecaying light and keeping them in a magnetized state.

Spirit is self-born. Spirit is ever conscious. God's attention is equally distributed everywhere and is fully concentrated everywhere. We human beings, made in God's own image, have latent within us the power to concentrate our attention and to feel our existence everywhere. By properly following the laws of living and by faithful practice of Kriya Yoga, we can expand our consciousness and reach the ocean of cosmic consciousness or divine Spirit.

The Process of Expanding Consciousness

Every twelve years, the human body completes a cycle and as a result, at 12, 24, and 36 years of age we find distinct changes in a person. Physical changes also effect corresponding changes in mind. Disease and wrong living retard this normal process of evolution. Our brain develops during twelve-year cycles in such a way that it displays distinct kinds of mentality. Our superior intellectual powers grow in the process and manifest in our efforts to understand, analyze, and control events in space and time. It is an established fact that the degree of manifestation of mental development of a person corresponds with the development of his brain cells.

The brain is the supreme electrical powerhouse. All the centers are interconnected and act under the influence of the supreme center, the brain. The brain cells discharge electricity or life currents that pass on to different nerves, which respectively carry motor impulses. The rate and quality of discharge varies according to the brain and state of health. The base of the brain discharges at a different rate from the cerebral hemispheres. In health, the brain gives out a steady rhythmic discharge; in disease this varies. The emotional disturbance caused by anxiety is accompanied by excessive electrical activity of nerve cells at the base of the brain, which interferes with the rhythm of the discharge of the higher centers. (Diagram 16; page 198)

The electrical flow from the brain is the life of the organism and it is the medium through which all sensory reports reach the brain and cause thought reactions. When the divine electricity first descends into the body, it rests in the insulated altars of spine and brain. From the seven cerebro-spinal centers the life force branches out into sensory nerves, keeping the soul busy in material perceptions. By the practice of Kriya Yoga, consciousness and energy again become centralized in the spine; the yogi feels a sort of infinite joy there, proof of the presence of the Divine within.

The nervous system, among all parts of the body, is more specially connected with consciousness. The mind is thus identified with the neural process. Psychologists and neurologists believe there is a pattern of neural activity underlying every thought, every perception, every action. The nervous system is an extremely complex structure with two broad divisions, the central and the peripheral. The central nervous system is made up of the brain and spinal cord. Its function is to correlate and integrate, and make the various parts of the body work together. The peripheral division consists of nerve fibers passing from the receptors to the central nervous system and of fibers passing from the central nervous system to muscles and glands.

The nervous system may be compared with a telephone service. It keeps all outlying parts of the body in effective communication with the great central exchange, the brain. The nervous system is also composed of cells. But these cells are highly specialized and distinct from others, both in appearance and function. They have the special capacity to receive and carry electro-chemical messages or nerve impulses. One nerve cell may roughly be compared to a single wire in a complex telephone system.

In the human brain, billions of nerve cells are woven together. Each of these can send messages to near and distant cells by means of complex interconnections. Even the most sophisticated electronic computer is a poor comparison with the human brain. When, through concentration, all the fine cells and brain cells are turned to the cosmic source, they become magnetized. Our body is made up of trillions of cells. Every cell is like an intelligent being. We have to educate and train those cells to know all the things that are going on in the world. This world and universe, our thoughts and feelings, are but one atom of the Infinite projected onto the plane of consciousness. Our reason works within that narrow limit, defined by the network of consciousness and not beyond.

Therefore, some other instrument must take us beyond. That instrument, according to Swami Vivekananda, is inspiration. Shri Aurobindo conceives it as the supramental consciousness that lies beyond our mind. We can attain it only if we can rouse the higher principles, the supermind, that lie hidden and dormant within us. The supermind is the infinite divine mind; existence-consciousness-bliss, *sat-chit-ananda*, in the creative poise. Buddha emphasizes the importance of *bodhi*, or enlightenment. As distinct from sense knowledge, the Hindu thinkers use the term *aparoksha* for this non-sensuous immediate knowledge. Dr. Radhakrishnan conceives it as intuition. Intuition, as direct and absolute knowledge of Reality, is recognized by many Western thinkers, including Plato, Descartes, Spinoza, and Bergson. It is difficult to define intuition, because it is too near to every one of us. Every one of us feels it. Paramahamsa Yoganandaji says that in intuition we are in tune with Reality, with the world of bliss, with the unity in diversity, with the inner laws governing the spiritual world, with God.

This intuition is absolutely immediate. The knowledge of Self is an example of intuitive apprehension. Self-knowledge is inseparable from Self-existence. It cannot be proven, because it is the basis of all proof. It is the light which is not nature, which is not humanity, but made them both. So instinct, reason, and intuition are the three instruments of knowledge. Instinct belongs to the animals, reason to human beings, and inspiration or intuition to the Godman. But the germs of each are found more or less in all human beings and one form develops into another. Reason develops into intuition and therefore, intuition does not contradict reason, but rather fulfills it. Things that reason cannot get at are brought to light by intuition and they do not contradict reason. As Swami Vivekananda puts it, "The old man does not contradict the child, but fulfills the child."

But intuitive knowledge is not confined to the limited region of our little self. By *sadhana* (spiritual practice), it can be expanded to grasp the entire Reality. As thought can be cultivated, so intuition can be developed. Every person has the power of intuition, as he has power of thought. The quickening of human evolution is caused by the development of intuition through concentration. All knowledge comes from the inner source, from the soul without limitation. One lifetime is not enough to learn all mysteries of the creation. The best way to know real Truth is to make use of the all-knowing power of intuition given to us by God. We can quicken our evolution by increasing the power of concentration and be liberated from animalistic life or the life of being human automatons. The intuition of the human race can be quickly developed only through intuitive meditation and not by the endless process of formal man-made education.

Intuitive meditation is possible through the scientific process of Kriya Yoga. This is India's unique and immortal contribution to the world. Kriya Yoga is an instrument through which human evolution can be quickened. The saints of India discovered that any bodily effect on the brain is a slow process, but a change effected by the brain on the body is immediate. Therefore, a process of sending the life force around the spine and brain produces an immediate effect and quickens evolution. Taking the body as our laboratory, we can make systematic experimentation and can realize the profound significance and efficacy of Kriya Yoga.

Just as a thrilling sensation is felt in the living organism through contact with an electric current, similarly, divine illumination, divine sound, and divine vibration are experienced in the body of a devotee soon after the practice of this scientific Kriya Yoga. This is the experience of awakening superconsciousness — the intuitional state of meditation. We are seeking an experience of God that is tangible. From this direct experience, devotion to God becomes deeper; we feel within the presence and realization of the Supreme Lord. If we can maintain this superconscious stage all the time, then we can attain quickly the cosmic conscious stage.

Every time we practice Kriya under the direct guidance of a realized spiritual master, our entire system undergoes a change. Our brainpower and mental receptivity are expanded. The Kriya technique can give us mathematical results proportionate to our intensity and depth of practice. It is highly effective to quicken evolution and is the essence and scientific synthesis of all yogas taught in India. This is not only an ancient science, but a profound philosophy of life that, when cultivated, can best mold and lead the life of humanity on this Earth.

III

THE SCIENCE OF KRIYA YOGA

"Science of Kriya Yoga" includes two important terms: science and yoga. Yoga means the union of the individual soul with the universal Soul or the union of the human being with God. The ordinary meaning of the word yoga is union. But it metaphysically means the realization of the identity of the Self with Brahman. Yoga aims at the realization of the all-pervasive existence of God. The physical body of a human being is a part of nature. The five senses of a person keep him enchanted and engrossed in the external world, as a result of which he loses the sense of good and evil. Like the fatal fascination of the moth for fire, the five senses drag one to the apparent charms of the external world and binds one to the miseries of such attachments. Being irresistibly drawn to the pleasures of the world, one loses all moral and ethical values, and evil tendencies get the upper hand. But if the sensory stimulus is stilled and the mind is tuned to divinity, a person evolves higher and higher until he transcends animality and rationality, and manifests his inherent divinity. Yoga is also the science of mental discipline. Perfect control of the modifications of consciousness is the aim, which is attained in different degrees through various forms of *samadhi*. The *samadhi* stage is the culmination of *dhyana* (meditation), when the whole mind is transformed into the higher state of the Divine.

Ancient Yoga

The spiritual discipline of yoga is very old and is still one of the main forms of *sadhana*. It is an independent spiritual discipline and is competent to achieve the highest good by itself.

Many sects rely entirely on yoga. However, it is not a sectarian discipline, but a universal one and is adopted to some extent by all sects. Its chief merit is that it is practical and free from all dogmas and presuppositions. It, therefore, does not conflict with any sect or religion.

Kriya Yoga includes techniques that are entirely scientific, every step being based upon experimental realization. Yoga and science are inseparable, just as religion and science are necessary complements. The scientist sets the task of controlling the physical forces, whereas the yogi is concerned with the mental forces. A scientist is an unconscious yogi whose mind works in external grooves. The yoga philosophy is one of the six orthodox Hindu philosophies; it is unlike the innumerable other philosophies of the world, because it is an entirely practical philosophy. It is an exact science based on immutable laws of nature.

Experience is the basis of all knowledge. The scientist experiments and arrives at conclusions that are easily accepted, because they agree with the experience of others. The conclusions of the scientist are based upon the universal experience of humanity. The science of Kriya Yoga places before humanity a practical and experimental technique that enables us to verify the truths propounded in the scriptures. Concentration and meditation, which are gained through the practice of Kriya Yoga, provide the techniques to realize the Truth.

Kriya Yoga is the most scientific technique to save humanity from misfortune and ultimate destruction. It is the essence of all the schools of yoga, though it is not similar to any of them. The procedures of the ancient *rishis* (sages) were extremely difficult and although they led to the realization of Brahman, they made yoga exclusive. The ancient yogis practiced fasting and other forms of penance that included many painful physical postures and exercises practiced for hours together. By long retention of breath and closure of the nasal passage, pain was usually felt in the heart and lungs. They renounced family ties and tried to realize God in seclusion. Thus, householders were automatically excluded from spiritual practice. Unlike these disciplines, Kriya Yoga is easy to practice and does not produce any discomfort. It can be practiced by people of all walks of life, irrespective of age.

Different Kinds of Yoga

The word yoga is derived from the Sanskrit root *yuj*, which means to join. The science of Kriya Yoga teaches the method of merging the individual will with the cosmic will by controlling the mind and its modifications, thereby attaining liberation. On the physical plane, yoga bestows good health and physical efficiency; on the mental plane concentration, balance of mind, and peace. On the spiritual plane, it guarantees liberation from the chain of birth and death, and offers eternal bliss, immortality, perfection, and everlasting peace. The ultimate objective of yoga is not only individual liberation, but the transformation of the entire human race. It aims to instill a divine nature and life into the physical, mental, and spiritual life of humanity. Yoga has several branches: Raja Yoga, Hatha Yoga, Mantra Yoga, Laya Yoga, Dhyana Yoga, and many others. Kriya Yoga is the essence of all yogas.

Hatha Yoga is preliminary to Raja Yoga and deals with the control of the body by *pranayama, asanas, bandhas,* and *mudras*. *Hatha* is composed of two syllables, *ha* and *tha*, which mean union of the sun and moon, or *prana* and *apana vayus*. Hatha Yoga is inseparable from Raja Yoga, which relates to the control of the mind. The various yogis begin *sadhana* on different planes: the Hatha yogi on the physical, the Raja yogi on the mental, and the Jñana yogi on the intellectual.

The system of Hatha Yoga includes a number of physical exercises that aim at rendering the body fit for meditation. By these exercises, the body is tuned so that it absorbs a greater quantity of cosmic energy. Kriya Yoga incorporates the most effective technique of Hatha Yoga, known as *mahamudra*. This technique disciplines the body and helps in rousing the untapped spiritual energy and uniting the soul and the spirit. Kriya Yoga accepts only the essence of Hatha Yoga and avoids all exercises that are exclusively physical.

Rising to a higher plane we come to Raja Yoga, which aims at the control and purification of the mind and the stilling of all thought waves or mental modifications, thereby making the mind fit for concentration and meditation. The science of Raja Yoga, as formulated by Sage Patañjali, the foremost exponent of yoga, is also known as Ashtanga Yoga or the yoga with eight limbs. The eight stages are *yama* (self-control), *niyama* (religious observances), *asana* (physical postures), *pranayama* (control of breath), *pratyahara* (withdrawal of the senses), *dharana* (concentration), *dhyana* (meditation), and *samadhi* (wisdom state).

Yama is related to morality and constitutes non-injury, truthfulness, non-covetousness, and continence in thought, word, and deed. *Niyama* comprises purity (internal and external), contentment, austerity, study of scriptures, and surrender to God. Observance of *yama* and *niyama* will bestow peace of mind and detachment, as well as compassion for all creatures. Successful completion of all the stages will lead to *nirvikalpa samadhi*, which, when constantly practiced, leads to liberation.

Raja Yoga has been called the royal road. Its technique is the best and most inclusive. The main technique of this science is *pranayama*, the control of the sum total of cosmic power. Kriya Yoga adopts this technique, as it is the easiest and most scientific. Kriya Yoga has taken the essence of Raja Yoga and has avoided all the lengthy methods.

The eight-fold path formulated by Sage Patañjali is the method that yogis can follow, basing their spiritual attainment on the rock foundation of *yama* and *niyama*. Many religious people are content to simply follow these rules, thinking that this is the whole of spirituality. But the practice of *yama* and *niyama* gives only inner satisfaction and some good karma; it does not lead to freedom. Only when *nirvikalpa samadhi* is attained has the goal been realized and the yogi can do away with the process of *yama-niyama*. Having reached the goal, the path becomes superfluous.

After *yama-niyama*, one has to master *asana* or correct physical postures. By the mastery of *asana* one rises above the physical consciousness and enters the mind. A person ceases to identify with the mortal frame and evolves higher. Correct posture means a body free from restlessness and an erect spine enables consciousness to flow from the lower centers to the higher and finally into the brain.

Self-control, mental and physical calmness, are achieved by the practice of *yama, niyama*, and *asana*. The seeker can sit in the posture for hours. By *pranayama* he is able to control the heartbeat and pulse, as well as the life force and the mind. By *pratyahara* he withdraws the mind from the physical world and his sense organs. This is the beginning of the real practice of Kriya Yoga. The practice of *dharana* enables him to concentrate the withdrawn mind upon one point. In *dhyana* this concentration becomes unbroken and he intuitively gains a conception of God. Ultimately, complete union with God is achieved in *samadhi*.

In ancient times, the saints of India practiced Ashtanga Yoga and by the mastery of the eight steps freed themselves from illusion, delusion, and error, thereby realizing the Truth. They realized the truth propounded in the Bhagavad Gita (2:48), "Yoga is balance of mind." This yoga was a technique of Self-realization, the practice of which brought bliss. Just as the essence of milk is separated and floats to the surface by the addition of lime juice, similarly, the practice of this technique enables one to transcend the world while living in it and achieve oneness with God.

The essence of the yogic techniques was resurrected and spread in all countries under the name of Kriya Yoga. Kriya Yoga is a developed form of the technique described by Sage Patañjali in his treatise on yoga. It is based on physiology, psychology, astrology, philosophy, and the direct experience of realized masters. The body is like a plot of land and Kriya Yoga cultivates this land for the development of the body, mind, and soul. If learned from an accomplished master and practiced regularly, a person gains control over the mind, heart, and soul. This gradual process enables one to reach the heights of Self-realization and attain infinite bliss.

Karma Yoga means the practice of detachment in all actions. Unselfishness produces detachment and indifference to the results of actions. It is the main teaching of the Gita. Karma Yoga means union with God through selfless actions. Human life is very precious and its goal is Self-realization. For the person of action, Karma Yoga shows how to perform actions so that Self-realization can be attained. Every act is spiritual, if the motive is pure. Work is worship. Service to humanity without egoism or expectation of any return is Karma Yoga. Kriya Yoga aids in the development of this attitude. By the practice of Kriya, a person gains divine experience and perceives that, though he is acting, God is the sole doer. Thus, Kriya Yoga includes the essence of Karma Yoga and can, therefore, be practiced every moment of the day, during all activities. The process of respiration is the life of a human being. By being conscious of this process, the yogi will perceive that all activities on the gross plane are the manifestation of that subtle action of *prana*. When by detached actions the mind is purified, true knowledge is realized through it. Therefore, the mind has to be purified at all costs. The Gita teaches that one who has purified the mind by the practice of Karma Yoga gains direct knowledge of the Self, which leads to liberation. All actions transform ultimately into knowledge.

Jñana Yoga teaches that God is everywhere and in everything. It does not differentiate between the Self and God. When the Jñana yogi realizes the Truth, he feels that the universe is full of God above, below, and in between. He is in all beings and all beings are in Him. He is Brahman, the one spirit of the universe. It is the body that eats and drinks and experiences pleasures and pain. He is not the body; He is It. He is the witness in health and disease. He is existence, knowledge, and bliss. He is the essence of all knowledge. He is eternal and unchanging. By the practice of Kriya Yoga, one gets direct divine experience of light, sound, and vibration and becomes established in God consciousness.

Concentration is the means to all knowledge. It is difficult to say where concentration ends and meditation begins. Meditation follows concentration. Concentration is to fix the mind firmly on a point whereas meditation is to go beyond mind. Dhyana Yoga is the basis of all yogas. On the substructure of Kriya Yoga the superstructure of concentration, meditation, and *samadhi* are successfully built. The knowledge of the Self dawns with the attainment of *samadhi*. Only then real devotion to God follows.

Japa means the repetition of some mantra or a name of the Lord. Mantra Yoga is the union of the embodied soul with the deity by the chanting of the *bija mantra* (root sound) of the deity. These sounds produce vibrations in the physical and astral worlds. Laya Yoga is the complete absorption of the mind. There is a technique in Kriya Yoga that is the essence of Laya Yoga: the mind is absorbed in the divine *om* sound, which is the cosmic sound of vibration within.

There is also Japa Yoga in Kriya Yoga. By the practice of Kriya Yoga, we can switch off our physical sensations and automatically perceive the invisible stage. In that stage we hear divine sound. We want to unify our mantras by mentally chanting them while hearing the divine sound. Then we cease to chant the mantra mentally and the divine sound is transformed into the *ishta mantra*. After that — by the help of the calmness, even while remaining in the physical world — we can hear the sound of the mantra in the vacuum. In the Hindu scriptures, Japa Yoga is described as mentally chanting mantras; but this Kriya Yoga *japa* is higher, because we are able to hear the talk of God as the divine sound and remain absorbed in it.

Kriya Yoga

The difference between Kriya Yoga and other traditional yogic practices is similar to the difference between the prescription of a modern, qualified doctor and village quack. The meticulous austerities and painful processes associated with many traditional yogas are totally absent in Kriya Yoga technique. The scientific technique of Kriya Yoga is taught by my authorized *acharyas*. This spiritual practice taught by Lahiri Mahashaya is most suitable for householders. The simple and easy breath control prescribed in the Kriya technique restores lost equilibrium and paves the way for salvation. But its practice needs the guidance of a Self-realized guru. The pure oxygen breathed in this process purifies the inner mechanism of the body, activates the limbs, and increases the appetite. It gives strength and youth to the body and memory, patience, and brilliance to the mind. It purifies the body, mind, intellect, and life simultaneously. No dietary restrictions are needed for this process. Sincere practice of Kriya enables one to experience the touch sensation, sound, vibration, and light flash of the divinity inside one's own body and helps to elevate the mind into supramental consciousness. This is not

Japa Yoga, nor is there any strain in holding of the breath. This Kriya Yoga is a very simple yoga and the highway of common religions. It is the quickest means of success. It gives mathematical results. This Kriya Yoga is an easy, cheap, simple, and sure practice.

This technique can be practiced without any restrictions of caste, creed, age, or gender. Any boy or girl above thirteen years of age can practice; even a person of seventy-five will derive a good deal of benefit from it. This Kriya Yoga will enable one to develop a healthy brain, keen mind, and prompt understanding.

Kriya Yoga definitely brings the message of hope to the hopeless, joy to the joyless, strength to the weak, understanding to the dull headed, peace to the brokenhearted, energy and ability to the fatigued, and salvation to the spiritual seekers. If these benefits and divine powers are not achieved after practicing Kriya Yoga, then know for certain that it is not the real Kriya Yoga technique.

"Kriya Yoga" are Sanskrit words, a combination of two root words. One is *kriya* and the other is yoga. In the word *kriya* there are two syllables: *kri* and *ya. Kri* means to pursue your work in daily life and *ya* means to be ever aware of the invisible God who is abiding in you and is directing and accomplishing work through you. Thus, the word *kriya* signifies that you lead your daily life as directed from your brain and at the same time, watch the invisible God who inspires your brain to direct. Without the invisible Being, your brain cannot function. A dead person cannot think because the invisible soul is not there. So it is necessary to remember that each and every thought comes from the invisible Self within. If you perceive that the indwelling Self is the sole doer in you, that He Himself is functioning in the body, then Self-realization is attained.

The second word, "yoga," literally means union of the visible body with the invisible body. This union is always present in everyone. No one can separate the invisible body from the visible body. The invisible body means the living soul who sees through the eyes, hears through the ears, smells and inhales through the nose, talks through the mouth, walks with the legs, and does all the actions through the body. The invisible body is the most important, for it controls volition. Yet, without the visible body, the invisible body cannot function nor operate in the material world.

Here the question arises: if the invisible body — the living God — is always within us, why do we not perceive this living presence of God in all actions? The answer is that the invisible body is lying hidden in the jungle of matter. With the Kriya Yoga technique we can cut through this jungle and cultivate the wasteland that is remaining in the spinal column. Then the dormant spiritual energy, *kundalini*, awakens and we realize the eternal presence of the living, yet invisible, God who is functioning through all our actions.

The invisible body, by its extroverted nature, deludes us into a material consciousness that is composed of the sensations received through the five sense telephones (eyes, ears, nose, skin, and tongue) and also through the mind, intellect, and self-centered thought. These are our enemies. They are continually pulling us down into the quicksand of delusion, illusion, and error. The result is that we cannot perceive that God is within us. But, if we cultivate superconsciousness and awareness of the inner Self through the proper Kriya Yoga technique, we will know that the visible body is only a projection of the invisible body.

Normally, human beings do not believe in God. Even if they do believe, they are still often filled with doubts. They remain engrossed in the material world. It is practically impossible to make them finally believe that God is animating their entire being by abiding within them.

When you go to a movie, the first thing you see is the light on the screen and then the picture in this light. You become amused and absorbed with the picture, although the story told in that movie is not real. But you do not see the operator who is in the projection room. Similarly, we are all engrossed with this mundane cinema of real life. We do not realize the presence of the living operator who is always present on the top of our head. He is the real, invisible God in every human being.

Concentration and the Sublimation of Life Force

The mind is always restless and leads us into illusion, delusion, and error. If you can introvert the five sense telephones with the help of Kriya Yoga, you can remain in the pinpointed state of concentration. With the mind, intellect, and thought under control, superconsciousness and cosmic consciousness can be attained.

This Kriya is based only on natural inhalation. There is no painful holding of breath or plugging of the nose. A Kriya yogi does not have to practice the various *asanas* or physical exercises. Normally, every person takes eighteen natural inhalations in a minute. During the sexual act the pace of respiration is accelerated and increases from twenty-four to thirty inhalations per minute. The heart also beats faster. During the time of anger the breathing is even faster. One breathes thirty to forty times per minute or even more, which is dangerous. A heart failure can be the consequence of extremely violent fits of anger. It is said that an elephant breathes only ten times a minute and so lives a long life. Crocodiles and tortoises take four inhalations a minute, and it is said that they live for more than a century. Through this Kriya Yoga we can increase not only our life span but also preserve sound health and an alert mind. During sleep we breath only ten to twelve times per minute, and the result is complete rest of the body and mind. That is because we completely forget our sense of the body and receive calmness. A sleeping person is almost a yogi; there is no body consciousness, but there is also no divine consciousness. If a person practices Kriya yogic breathing — deep, slow, and relaxed as in sleep — then surely he will get mental calmness. He will then enter into the center and will perceive divinity within.

When practicing Kriya, we take deep inhalation and sufficient oxygen goes into the lungs, heart, and brain. Oxygen is the nutrition of the brain and, therefore, increases mental excellence, prompt understanding, ready wit, and quick receptivity.

The oxygen purifies the impure blood and the purified blood carries hemoglobin to the whole system. In every human being there are more than 72 billion vessels and fine tissues. This hemoglobin constantly passes through the blood vessels. The blood contains numerous chemicals: potassium, sodium, magnesium, zinc, phosphorous, copper, sulphur, and more. These chemicals are passing through the whole body in solution. The word globin means protein in solution. Albumin, globulin, and fibrinogen are the three proteins running through the blood vessels keeping the body healthy and lustrous.

The Kriya Yoga technique is the combination of the three principal yogas: *kaṛma, jñana,* and *bhakti.* Bhakti Yoga means the yoga of divine love. After prayer or worship, devotion or meditation, if a person does not feel divine love, then there has not been real prayer or meditation. It is, of course, difficult to gain divine love. But, through the guidance of a realized master or guru and through the practice of the Kriya technique, one can acquire *bhakti.* If a person has poor appetite, he should visit a doctor, get a prescription and use the medicine in order to increase the appetite. But, if the patient only reads the prescription, memorizes it and recites it loudly — no matter if he recites it a thousand times — he will not gain any benefit. One cannot achieve God-realization by only reading lessons or religious books and going to churches, temples, and mosques. The sick person has to follow the doctor's advice, purchase the medicine and take the medicine according to the doctor's instructions; then surely he will be cured. Similarly, if you follow the spiritual guide 100%, then surely you will get extreme calmness, which is godliness. Through this calmness you can reach God at the cross inside the brain where the light of God and the light of Christ consciousness are always shining. So you require seclusion, because seclusion is the price of greatness. If, without distraction, you follow the advice of a realized Kriya yogi, then you can reach God very quickly. This Kriya Yoga technique is the quickest means of success. It will lead to the acquisition of balance of mind, amity, and love. Through this you can always remain in the third circuit (i.e., inside the cranium above the pituitary), which is the Kingdom of God. The longer you remain there, the more you will hear a constant divine sound and feel a constant touch sensation of God and visualize an effulgent divine light that altogether will lead you to a blissful sojourn in the Kingdom of Heaven.

In darkness you cannot walk properly on the road. However, if you carry a light in your hand, you can go everywhere without difficulty. In the same way, when you perceive constantly the divine light in your body, you can constantly feel cosmic consciousness in you. When the battery of a motorcar goes down, you take the battery for recharging; then afterwards you can again drive the car even in the darkest night on a serpentine road. So, every morning if you charge the used-up battery of your system through the practice of Kriya Yoga, then throughout the day you will experience the presence of God within and feel that His power is guiding you in every action.

All religious organizations teach how to attain salvation. One says to pray jointly and loudly, while another says to offer flowers and fruits at the altar and chant mantras and hymns so that one can perceive God. Others say that only by chanting the names of Rama, Krishna, and Shiva will you be realized. But the Kriya Yoga system (as taught by Lahiri Mahashaya, Shriyukteshwarji, and Paramahamsa Yoganandaji in India) aims not only at salvation or Self-realization, it also secures simultaneous development of body, mind, intellect, and soul.

This is the scientific age and educated people do not accept fanatic ideas, orthodox views, dogmatic moods, blind faith, or religious play. They possess the yearning for God-realization, but they do not like to attach the wheels of a bullock cart to a motor car. Comparably, the pattern of religion practiced during previous centuries cannot be satisfactory to the temperament of the modern times. Science aims at the acquisition of supreme knowledge and ultimately, cosmic consciousness. The Kriya Yoga technique is a scientific technique. Through deep and steady inhalation, you feel God in the pituitary gland and fontanel. If you keep pinpointed attention there, you will feel heaviness, which is the touch sensation of God on the top of your head. It is said to be like a cash payment; each inhalation gives you the immediate sense of creeping heaviness on the top of your head. Also, by the intake of more oxygen with deep inhalation, you will get physical, mental, and spiritual development.

It is necessary to withdraw the senses from the body and, thus, get God consciousness, cosmic consciousness. So, if you pray loudly in the mosque, temple or church, your attention will remain tied to the words of the prayer or to the rhythm of the chant, and you will not be able to withdraw your senses from the material world. But Kriya is such a powerful technique that any person irrespective of caste, creed, or color can practice it and will immediately obtain extreme calmness. The aim of every religion is to get calmness and go into the center of the sensorium. With the Kriya Yoga technique, we can be peaceful, remain in the center, and realize the Self.

Many people like to have their horoscopes read by an astrologer. It is a frailty of human nature to seek to know the future. Kriya Yoga will enable us to become free from the bad influences of stars and planets that are located in the six spinal centers. In ascending order, the centers from the coccygeal to the medulla oblongata are called the summer solstice of six months; in descending order, from the medulla oblongata to the coccygeal is the winter solstice representing the other six months of the year. In these six plexuses the signs of the zodiac with the nine planets and twenty-seven stars are located. By practicing Kriya Yoga and praying devotedly to God to go up and come down the spine using inhalation and exhalation, He will destroy the bad effects of stars and planets. Divine grace will certainly exercise influence over the six centers and make us free from troubles and will give integral advancement. (Diagram 3; page 92)

The inherent nature of the mind is restlessness. To master the mind, deep inhalation is required. So, when we practice Kriya Yoga, within a short time automatically we will feel that the mind is transformed into cosmic consciousness. Then we experience superhuman perception, and be ultimately transported to the divine plane. If a person does not strive for salvation or Self-realization, he will be confronted with various troubles, worries, anxieties, pitfalls, and shortcomings. These dangers and difficulties will turn the mind towards God. But by prayer alone, one cannot reach God very quickly. Self-realization is the ultimate goal of every human being. So, if a person practices this scientific technique regularly and sincerely, he can surely attain the God-realization that is Self-realization.

Do not wait for tomorrow. The immediate present is the time to earn God, that is, to realize that God is abiding within you and everywhere around you. You should feel that God is inhaling through your nose and that is why you are alive. Inhalation is the living God in every human being, because once this breathing stops life ends. This breath is God. We are indebted to God, who is always inhaling through us, keeping us alive, and giving us the opportunity to realize Him. No one knows when death will come. So, it is wise to practice Kriya Yoga and learn to keep constant attention on the natural inhalation, which is God Himself. To maintain this constant attention, one must meditate, meditate, and meditate.

The Kriya Yoga technique enables one to watch God through every action. The more you practice, the more you will feel that God is inspiring you to do the work. Then you will be able to watch God all the time. Kriya Yoga enables one to be calmly active and actively calm. If you can think of God in your everyday action, then you can remain in a state of perpetual Self-realization and be filled with eternal joy. By Kriya Yoga you can establish yourself forever in the Infinite and you can feel God before, during, and after every action.

Kriya is derived from the root *kri,* which means "to do." We are to do our duty and perform all necessary actions. *Ya* signifies the doer, who is the invisible, subtle power in us. In every action, in every disposition, we are to realize this power. Whatever a person does, whatever he thinks, this power is the basis. The scriptures say that the union of the embodied soul with the Self is yoga. The individual is united with the all-pervading cosmic power. This is the divine power and the union is always present. If there is no union, it means death. But being engrossed in illusion, delusion, and error, one does not perceive this union. By the practice of Kriya Yoga one will perceive it and become free while living in the body, a *jivanmukta* (one who is free from the cycle of birth and death).

Kriya Yoga is a scientific technique that closely follows the method of Sage Patañjali. There is no need to abandon family life and go to the forest, nor is there any need to change one's eating habits. Also, there are no physical sufferings to be undergone. Most people labor under misconceptions that yoga means physical feats, control of breath, and so on. But yoga, particularly Kriya Yoga, is different. There are various phases of Kriya Yoga. In the first phase, the restless and unstable mind becomes calm and directs itself to the Divine.

By the practice of Kriya Yoga we attain a new goal of happiness, awakening, and Self-realization that enables us to live according to the highest existence. One will feel the presence of God and perceive Him in every object, every thought, and every feeling. By achieving his own Self-realization, one will understand that Kriya Yoga is the best that India has given; it offers the most scientific and easy technique of liberation.

A rusty wire is charged when connected with electric current. Similarly, if the extrovert human mind is charged with wisdom, science, and super wisdom, then ignorance vanishes within a second and life is illumined with divine light. The scientific means of transforming the physical consciousness into divine consciousness is called Kriya Yoga.

In order to know Brahman, one has to become Brahman. The scriptures say that one has to become God in order to worship God. Only by transcending human limitations and becoming established in the Divine, is realization possible. Just as one has to change the station of a radio to hear something different, one has to switch over to divine consciousness from human consciousness. Unless the outgoing and extrovert nature of the mind is controlled and is withdrawn into itself, concentration for Self-realization is not possible. Then will come the realization of the omnipresence of God and, ultimately, fulfillment of life. Then one will realize the Truth taught in the Bhagavad Gita, Upanishads, and other scriptures. It is for this that one has to practice a technique that will provide constant divine consciousness.

One Cycle of Kriya
Completes a Solar Year of Spiritual Evolution

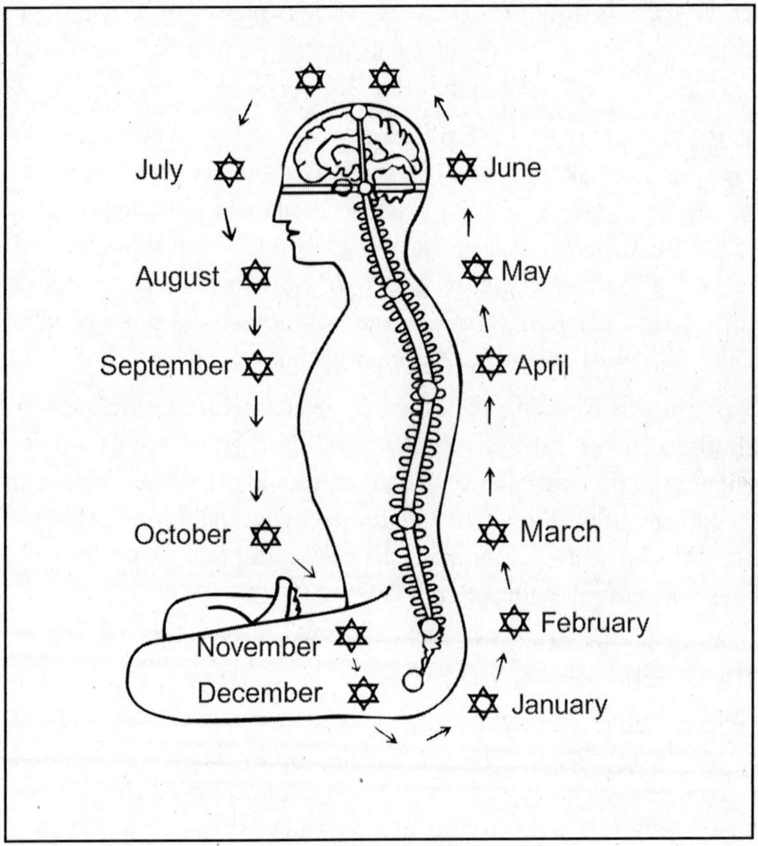

DIAGRAM 3 - One cycle of Kriya completes a solar year of spiritual evolution. When the inner sound, light, or vibration is circulated in a microcosmic orbit up the spine and down to the front of the body, this concentrated divine force acts like an internal sun that enables the Kriya meditator to complete an entire year's karma.

One Cycle of Kriya
Includes the Different Phases of Each Lunar Month

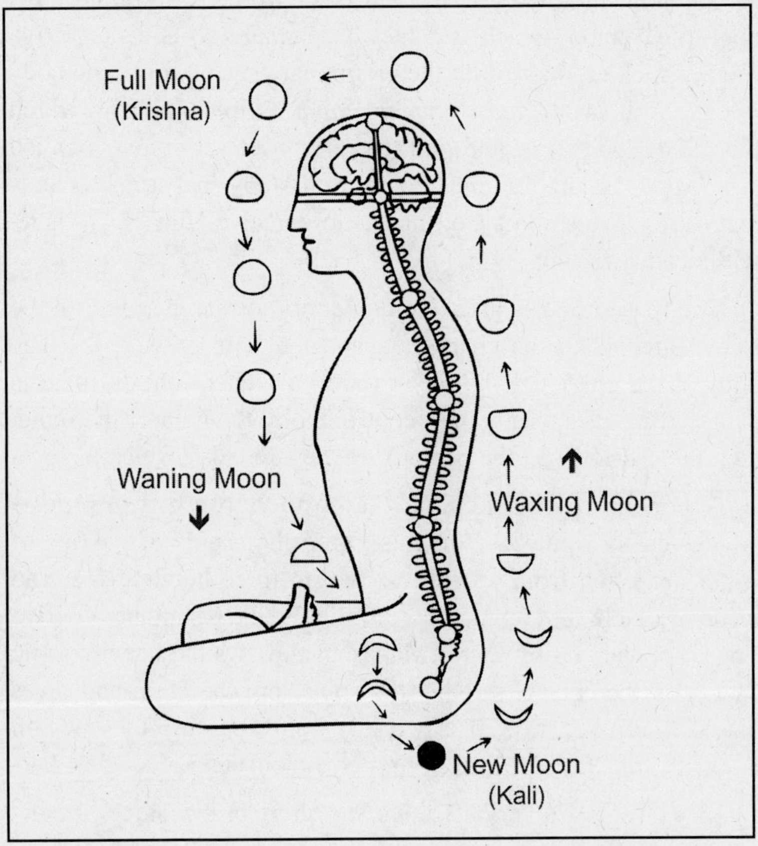

DIAGRAM 4 - One cycle of Kriya includes the different phases of each lunar month. The moon cycle represents the changing desires of the human mind. Kriya Yoga balances desire for money, sex, love, or food by drawing their elemental essence up the spine into the crown and back down into the coccyx. Kali, the dark goddess of the 15th or new moon, symbolizes shakti power coiled at the base of the spine. Kala is time, i.e. soul (Isha) who has mastered time and, therefore, death. Krishna symbolizes the full light of soul consciousness.

In his Yoga Aphorisms (Sadhana Pada, 1), Sage Patañjali says, *tapaḥ svādhyāya iśvarapraṇidhānāni kriyāyogaḥ*: which means "Mortification, study, and surrendering the fruits of work to God are called Kriya Yoga." In other words, working towards yoga (i.e., union, which is achieved in *samadhi*) is called Kriya Yoga, which consists of all the preliminaries. Control of the body is called physical *tapas*, but real *tapas* is inhalation by which the mental wave is controlled. Repetition of scriptures is called *svadhyaya,* but its real meaning is Self-study that leads to Self-realization. Worship of God means to perceive Him everywhere, within and without.

The sense organs can be compared to horses, the mind to the reins, intellect to the charioteer, and the Self to the rider. The body is the chariot. If the horses are not under control, there is danger. But, if the senses are controlled by the help of the mind, then the chariot (i.e., the person) reaches the goal, which is yoga.

A person bores a hole in the earth into which a pipe is connected to a pump. With this pump thousands of gallons of water are lifted from a depth of two to three hundred feet and made available for common use. Similarly, the technique of Kriya Yoga, popularized by Lahiri Mahashaya, draws the latent cosmic energy in the coccyx through the spine into the brain and gives one divine realization. The worldly consciousness of a person is easily transformed into divine consciousness.

Kriya Yoga is a very effective and shortcut technique of Self-realization. This is the best highway to the spiritual kingdom, the grand road for Self-realization. By the practice of Kriya Yoga, a person transcends human consciousness and reaches the divine abode at rocket speed. Living in the world amidst all worldly activity, the practitioner realizes the omnipresent divine existence with the help of divine consciousness and light.

It is not through the study of the scriptures, but through spiritual practice under the direct guidance of a guru that one realizes the Self. Kriya Yoga greatly reduces the time required for emancipation and makes it possible in one birth. It also purifies the blood and keeps the body healthy. Just as light dispels darkness, similarly, by the practice of Kriya Yoga, ignorance disappears and the light of wisdom shines. With the attainment of wisdom, one goes to the next stage (i.e., union with Brahman). At this stage divine blessing flows and the divine play (i.e., *lila*) is revealed.

The knower of the Self becomes the Self, the knower of Brahman becomes Brahman. By the realization of the Self, all divine qualities are attained and the manifestations of God are known. As piece of wood coming into contact with fire acquires its qualities, likewise, by union with Brahman the aspirant acquires the qualities and power of Brahman, going beyond which he attains supreme bliss. Material powers are nothing compared to this divine realization. Compared to the science of Self-realization, all other sciences are like helpless, ignorant infants.

Like the truth of the research of physical sciences, the beneficial results of Kriya Yoga can be tried and proven in everyday life. Its results can be directly experienced and verified. Just as a person gets a shock by touching a live electric wire, so also, one can experience within oneself divine light, divine sound, and divine vibration by the practice of Kriya Yoga. Such direct and immediate experience deepens love for God; His existence within and all around is felt. Constant meditation brings about the fulfillment of the mission of human life.

The practice of Kriya Yoga is based upon scientific principles and is dependent upon inhalation and exhalation, resulting in concrete supramental development. The essence of Vedanta teaching can be realized through the practice of Kriya Yoga. The main objective of all the yogas and *sadhanas* is to make the practitioner introvert and the Kriya Yoga technique helps in the quickening of this process.

Through other techniques of yoga *sadhana*, the rousing of the untapped spiritual energy (*kundalini shakti*) and the achievement of a balanced yogic mind is not easy. But in Kriya Yoga this becomes possible within a very short period, allowing the *sadhaka* to maintain a divine state of mind. When the *kundalini shakti* is awakened, the devotee gains some extraordinary tangible perception — the vision of divine light, hearing of cosmic sound, and the experience of divine vibration in the whole spine and cerebral region. Through the guide or guru, the aspirant of Kriya Yoga acquires such experience at the initial stage of practice.

The Kriya Yoga technique is highly effective and mathematical in its results. The spinal cord is the vital organ of human physiology. The spinal channel, known as *sushumna,* plays a vital role in the practice of Kriya Yoga. The spinal cord is the divine passage through which the *kundalini shakti* moves upwards to reach the divine cave in the fontanel. The divine current, which moves upwards and downwards through the *sushumna* from the coccygeal center to the fontanel, creates a divine magnetic field inside the whole spine and absorbs all the external and extrovert propensities, replacing them with divine calmness. We have in us two types of forces: centrifugal and centripetal. The centrifugal forces, which draw us always to external objects, are controlled and made introvert and lead to the stage of *samadhi* (the stage of cosmic consciousness).

However extroverted a person may be, Kriya Yoga will turn his external forces inside and make his path of *sadhana* very easy and successful. Even in the midst of worldly worries and troubles, one can realize God like Shyamacharan Lahiri, the father of Kriya Yoga in modern times, and experience freedom from all worldly attachment.

There is no other food restriction except that one should not indulge in taking liquor or any intoxicating drug that is harmful to the nervous system and health. There is an effective physical posture practiced in Kriya that has direct control over the digestive system and helps in easy assimilation of food. (Diagram 12; page 178)

By the practice of Kriya Yoga, inner and outer purification naturally occurs. Whoever is God conscious is always pure. God is abiding in every human being. If we search for Him within our whole system, our mind cannot be attracted to external pomp and grandeur.

There is a very important part of the Kriya Yoga technique that gives all-around development to the one who practices it. This precious technique, when practiced correctly, gives necessary stimulation to the principal glands important for physical health. With the practice of this technique one gets pressure on the liver, which increases the digestive secretions in the system; food is digested quickly and constipation is banished. By putting pressure on the adrenal glands, one gets salts that give strength to the heart and cures gastric troubles. The pressure on the pancreas sends insulin into the system and diabetes is avoided. By this technique, duodenal troubles also disappear. This technique gives pressure on the kidneys, which prevents urinary problems. With its practice, one gets sufficient pressure on ascending, descending, transverse, sigmoid colons, and the rectum is massaged. Also, the sex organs receive pressure, which prevents impotency. The testicles secrete several hormones. These hormones affect the meninges that lie just below the skull and vertebral column and can give man energy and agility. These hormones also make man strong, brave, hardy, enduring, and make the semen vigorous and healthy by which a man can have healthy children.

The thyroid is a master regulating gland. It, too, receives massage with this technique. In consequence, the thyroid gland functions normally and that in turn prevents serious diseases. The pituitary gland is the master gland of all glands in the human body. When it is attuned, the secretions of the other endocrine glands become perfectly balanced and regulated. Kriya Yoga practice balances secretions from all glands.

Endocrine glands are found in the womb of the female, the ovaries. By the practice of the Kriya Yoga technique a woman puts pressure on these glands, which produce two types of secretions: estrogen and progesterone. Estrogen gives luster, beauty, and youthfulness to the woman. Retarded physical growth and lack of breast development can be cured with the help of this hormone. The hormone progesterone helps the woman in her pregnancy and lubricates the whole system during the conception of the child.

While practicing this technique one has to bend the head and body, which gives circulation to the fine tissues of cerebrum and cerebellum. Circulation is increased in the whole nervous system, including the entire spinal cord and various plexuses, which gives subtle inner perception and God-realization. There are three channels inside the spinal cord, named in the Sanskrit *shastras* as *ida, pingala,* and *sushumna.* By the practice of this precious technique, *ida* and *pingala* separate themselves from *sushumna* and the passage in *sushumna* is clearly opened. This is said to be the awakening of the *kundalini shakti.* This spinal channel is the royal road through which the indwelling Self, God, is constantly functioning in the human being, going up and coming down the spine and giving various dispositions and inspirations. We can say that our soul is hidden in the jungle of matter and with the Kriya Yoga technique we can free the soul from bondage. We can then cultivate the fallow land in the *sushumna* by Kriya breathing and continually live in cosmic consciousness. If a person does not practice the technique of Kriya Yoga, the master gland, the pituitary is not stimulated sufficiently. Taking hormonal injections will not secure God-realization. But the regular practice of this technique will automatically take us to the third circuit in the brain wherein lies the pituitary, which is the real abode of God.

In our physical body there are three knots or *granthis.* The first knot is called *brahma granthi,* which is between the coccygeal and navel centers. Unless this knot is opened, one cannot realize the Truth, the realization of the living God abiding in one's own body. Since human consciousness is in the *brahma* knot, it remains completely absorbed in material and sensual desires.

The second knot is called *vishnu granthi,* which starts from the navel center to below the pituitary. There the five sense telephones are always busy with the external world and the mind is not able to achieve God-realization.

The third knot, *rudra granthi,* remains between the pituitary and fontanel. If a true seeker with sincere desire withdraws the senses from the coccygeal center and remains concentrated above the pituitary, then surely he will perceive that God is dwelling in the cranium. At that stage he will get constant God-realization. In every activity he will feel that God is the only doer. Then he will constantly think of Him. No matter where the compass of his actions turns the needle, the concentrated subconscious attention will always point to north, the presence of God on the top of the head.

The next important part of the technique is called Kriya proper. As already explained: God is constantly going up and coming down the spinal cord, destroying the bad influences of the planets and stars inside the spinal canal. A rusty wire has no power; but if you plug this rusty wire into the electric socket, then immediately you will see it electrified and alive with powerful energy. Similarly, by magnetizing your spine through Kriya, you can change your life force into all accomplishing, radiant divine force that in turn hastens physical and mental evolution. You will also constantly realize the living God abiding within you. The ladder of the spine is the only way to true ascension and upliftment to God consciousness.

"What the mind cannot comprehend, but what constitutes the mind, know that alone to be God. What speech cannot reveal, but what reveals the speech, know that alone to be God" (Kena Upanishad 1:6). So, the Kriya Yoga technique can lead us beyond gross sense perceptions and can give us extreme peace and calmness, which is godliness. The more one practices this technique faithfully, regularly, and sincerely, the more one will experience *savikalpa samadhi* (superconscious stage) and *nirvikalpa samadhi* (the cosmic conscious or pulseless stage).

There are six stages of Kriya technique through which a *kriyavan* can control the different centers and get Self-realization. These should be learned from a realized yogi and practiced under his direct guidance and supervision. After completion of these six steps, cosmic consciousness will automatically dawn. Then your life will be full of bliss and the goal, which is the achievement of the Supreme Reality, is attained.

By first Kriya you can convert your mind into consciousness and get calmness and the triple divine qualities of light, sound, and blissful vibration. Also, the devotee gets sound health, sound mind, and the intellect is transformed into knowledge. By the help of first Kriya, the *kundalini shakti* comes up from the coccygeal center to the pituitary and above. You can practically feel that some divine current and divine light are coming up and going down the spine. When a person practices meditation and the mind, intellect, thought, and ego do not remain in him, then he hears the divine sound, the invisible talk of God. Through practice, he hears this sound continually. This is called *anahata dhvani* (non-stopping sound). In first Kriya the meditator can get *subhechha samadhi. Subhechha* means divine desire for soul culture. This arises in first Kriya when the meditator gets supersensation in the body and great calmness.

By practicing second Kriya, you can perceive the triple divine qualities in each center. Gradually, that power comes up the spine and in each center there are different types of divine sound. You also get dazzling flashes of light, vibration, and the twelve types of divine sound coming from the high heaven, the vacuum, filling the whole brain. It is a great gain for the Kriya practitioner when second Kriya is completed. Whenever he is in practical life and doing any work, then he can feel the soul is functioning in that particular center. Immediately, he can feel that, when any disposition is coming in any center, it is coming from God. But when evil propensities are coming in a particular center, he can remove these propensities. The *samadhi* of second Kriya is called *vicharani samadhi.* This means that cosmic consciousness is roaming from one center to another.

The practice of third Kriya is inside the cranium, in the third circuit. The cranium is the divine kingdom. By the practice of third Kriya the meditator can remain free of the worldly sense. During meditation the only perception is of the triple divine qualities rotating inside the cranium. It feels as if the soul is separated from the body and is floating in the vacuum. In this stage the devotee feels that the soul is all-pervading and is going up to the high heaven. While the disciple remains busy in worldly activities, he feels as if some super power is doing work through him; he remains detached. The *samadhi* of third Kriya is *tanu-manasa samadhi.* This means that the mind is not roaming in the biological sense, it is roaming only in the real philosophical sense and perceiving God consciousness.

By practicing fourth Kriya the disciple feels some special movement of the soul inside the forehead, pons, thalamus, hypothalamus, pineal gland, and in front of the pituitary. He feels that the light is rotating around from the high heaven to Earth. That is called *asamsakti samadhi*. That means that you are roaming in cosmic consciousness.

In fifth Kriya the devotee mostly feels divine sensation in the cerebellum. He gradually comes near to the pineal gland and tries his utmost to enter into it. This is called *sattapatti samadhi. Satta* means soul. *Apatti* means appearing. Soul is appearing and trying to enter into the pineal gland. That means he is almost near *nirvikalpa samadhi.* It is also called *padartha bhavini samadhi.* That means he is almost merging in wisdom. In this stage he has no sense of the universe. He feels that the door of God is almost open, but cannot yet enter.

Sixth Kriya is in the divine kingdom. The devotee gets constant God consciousness in worldly activity. He does everything, but always remains near the door of God. At any moment he can get *nirvikalpa samadhi.* This means that he is in the world and not in the world. When he gets this *nirvikalpa* stage, immediately he gets pulselessness. That is called *turiya samadhi,* which means to merge in God.

God has created human beings in His own image. So, we can know God only through Self-realization. But this is not possible in a state of mind full of waves of disquietude arising from the identification of the Self with the changing states of body and mind. This gives a distorted image of God, like the image of the sun on the unsteady surface of water.

According to the great Muslim mystic poet Santa Kabir, "God is the Breath of all breath." Breath or *prana,* is the life energy in us. The cosmic life force is the source of life of all living things and the cause of creation of all the stars and planets. Cosmic consciousness is also intimately linked with the individual consciousness. But this link becomes less and less intimate when we become more and more individualistic, selfish, and body bound.

As the life force in man moves outward, sensations and thoughts distort the calm image of the Self or soul. The presence of breath in a person is life and absence of it is death. Hence, the method that teaches us the process of Self-realization through the control of life force must be scientific and best of all. The Kriya Yoga method has proved to be most effective and teaches us to turn the life force inward. It takes us straight to the consciousness of the Self, the blissful God. The main thing in this process is to understand thoroughly the mystery of the life force that sustains the human body organism, causing it to vibrate with life and energy. Normally, the life force is conducted down from the medulla oblongata through the inner spinal centers to different physical regions and senses. The life energy at the base of the spine in the coccyx is known as *kundalini*. Through the Kriya process the current from the senses can be withdrawn and directed into the spinal passage. This will lead to the awakening of *kundalini*.

When *kundalini* is awakened, the current reverses its outward flow to the senses and flows inward towards the brain. Reverse action is also noticed in the different chakras or the physiological centers in the spine. The lotuses in the different chakras, with their varied number of petals that symbolize the amount of energy emitted by each center, start reverse action. The petals turn up towards the brain instead of dropping towards the coccyx. Thus, the yogi consciously directs this life current towards the infinite, or cosmic, life force.

During the dreamless sleep, the human mind is withdrawn from outer distractions and thoughts in the subconscious remain dormant. This is a negative state. Conscious withdrawal of the mind from outer distractions and body consciousness and the focusing of attention on a single object of thought results in a state of positive and real concentration. The power of the mind is like dissipated rays of light that illuminate when concentrated. Such concentration may be accomplished through the practice of Kriya Yoga.

Mind is the Lord of all passions, but breath is the controller of the mind. If breath is restless, one becomes consumed with lust, anger, greed, and loses the power of judgement and discrimination. If breath is properly controlled through the scientific process of yoga, realization is possible even during this lifetime.

The medulla oblongata is the seat of life energy in the human body. When, through the practice of yoga, we increase our power of perception, feeling, and intuition, we always feel divine light, sound, and touch sensation of superconsciousness and realize the truth — that this body is the shadow of God. The life current existing in the nervous system becomes purified and, consequently, the divine passage in the spinal channel is opened. The life energy from the coccygeal center passes to the medulla oblongata, pervading the cerebrum and cerebellum. As a result, all mental propensities reach the stage of equilibrium. Life becomes meaningful, filled with celestial bliss, and with direct perception of divine effulgence.

Every soul is destined to be perfect and every being in the end will attain the state of perfection. External influences and vibrations effect some amount of development in the whole universe, including the human mind and soul. As the life energy moves around its nucleus by the cosmic force, everything in the universe undergoes automatic evolution. The passing of cosmic current once around the spine will, similarly, give us the equivalent result of one year of solar evolution, if we consciously direct it in a scientific way. (Diagrams 3 & 4; pages 92 & 93)

One complete revolution of the Earth around the sun produces one year's effect upon a human being. This normal time of human revolution can be quickened by revolving the life force around the elliptical path of the spinal column and its six centers, upward from the coccyx to the pituitary and above, and downward from there to the coccyx. The soul is the central sun and the spine with its six centers makes twelve points corresponding to the twelve signs of the zodiac.

Kriya Yoga is a scientific technique. The practice of this yoga annihilates all the unusual and unreasonable elemental propensities ever present in the spiritual centers of human body. It awakens the *kundalini* and restores equilibrium. It enables one to dispel delusion and ignorance, and discover the divinity within one's own Self. Practice of Kriya Yoga simply opens an apparently sealed way to divinity that resides in the human body. Once this reality is discovered, all other outward mantras and worship become futile. The Kriya process quickens the realization of the formless in the form and frame of the body. Close personal contact with the guru makes this realization easier. The Earth moves around the sun in twelve months and absorbs sufficient energy to undergo necessary transformation. Similarly, spiritual consciousness equips one with required energy for spiritual change. The northern declination of the sun starts with vernal equinox and the southern declination with autumnal equinox. Each declination takes six months. In the human physiology there are six plexuses from the coccygeal up to the soul center or the divine cave. The awakened *kundalini* ascends and descends through the *sushumna* nerve, which is similar to the sun's northern and southern declination. In the human body the soul is the sun around which the *kundalini shakti* moves. In Kriya Yoga, this movement of *kundalini* once around *sushumna* is equal to one year of spiritual practice elsewhere.

Every night during sleep our attention remains unconsciously disconnected from the senses, providing rest and refreshment to body and mind. The rejuvenating effect of sleep can be accomplished consciously by regulated Kriya breathing, while the body is quiet in a meditation posture. Activity of mind, organs, and muscles is stilled without any loss of consciousness. By slowing down the functioning of the heart and preventing the outward dissipation of life currents through the sensory nerves, Kriya practice prolongs the life span.

During Kriya practice the breath does not actually circulate in the spine, but the increased life force derived from transmuted breath is mentally directed by visualization and willpower to circulate continuously up and down the spine. The magnetic pull of circulating current draws the bodily currents away from the sensory nerves and organs.

Oxygen is nutrition to our whole system. It creates new blood corpuscles and through them gives vitality, luster, beauty, good health, rejuvenation, and regeneration to the body. Through Kriya Yoga, oxygen changes into its basic constituents of atomic energy, which in turn transforms into subtle life energy. By continuous regulated breathing, as prescribed in the Kriya technique, the entire carbon-waste content of the body is burned away. When that is accomplished, there is no more dark, impure, poisonous blood to flow in the body and no impure blood is pumped into the lungs for purification. Hence, this gives rest to the heart and lungs.

The purpose of burning the carbon is to quiet the heart. The purpose of quieting the heart is to control the five sense telephones and direct the energy from them to the spine. The condition of sleep produces unconscious quietness and peace. The Kriya technique leads to an ever-increasing, ever-new joyous state of awareness culminating in breathlessness. Hindu yogis state that the spiritual potency of this current actually changes the atomic composition of the body cells.

Breathlessness is deathlessness. Many people erroneously believe that *pranayama,* or control of life force, is accomplished by control of breath. The opposite is true. Control of breath is a result of controlling the life force. Trying to control the life force by holding the breath in the lungs is unscientific and unpleasant. Holding the breath in the lungs for an uncomfortably long period causes harmful pressure on the heart, lungs, diaphragm, and arteries, and should, therefore, be strictly avoided.

The real meaning of *pranayama*, according to Sage Patañjali, is the gradual unforced cessation of breathing. Discontinuance of inhalation and exhalation can be brought about by Kriya Yoga, a form of *pranayama*. The blood is decarbonized and recharged with oxygen; the atoms of this extra oxygen are then transmuted into life current, rendering breathing unnecessary for a certain period. *Pranayama* results in breathlessness, which calms the heart and lungs, and increases longevity. In the breathless state the life force, which ordinarily depends on oxygen for its manifestation and perpetuation in the human body, is freed from its slavery to the breath or oxygen and moves toward spirit.

The Kriya technique is the scientific and mathematical way of changing the material body consciousness into cosmic consciousness. The correct practice of one Kriya is equivalent to one year's progressive evolution. Every inhalation and exhalation in a systematic and regulated way with the feeling of divine touch sensation and sound vibration completes one Kriya. In higher Kriyas, the evolution is cumulatively quickened by twelve years' progression. Thus, it is possible to attain the breathless and cosmic conscious stage in one or two Kriyas. The realized gurus who have mastered the higher technique of Kriya Yoga can easily attain this stage of cosmic consciousness. However, they rarely display it, keeping it reserved for their sincere devotees to infuse in them divine powers and confidence for their quicker evolution.

This quickening impulse cannot be derived from books. The soul can only receive such impulse from another soul and from nothing else. To quicken the spirit, the impulse must come from another soul. The person from whose soul such an impulse comes is called the guru (the teacher), and the person to whose soul the impulse is conveyed is called the student.

Kriya Yoga is the quickest means to success. The speciality of the Kriya Yoga technique is that it effects simultaneous development of body, mind, and soul in the shortest possible time. It is an easy, but vitalizing process. It is a spiritual omnibus with room enough for persons of all tastes and cultures. It is a living progressive spiritual path whose adaptability is the sign of its vitality. Not only in an individual life, but also in the life of the whole human race, the Kriya Yoga process will definitely play a very effective role in mitigating suffering and will work as a panacea for material, psychological, and spiritual problems.

IV

THE THEORY OF KRIYA YOGA

The 25 Elements of Every Human Body

Each human body is made of 24 natural elements *(prakriti)* plus one cosmic element, the soul or *purusha*. The 24 natural elements are:

- five organs of perception (*jñanendriyas*) — eye, ear, nose, tongue, and skin;
- five types of perception from the five sense telephones — sound, sight, smell, taste, and touch sensation;
- five organs of action (*karmendriyas*) — *vak* (talk), *pani* (hand), *pada* (leg), *payu* (rectum), and *upastha* (genitals);
- five subtle elements (*tattvas*) — *prithivi* (earth), *apas* (water), *agni* (fire), *vayu* (air), and *akasha* (ether or vacuum); and
- four inner instruments — *manas* (mind), *buddhi* (intellect), *ahamkara* (ego), and *chitta* (by which we perceive natural phenomena).

The aggregation of these 24 gross elements is called *prakriti*.

Kriya Yoga technique is such a powerful technique that, if you practice it for a short time, you can change the 24 gross elements from the physical (bodily sense) into the divine stage, which is called *paraprakriti* or *paravastha* (cosmic consciousness). In the yogic scriptures it is called *samprajñata samadhi*, which means consciousness about cosmic consciousness.

Along with the 24 gross elements, there is one *purusha*. *Purusha* is the power of God. He is the conductor of the life

The Placement of the Seed Syllables Within the Human Body

The Sanskrit language, from which all other languages have been derived, was formulated from the sounds of the 50 seed syllables.

All the seed syllables of the lotus petals are a manifestation and an aggregation of the seed syllable *Om*, which is the power of God.

हं	ham	क्षं	ksham
अः	ah	अं	ang
अं	aung	आं	aang
औं	oung	इं	ing
ओं	ong	ईं	iing
ऐं	aing	उं	ung
एं	eng	ऊं	uung
ॡं	llring	ऋं	ring
ऌं	lring	ॠं	rring
ठं	thong	कं	kong
टं	tong	खं	khong
ञं	neong	गं	gong
झं	jhong	घं	ghong
जं	jong	ङं	wong
छं	chhong	चं	chong
फं	phong	डं	dong
पं	pong	ढं	dhong
नं	nong	णं	nong
धं	dhong	तं	tong
दं	dong	थं	thong
लं	long	बं	bong
रं	rong	भं	bhong
यं	yong	मं	mong
सं	song	वं	vong
षं	shong	शं	shhong

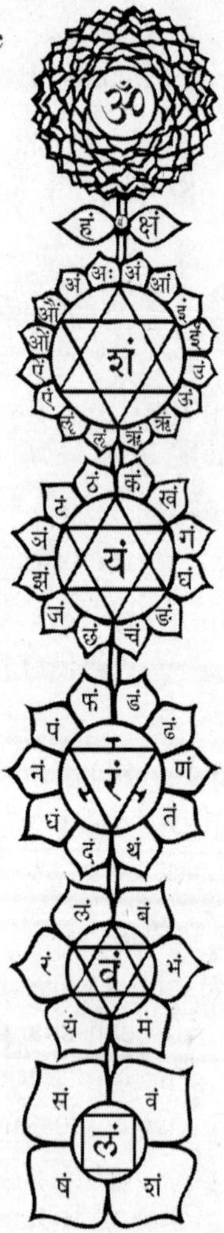

Diagram 5

force of every human being. He remains compassionately detached within each human body and is called the invisible body. Without the soul, the 24 gross elements of *prakriti* cannot do anything. There is also marvelous delusion, illusion, and error that is given by the *purusha* to every gross body, which is called *kundalini*.

In the Guru Gita (74) it is said:

piṇḍaṃ kuṇḍalini śaktim
haṃsa iti udāḥṛtaṃ
rūpaṃ binduṃ iti jñeyaṃ
rupātītaṃ niraṇjanam

The gross body of every human being is called *pindam*, but the *kundalini shakti* remains in a latent form in the whole body. Until and unless you can withdraw the senses from the coccygeal center to the sacral center, the sacral to the lumbar, the lumbar to the dorsal, the dorsal to the cervical, the cervical to the medulla oblongata, and the medulla oblongata to the cortical center (i.e., fontanel), you cannot perceive the indwelling divinity. The sounds of the fifty letters of the Sanskrit alphabet are in the spine between the coccygeal center and the pituitary gland. The first letter *ham* is in the pituitary gland, and the last letter *sa* is in the coccygeal center. If all of these letters are withdrawn and consciousness is locked in the pituitary, this is the *hamsa* stage. In the *hamsa* stage, a person cannot talk. He can only perceive divinity in the whole body. The gross body is *ham*, and the power of God is soul or *sa*. *Ham* is a dead body; it cannot inhale without *sa*, the invisible body or soul.

In the Gheranda Samhita (5:83) it is said, *haṃ kāreṇa bahir-yāti sakareṇa viśet punaḥ*. This means that the exhaled air is *ham* and the inhaled air is *sa*. *Sa* is the soul. Again, it is said in the Shiva Svarodaya (verse 51), *haṃkaro nirgame proktaḥ sakarāstu praveśane*. This means that when the air is exiting through the nose, it is *ham*; when the air is entering on the inhalation, it is *sa*, because the soul is He who can inhale. Therefore, to reverse this order of *ham* and *sa* does not tally with the scriptures.

Rupam bindum eti jñeyam means that, in order to awaken *kundalini shakti,* one must fix attention on a point in the vacuum, a point having no length and breadth. *Vinā tāl jahān kamal khilāne te hi carahi haṃsa keli-kare.* Sant Kabir, the Indian mystic philosopher who is considered one of the world's greatest poets, described his spiritual achievement, "It is as if my spinal canal is just like a pond where in the coccygeal center I am perceiving a four-petalled lotus; in my sacral center, a six-petalled lotus; in my lumbar center, a ten-petalled lotus; in my dorsal center, a twelve-petalled lotus; in my cervical center, a sixteen-petalled lotus; in my pituitary, a two-petalled lotus. The latter is called *hamsa* (swan) and means 'I am He.' Therefore, I am perceiving the *hamsa* in my whole body." The thousand-petalled lotus remains in the cortical center. There are a thousand propensities inside the brain because of its vastly complex networks of nervous tissue. This is symbolized by the thousand petals. (Diagrams 5 & 6; pages 110 & 120)

Inside the gross body, there is the invisible body, *purusha. Purusha* does everything and is similar to the electric current of the body by which the gross body *prakriti* (combination of 24 elements) is functioning. The eyes see, ears hear, nose smells, the mouth talks. Because of these five sense telephones the mind thinks, "I am the doer. The soul is not the doer." This is *maya* (delusion). When the mouth talks, or the hand works, or the leg walks, or the rectum evacuates, or the genitals function, these working organs do not give us the perception that the soul is the only doer. We think that we are the doer. This is the main error of human beings and is the inevitable result of the gross human body.

The five gross elements of every human body are: vacuum, air, fire, water, and earth. There are five kinds of vacuums between the pituitary and fontanel inside the human body: *chidakasha, parakasha, daharakasha, atmakasha*, and *mahakasha.* (Diagram 7; page 121)

Vital Airs and Chakras

In every thought, our vital air (*prana*) and the quantity and quality of inhalation changes. There are fifty types of air in the body, but the *Yoga Shastras* have classified them into five types of airs: *apana, samana, vyana, prana*, and *udana.* In the coccygeal and sacral centers, there is *apana* air. In the lumbar center is *samana* air; in the dorsal center is *vyana* air, in the cervical center is *prana* air, and above the cervical center is *udana* air. The air we inhale is called *prana* air. When it comes in the lungs, it is called *vyana*. During the time of sexual satisfaction, the heart rate increases. That is also *vyana* air. After food, we take a special type of inhalation and exhalation by the help of which we can digest our food. That air is *samana* air. When we take food, we sometimes feel some wind is moving. That wind is also called *samana* air. After that, the air enters in the colon and discharges through the anus. That air is called *apana* air or *anila* air. During meditation when we sit in *paravastha*, inhalation and exhalation become very feeble. That air gives us triple divine qualities in our whole body. That is the real air for calmness, divinity, and godliness. That air goes in the cranium from the pituitary and is called *udana* air. *Prana* air is the king of all airs, because without *prana* air (inhalation), a person is a dead body. That *prana* air is divided into five main airs and then further into fifty types. (Diagram 8; page 127)

The *udana* air gives us supreme God consciousness, because it is coming from the cortical center and remains between the medulla and fontanel. The two vagus nerves and other cranial nerves allow the storehouse of the brain to perceive awareness of external stimuli and this leads us to the physiological sense. In the cerebrum and cerebellum there are so many nerves. The two vagus nerves (salsai and gairus) originate from the medulla. Using them, we can switch off the ignorance of our mindstuff and can switch on our finest purified sensations.

These nerves form convolutions in the brain, where we get the finest intellect, power of reasoning, intuition, foresight, and divinity. Also, by the help of these nerves, people can control their lungs with deep inhalations and can reduce their heartbeat and give rest to their tissues and cells. By the Kriya Yoga technique, everyone can remove nervousness, weakness, fatigue, anger, sorrows, fear, and premature death, and can perceive divinity inside the cerebrum and cerebellum. Also, with the Kriya Yoga technique, a person can perceive and realize three divine qualities and feel true love and regard. This is why the yoga scriptures give special importance to the *udana* air in the brain.

The coccygeal center is called the earth center, the sacral center is called the water center, the lumbar center is called the fire center, the dorsal center is called the air center, and the cervical center is called the vacuum center. From the cervical center to the crown of the head is also called the vacuum center because five vacuums are there.

In the *Yoga Shastras*, the coccygeal center is called *annamaya kosha*. It is also called the wealth center, because all material wealth is of the earth (i.e., food grains, metals, diamonds, petroleum, uranium). The sacral center is called *pranamaya kosha*, the life center, because every human being is born by sex pleasure and life remains in every human body. The lumbar center is called *manomaya kosha.* The mind is formed in the lumbar center. In all matter and in particular in every foodstuff, there is energy. This is the power of God and that energy enters the stomach as foodstuff where it is digested by the *vaisvanara agni* (divine fire). Therefore, people get energy from the material world and matter. If we only take food, we cannot get energy. But when we combine the life force and the soul-fire, we can then have real energy in our whole body and mind.

In the lumbar center there are two kinds of mind. It is written in the Amritabindu Upanishad (mantra 2), *mana eva manuśyāñāṃ kārañaṃ bandhamokśayoḥ.* The mind can lead a man to hell in the coccygeal and sacral centers, which only give money sense and sex sense. The general mass of people on Earth are engrossed in business, industry, wealth, power, pleasure of senses, cars, houses, extreme happiness, or extreme sense pleasures. Their minds and brains remain captive in the jungle of matter. Thus, there will always remain anxieties, worries, sorrows, frictions, avarice, anger, greediness, difficulties, danger, doubts, and suspicions, and, consequently, they will suffer from nervousness and disease.

By the practice of Kriya Yoga they can withdraw their thought waves and mindstuff into knowledge, their knowledge to consciousness and consciousness to superconsciousness. Also, by the practice of Kriya Yoga, a man can withdraw his *manomaya kosha* from the coccygeal and sacral centers to above the lumbar center and get superconsciousness, peace, solace, and joy in life. This is why in the above *shloka* it is written *karanam bandha moksayoh.* If you convert your mind into consciousness above the navel center, then you will feel that you are not the doer. You will feel that the soul is drawing inhalation directly to the lungs in the heart center. The dorsal center is the heart center and in yoga scriptures it is called *vijnanamaya kosha.*

Since people are absorbed in the visible body, they think, "I am inhaling." But the moment they come to a proper environment, that is, to a realized guru, a realized Kriya Yoga master, they will learn that a dead man cannot inhale and that the supra-electronic life force, oxygen, is being pulled by the inner mechanism, the soul. This is what sustains human life.

In Our Every Disposition, Our Inhalation Changes

If the general mass of people come to a real Kriya yogi, they will be taught the truth behind their inhalation. In our every disposition, every mood, our inhalations vary. When one enjoys the sex sense, the heart pumps more and more. When one becomes angry, the heart beats even faster. When one has fear, the heart beats most rapidly and may at this stage cause heart failure. But when we sleep, our heartbeats become slow and calm, and, by the help of slow inhalation, anxieties and thoughts disappear. The real Kriya yogi teaches the students how to get extreme calmness by the process of inhalation. The moment they take calm inhalation, as taught in Kriya Yoga, they get the breathless stage that is the deathless stage. At that time the heart takes a rest, as do the brain and the mind, and the practitioners can work nicely and live longer lives.

Mind is the principal thing of every human being that comes from the energy of food. That is why in the Bhagavad Gita (6:17) it is written, *yuktāhāra-vihārasya yukta-ceṣṭasya karmasu yukta-svapna-avabodhasya yoga bhavati duḥkhahā*. This means a moderate diet, moderate sex pleasure, moderate work, and moderate contemplation will enable man to have a calm mind and God-realization.

The power of the mind is very fast. It is faster than airplanes or rockets. By plane you can travel a long distance within a very short period, but your mind can reach any distance within the twinkling of an eye. With a single sentence, a person can have extreme joy or extreme sorrow. For example, if we get good news, immediately we have extreme joy, but if it is bad news, immediately our mind feels severe pain. Even if we hear news that is false, that someone close is dead, just hearing this news we may faint, or become unconscious, by the help of the mind. The Kriya Yoga technique given by a Kriya yogi teaches how to switch off the mind, how to remain free from sorrow, free from the pleasures of the senses and how to switch on our knowledge body and go from knowledge to superconsciousness.

How to Switch Off Your Mind

Concentration of mind requires two things: (1) good environment and (2) removal of objects of distraction. A quiet place is not always required for meditation. When a person practices Kriya Yoga, he can switch off the five sense telephones and get quietness or calmness wherever he is.

The activity of the lungs and heart is caused by physiological changes of a biological and biochemical nature. These activities are controlled by the life force (*prana*), which is the electrical power in the sensory motor nerves. The storehouse of *prana* is in the brain, but it is guided from the medulla oblongata to the vagus nerves and other cranial nerves, which then give direct power to the heart, lungs, diaphragm, and every part of the body: the cells, molecules, tissues, and atoms.

The gross body always feels, "I am all in all, the invisible body is nothing to me," but when a person comes to a divine environment, the master teaches physiology and psychology side by side. He will learn that the knowledge body has thorough control over the mind and, according to the guidance of a real Kriya yogi, will learn that the physiological forces are controlled by the three super powers:

- *dharana* perception and conception of the soul;
- *dhyana* the formless stage; or *adhyatma avastha* in which there is no mind, intellect, ego or thought; and
- *samadhi* the merging in the soul.

Then the person can perceive that the invisible body is the real conductor of the visible body. Psychological forces are the force of the soul, that is the invisible and real "I" (*purusha*), and physiological forces are the force of the visible and unreal "I" (*prakriti*). So, by the guidance of a good master, the person who practices Kriya Yoga can control the lungs and heart and can withdraw the mind from the external world.

What Kriya Yoga Can Give You

Each person has some control over the breath and lungs, but no control over the heart. Controlling the lungs by the philosophical Kriya Yoga technique, without pressing the nose or creating any disorder in the heart, a person gradually controls the tissues, molecules, muscles, and atoms. The heartbeat and breath become weaker and slower. By the help of this, we can withdraw all thoughts and anxieties from the mind and brain, and cool the brain. For example, when a pet dog runs for a long period, its tissues, muscles, and molecules become tired, the dog takes rest and its mind becomes extremely cool; it sleeps immediately. Similarly, by the Kriya Yoga technique we can make our brain and mindstuff free and with this single-minded state we can work perfectly.

Kriya Yoga is based on physiology, psychology, astrology, and philosophy. Its power is a great mystery. It places value on the mundane and the spiritual world equally. Kriya Yoga power enables a person to get success in any field. It gives all-around development. To the person remaining in the family and in the world, Kriya Yoga can give extreme inner peace, divineness, and repose.

The tremendous power within each person is the Lord's own power of creation. By that power, anyone can perceive God, even through his delusion, illusion, and error. The realized master can awaken the *kundalini shakti* during the time of initiation. That is called *shaktipata.* The student will get constant awareness of the soul within. That power gives skill and success in any field of research and beautiful tact in practical life.

People get extreme energy and sound health because of the scientific nature of this technique. They take sufficient oxygen, which is the nutrition of the brain, lungs, heart, and the whole system. Impure blood is purified by the oxygen. Kriya Yoga can heal a sick mind and a sick body. If anyone eats any germ, he can digest it. He can get sound health by Kriya Yoga. Kriya Yoga gives long life, peace, prosperity, fame, and salvation. Educated and illiterate, men and women, boys and girls above thirteen years, rich and poor, employers and employees can practice this Kriya Yoga to get balance of mind, prompt understanding, ready wit, amity, affection, and oneness. Balance of mind is controlled by the lungs and heart and by deep breathing.

Ignorance and knowledge are both coming from the heart center. If we cannot control our breath, the heart and lungs, then we cannot switch off our mindstuff from our brain. However, if we can control our breath by Kriya Yoga, we can go into divinity and can reach *vijnanamaya kosha.* So, the heart center is called *vijnanamaya kosha.*

In the yoga scriptures it is said, *indriyānām manonāthaḥ manonāthastu maruta māruta-stu laya-nāthaḥ sa laya nādam āśritaḥ*. It means the master of our five sense telephones is mind and the master of mind is deep inhalation. Through Kriya Yoga, we can switch off our mind center and switch on our knowledge center. Mind gives ignorance. Mind cannot judge anything. Mind brings destruction, so the mind is blind. Knowledge, however, leads to calmness and perfection; knowledge leads our life from darkness to light. When the air (inhalation) is controlled, then we attain the vacuum stage. When we remain in the vacuum stage, we hear divine sound, the talk of God. We

Placement of Seed Syllables

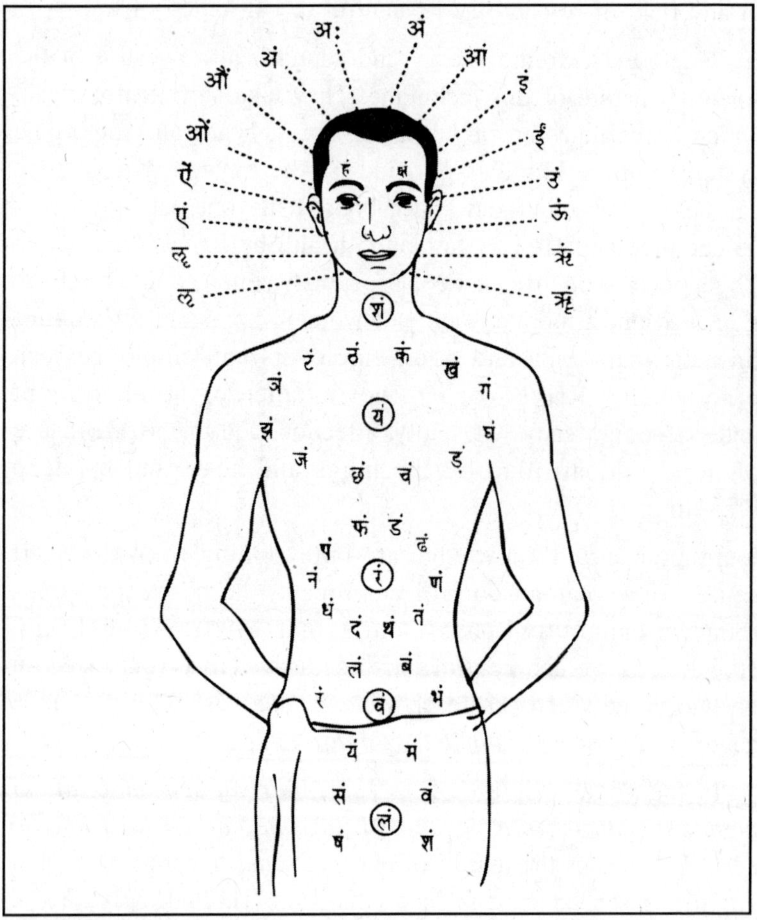

DIAGRAM 6 - The placement of the seed syllables within the human body. This is the actual positioning of all of the seed syllables in the lotuses within the human body. Thoughts and propensities of the "I am" or ego nature are produced by the 48 seed syllables that are remaining in the petals of the five lower lotuses. Kriya Yoga teaches how to remove them, whereby one attains liberation and cosmic consciousness.

Five Vacuums in the Cranium

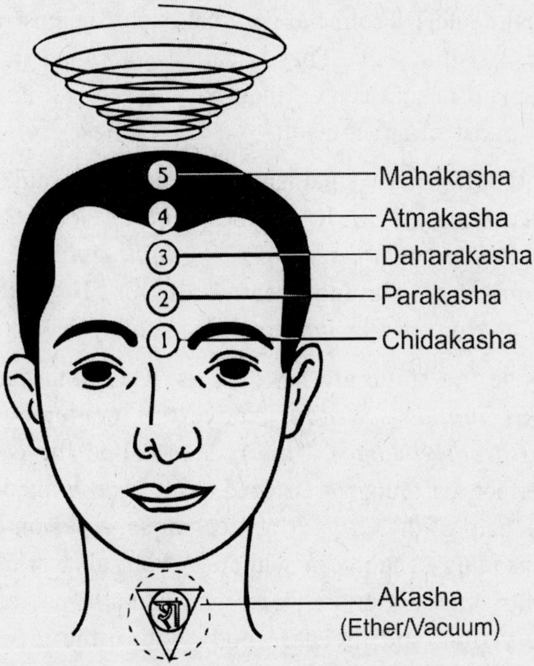

1. Chidakasha: life force of human beings in the pituitary.
2. Parakasha: inner fire born of meditation above the pituitary; no mind, body, ego, or intellect remains.
3. Daharakasha: nothingness, superconscious state below the fontanel.
4. Atmakasha: cosmic conscious stage at the fontanel.
5. Mahakasha: great emptiness, wisdom stage of *nirvikalpa samadhi*; merged in the pulselessness above the fontanel.

DIAGRAM 7 - Five vacuums in the cranium. Sunyam, the five stages of the meditative emptiness, have a common matrix of akasha, which means vacuum or empty space. Akasha also means sky or ether. As the highest of the five primary gross elements, it occupies the space from the neck to the pituitary.

can even feel the truth, emptiness, and divine vibration all over the universe. We can see illumination everywhere; at that time we gradually go from the dorsal center to the vacuum (i.e., cervical center). From the cervical center begins the real abode of the invisible God. That is called *anandamaya kosha*. If we can remain in that center, then we can feel extreme detachment in the midst of attachment.

In the Taittiriya Upanishads (2:6:1) it is said, *so'kāmayata bahu śyām prajāyeya*. It was the desire of God to become many. So, *idaṃ sarvam asṛjata yad idaṃ kiṃca tat sṛṣṭvā tad evānuprāviśat*. Having created all this, He entered into the creation. However insignificant something may be, it is He.

Inside the spine are six centers. The sixth center is called *sat-chit-ananda-svarupa*. Above this center is the fontanel (*sahasra-dala-padma*). This is also called the cortical center. All perfect reasonings are stored in the cerebrum and cerebellum. By the help of the Kriya Yoga technique, a person can remain in the reasoning center; can withdraw from all worldly sensations, thoughts, and anxieties; and can constantly perceive the union of the visible and invisible body within the gross body. That state is called *savikalpa samadhi* or *samprajñata samadhi*. That means superconscious *samadhi*. After this, a person can also attain the *turiya samadhi*, that is, *nirvikalpa samadhi*. In that stage the Kriya yogi remains in the divine rhythm. (Diagram 15; page 192)

Five Types of Air

In this universe there is no existence without air. Plants cannot grow without air, animal beings cannot live and grow without air, food cannot grow without air. Therefore, air is the supra-electronic force that is called life force. The air is the second creation of the Lord. It is invisible. The sky is the first creation of the Lord; it is also invisible. From the sky we get divine sound, which is invisible; from the air we get touch sensation, which is also invisible. (Diagram 8; page 127)

Five types of air (*prana*) constantly pass through the spinal canal, which the human being can use by magnetizing the spine to transform this life force into all-accomplishing radiant divine force. In the scriptures it is said, *āyur-vāyur, balavāyur, vāyur dhātā śarīriña, vāyuh sarvam idamviśvam vāyuḥ pratyakśa-devatā*. *Ayur-vayuh* means that everyone is alive because they inhale. *Balam-vayuh* means that oxygen comes through inhalation, which is why the blood does not clot and why there is strength in the body. *Vayur dhata sharirina* means no one survives if they do not inhale air. *Vayuh sarvam idamvishvam* means that we know that air is present all around us. *Vayuh pratyaksha devata* means that is why the air is called the living power of God.

The yoga scriptures teach that the four types of air that human beings constantly use in their bodies are:

- *Puraka* — the incoming breath;
- *Antah-kumbhaka* — the breath held inside after inhalation without locking the nose;
- *Rechaka* — the exhalation or outgoing breath; and
- *Bahir-kumbhaka* — the breath held outside after exhalation without locking the nose.

When the Mind Becomes Calm, Three Manifestations Can Be Felt

It is also written in Yoga Sutra of Patañjali (Samadhi Pada, 34), *prachhardana vidhāraṇābhyā vā prāṇasya.* This means that if you want to cool down your mind, you should take deep inhalation and exhalation. If a person under the guidance of a good Kriya Yoga master can practice this properly for fifteen minutes, then he should get three divine qualities in him. After this practice, the Kriya yogi reaches another stage of Kriya, which is called *nishcale nishcalo bhavet.* It means that he will forget his body sense, mind sense, and worldly sense. At that time he does not keep any attention on the breath and almost gets the breathless stage, which is the deathless stage. In this stage the heart beats very slowly and, thus, rests. By the help of this Kriya, people can get long life. In this divine state, people get real purification. This is real meditation. At this time people can only perceive three things:

1) illumination throughout the universe, light is the third creation of God;

2) a sensation of movement from the high heaven to the earth, which is the perception of all-pervadingness and the movement sensation of the soul throughout the gross body — this is called the *hamsa-sadhana*;

3) the divine sound, the *om* sound, can be heard in any of its varieties: as a rumbling sound, bumblebee sound, mosquito buzzing sound, roaring sound, church-bell sound, gong-bell sound, storm sound, violin sound, flute sound, conch-blowing sound, or sometimes a combination of all melodious and harmonious sounds at the same time.

Sant Kabir, one of the great yogis, described the condition of one absorbed in meditation, *rash gagan gufa me ajhar jharay bin baja jhankar uthi jahān, samājha pade jab dhyāna dhare:* "When a devotee is absorbed in the superconscious stage, then the sweet divine nectar rolls down from the fontanel and he hears the violin, flute, and other melodious sounds."

When a person practices Kriya proper, then his whole body and spine are magnetized, the life force is changed into divine force, and he feels the greatest energy throughout all his activities.

By the help of this technique, he gets physical, mental, and intellectual regeneration and rejuvenation. Sant Kabir also said, *binu chanda ujiari daraśe jahān tānhā jyoti najar pare:* When a person practices *jyoti mudra,* the last technique of Kriya, the five sense telephones are introverted and the moonlight, bluish light and white light are seen in front of the forehead. After that when he sits like Lahiri Baba with the forehead wrinkled, he can see divine light all over the universe. The light is the living presence of the soul. In the Upanishads, it is written in several places that fire is the real soul, and the soul is the real fire, and the air (oxygen) is the life of the soul. If you light a candle and cover it with a jar, then, within a short time, the light will be extinguished. Similarly, the soul-fire is in the cranium and the life force (in the form of air) carries oxygen that allows the soul-fire to remain in the body. If you hold your breath for five minutes, then surely your fire, that is, your soul, will not remain in the body.

The Real Meaning of the Fire Ceremony

The Hindus make offerings in a fire ceremony called *agnihotra*. They offer oblation on the fire and chant various mantras. For the real fire ceremony, where the five sense telephones cannot function, one does not require any material object such as wood, butter oil, and so on. The oxygen being inhaled and the divine soul-fire inside your cranium is the real fire ceremony. This can be felt by the practice of Kriya Yoga. (Diagram 9; page 128)

Butter oil is nothing but a type of matter. In the brain and mind of a yogi, so many material desires and ambitions remain. The yogi takes all the desires and ambitions and offers them to the unparalleled fire. Gradually, all the past thoughts, present thoughts, and worldly thoughts within the yogi are completely burned. All the whims and madness of the yogi are completely burned to ashes. The yogi, with his love, withdraws his inhalation; this is the butter oil. By the help of this, the yogi can burn all his desires in the spiritual fire inside the cranium. The power of God within the yogi is happy to see his sacrifice. This is, undoubtedly, a divine fire ceremony. The yogi gets the formless stage, thoughtless stage. In Christianity it is taught that the formless stage is the ultimate goal. This is also taught in Islam and Hinduism. It is taught by Kriya yogis. The air is the supra-electronic force that carries oxygen through the nose and offers oblation to the living fire. A person should constantly feel his inhalation and exhalation, which is the living power of God always within. Then he will get constant liberation in family life through his worldly actions. Kriya Yoga does not make a person lazy. It gives constant awareness of his inherent divinity.

The Hindus carry firewood, incense, fruits, and flowers to God for His satisfaction. Likewise, the Christians take candles, flowers, and donations to the altar. The Muslims enter the mosque with incense to satisfy God. However, the Kriya yogis convey their lives, that is, they offer their breath of life to the living fire that is the soul. The Kriya yogi constantly offers oblation to the fire and becomes very humble toward the soul, that is, the power of God. Lahiri Baba and Shriyukteshwarji said, "Through every human being, the power of God is taking 21,600 inhalations in a day. Of these, if a person can watch 1,728 inhalations and exhalations taken by the soul through the nose, this finishes the meditation of ten years."

There are seven centers in the cerebro-spinal system. Two lights are in each center: one for the gross body and one for the soul. Whenever a person earns money, he earns it from the first center, the coccygeal center, the money center. He will feel the existence of the soul there through the practice of Kriya Yoga. In every action, one sees the real actor; so, one light is for the actor and the other is for the action. Whenever a person feels the sex sense, he should also see the soul light in the second center, the sacral center,

Five Subtle Vital Airs in Every Human Body

Udana Air	Spiritual "up" breath of ether within the nostrils. Faint breath for God-realization. (neck chakra)
Prana Air	Out breath of water element. The soul exhales, releasing life force. (heart chakra)
Vyana Air	Mid breath of air. Heart breathing controls passion, anger, pride, appetite, sleep, meditation, and all qualities. (In the entire body)
Samana Air	Digestive breath of fire. Transforms food into energy and gives all-round development. (navel chakra)
Apana Air	Air and fluid discharge from two low centers. (lower chakras; anus and genital)

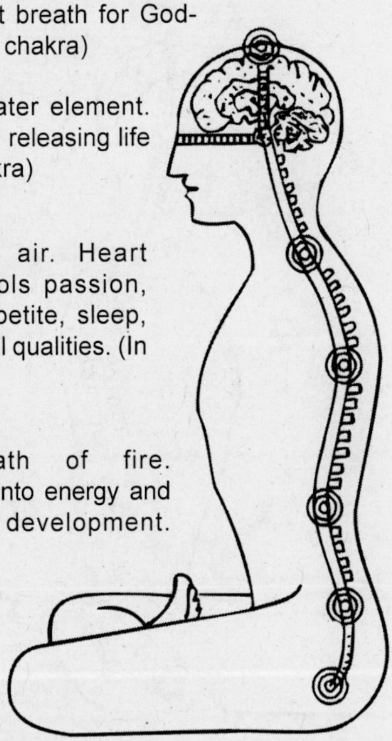

DIAGRAM 8 - Five subtle vital airs in every human body. Kriya Yoga meditation allows the practitioner to become aware of and regulate the five internal breaths.

The Seven Holy Fires in the Human System

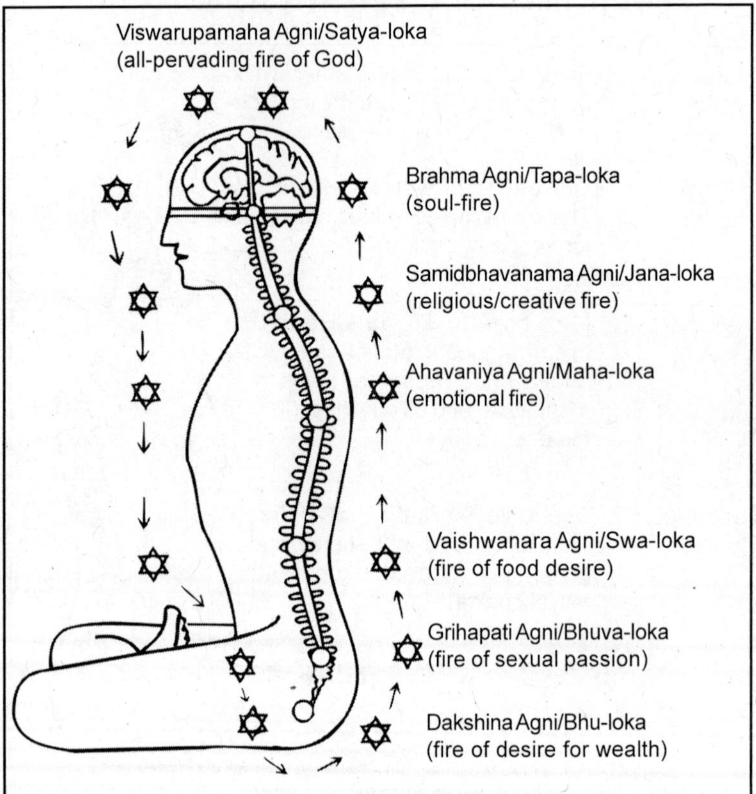

DIAGRAM 9 - The seven holy fires in the human system. A Kriya yogi watches the seven "fires" circulating up the cerebro-spinal canal and seven fires going down. These fires are the divine power of God. Outwardly, the fires take form as seven types of desire; inwardly, the fire is perceived as lights that lead to knowledge, consciousness, superconsciousness, and cosmic consciousness. By watching this God-fire in your every action, you can perceive God as the sole doer in the body. This solar or God-fire grants constant alertness in the soul and liberation from karma.

because without the soul he cannot feel the sex sense. By the Kriya Yoga technique, one can watch two lights in the third center, the lumbar center in the solar plexus, one light is eating and the other is feeding. Without the soul, a person cannot get the taste of food. By the practice of Kriya Yoga one can eat food while feeling that without the soul he cannot receive the taste of that food. By Kriya Yoga people can get constant liberation through taste.

In the fourth or dorsal center (heart center), there are also two lights, one for delusion and the other for dis-illusion. Without the soul, neither could exist. Similarly, two lights are in the fifth center, the cervical center at the throat. This is the vacuum center, which creates detachment so that people may cease functioning in the next moment. The soul is functioning in the friend, in the husband, in the wife, in the children; but, in the next moment it may not function. Any person can expire at any time. By the practice of Kriya Yoga people can constantly feel that the soul is remaining compassionately detached.

The sixth center is also called the soul center, and is in the medulla oblongata. Here are also two lights; one is for the biological sense and the other is for the psychological sense. If a person jointly feels both the physiological and psychological senses, then he can constantly have single-mindedness in his every action, because he is feeling the real actor there. Through his single-minded state, he can work in the world while perceiving that he is not the doer; God, the soul, is the doer.

The seventh center, the fontanel, is also a physiological and psychological center. There, people use reason and judge what is right and wrong. Mind, thought, and intellect function there; but people can twist their mind into consciousness, coil their mind into superconsciousness and transform it into divinity because of the many nerves in the cerebrum and cerebellum. As a result, people can be led from evil to good, from the wrong path to the right path, from darkness to light, from ignorance to knowledge, and from delusion to the constant awareness of the soul. The Kriya Yoga technique gives a marvelous power by which a person can remove his ignorance and perceive divinity in his every activity. Therefore, Kriya Yoga values both the mundane and the spiritual equally.

In the yoga scriptures it is written, *recakaṃ pūrakam tyaktvā yat sukhāt vāyur dhāraṇam prāṇāyāma ayam ity uktvā sa kevalam iti smṛtam.* This means when you practice *mahamudra*, there is deep holding of the breath and deep exhalation. After that, you get absolute rest and feel the divine sensation in each of the body parts. At that time, you do not watch the breath. You go almost into the breathless stage and your heart beats very slowly. This is called *pranayama ayam ity uktva.* That is called the real rest of *prana*, that is, *pranayama* (*prana* = breath; *ayama* = rest). *Sa kevalam iti smṛtam.* Resting the breath is called *kaivalya-pranayama*, which means constant awareness of the soul. Only by the practice of Kriya Yoga can a person get constant awareness of the soul, even when working in the material world. This was proved by Lahiri Baba in his life, for he was a family man working in an office. Yet, even then, he constantly perceived that the soul was working through him. It is written in the Jñanodaya scriptures, *cittādi-sarva bhāveṣu brahmatenaiva bhāvanāt nirodhaḥ sarva-vṛtyānām prāṇāyamas tad ucyate.* This means that the *manas*, *buddhi*, and *ahamkara* in the *chitta* will remain, but they will function only by the power of God (Brahman). If you perceive that the soul is functioning in all your dispositions and moods, then you are a real *sadhaka.*

In the Yoga Sutra of Patañjali (Sadhana Pada 1), it is asked, what is Kriya Yoga? The answer is given, *tapaḥ-svādhyāya-īśvarapraṇidhānāni kriyāyogaḥ. Tapas* ordinarily means the offering of oblation in the fire, but the metaphysical meaning, as stated before, is that the inhalation is the butter oil and the soul is the real fire. So, the Kriya yogi offers every inhalation (life) to the soul-fire. *Svadhyaya* means, ordinarily, to read such books as the Mahabharata, Bible, Bhagavad Gita, Quran, and Brahmasutra. These are the authentic books of Self-realization. Kriya Yoga is the applied part of all scriptures. To grasp the metaphysical meaning of *svadhyaya*, *sva* means inhalation, inhalation means soul, soul means He. *Adhyaya* means to study or seek or culture. Soul culture is real *svadhyaya.* In each human being, the soul is abiding to seek the soul. It is the duty of each human being to seek the soul within by Kriya Yoga. In your every action, the soul is the only actor; so, to seek the soul in your every action is *svadhyaya.*

In the Bhagavad Gita (3:5) it is written, *na hi kaśit kṣaṇam api jātu tiṣṭhatyakarmakṛt:* A person cannot cease for a single moment to do work. But, people cannot do any work without the soul. So, if a person seeks Him always within his mind, thought and intellect, knowledge, consciousness and superconsciousness, that is the real *svadhyaya*. The study of the soul is *svadhyaya*, the study of soul culture is *svadhyaya.* The practice of Kriya Yoga is *svadhyaya*, and the study of one's own Self is *svadhyaya.*

The above-mentioned *sutra* states, in *ishwara pranidhana*, *pranidhana* means to merge with. In the Mahabharata it is said that the invisible God is divided into eight stages: *ishwara* is on the fifth stage, between the cervical center and the pituitary. *Ishwara* means the soul, which is all-pervading in the universe. However insignificant a thing may be, it is He. But, if you do not meditate very deeply, you cannot perceive this truth. Kriya Yoga meditation is a metaphysical meditation by *tapas* (offering oblation to the real fire). The Kriya yogi feels that everything in the universe is burnt. He feels divine movement sensation in the whole universe, illumination of divine fire in the whole universe, sweet divine melodious sound from all over the universe, and he remains in the superconscious stage. By this the yogi gets extreme love, regard, and indebtedness to God. This love for God, called *ishwara pranidhana,* is very rare.

The Shandilya Bhakti Sutra (2) says, *bhakti sā parānurakti-īśvare*: This means the highest attachment to God. The great poet Tulsidas said, *kāmihi nari pyāri jimi lobhihi pyāri jimi, dām, timi hi raghunātha nirantara lagi more rāma*: "As the newly married husband loves his wife, as the newly married wife loves her husband, as the miser loves his money deeply, as the drunkard loves his wine deeply, similarly, one should love God." This can be accomplished by the Kriya Yoga technique. When a person completely loses worldly senses and gets so many divine perceptions in the whole body, perceiving *samprajñata samadhi* (conscious *samadhi* or *saguna samadhi*) and finally *turiya samadhi*, then he feels the greatest love for God. This is the real stage when a Kriya yogi can merge with Infinity.

V

KRIYA YOGA IN ANCIENT SCRIPTURES

> "I proclaimed this imperishable yoga to Vivasvan. Vivasvan told it to Manu, and Manu told it to Iksvaku. Thus handed down from one another the royal sages knew it until the yoga was lost to the world through long lapse of time," says the Blessed Lord in the Bhagavad Gita (4:1-2).

The imperishable yoga (Avyaya Yoga) is none other than Kriya Yoga, which was brought to mankind by the Lord God with His creation. The supreme mystery of Kriya Yoga was revealed by God Himself. Kriya Yoga is the spiritual practice based on breath control. God breathed into the nostrils the breath of life, which is mentioned in the Book of Genesis (the Torah). God also taught the science of self-control through breath regulation. This Kriya Yoga was brought again into mass practice by the great master Babaji Maharaj through his able householder disciple Shri Shyamacharan Lahiri, popularly known as Lahiri Mahashaya, or Lahiri Baba, in modern times.

The Vedas

The Vedas are the most ancient and holy scriptures of mankind; no one knows how many thousand years old they are. *Veda* in Sanskrit comes from the root *vid*, which means "to know." The Vedas are the treasure house of material and spiritual knowledge. There are several detailed discussions about yoga practice in the Vedas. Nowadays you hear of many kinds of yoga, but at that time, there was one yoga, the yoga of breath control, canalization of *prana*, which ultimately brought control of life. Yoga in the Vedas was nothing less than the meditation of Kriya Yoga.

It is written in the Vedas (Rig Veda 1:18:7):

yasmāt ṛte na siddhyati, yajno vipaścitaścana
sa dhīnān yoga minvati

Without yoga, the means to control thought (i.e., *praṇa karma*), no one can attain perfection. Yoga is the path of perfection and the key to success.

There are repeated descriptions of yoga (i.e., Kriya Yoga) in all the branches of the Vedas, including discussions about *chakras kvo trichakra*: Where are the lower three centers (Rig Veda 1:34:9).

In the Atharva Veda, it is said, *aśṭa cakra navadvāra devānam puram ayodhyā, tasyam hiranmayaḥ koṣaḥ svargojyotisa vṛtāḥ*: This human body is the chariot of the nine doors and eight chakras. It has *ayodhya*, the place beyond all the frictions, fights, and fluctuations. In between there is ever-dazzling covering of delusion, beyond which you will enter the kingdom of heaven.

The Upanishads

The Upanishads are the last part of the Vedas: They are many in number and contain divine wisdom. There are many meanings of the word *upanishad* (to remove all ignorance quickly, to sit near the truth, to sit near the master). However, in some specific verses of different Upanishads, there is clear indication of meditation and Kriya practice.

In Shvetashvatara Upanishad (6:11) it is written:

"The one God is hiding in every living being,
still then, He is all-pervading, the innermost being in all.
He does all the work (*kri*), abiding in all (*ya*).
He is the witnessing consciousness, formless and immortal."

In the Mundaka Upanishad (3:1:4) it is described:

"Brahman, God is the indwelling Self in all.
Verily He is the reality of life and illumination.
Realizing Brahman, man becomes enlightened.
There is none wiser than the one who has realized God.
He performs all daily works as the expression of his divine Self, and his enjoyment is infused with love of God.
He is a true *kriyavan*, the wisest among the wise men."

This verse contains three important words: *kriyavan* (the one who practices Kriya Yoga, the supreme meditation), *atmakrida* (through every action, enjoys as perceiver of the soul), *atmarati* (to love the soul, God, in every breath, in every moment, in every thought, disposition, and activity).

In the same Upanishad, at a different place (3:2:10) it is said:

"He is the *kriyavan*, lover of wisdom, devoted to God,
constantly hearing the divine sound (i.e., *Om*),
who practices the mystic rites of subjective meditation (i.e., Kriya Yoga), who has taken the vow of Self-illumination,
perception of divine light on the top of the head,
and he alone is rightly qualified to receive the
divine wisdom and God-realization."

The Bhagavad Gita

The Bhagavad Gita (in short, the Gita) is the handbook of yoga. From beginning to end, the Gita explains the science of meditation, right action, divine love, and realization. Each chapter of the Gita is also named as yoga. The concluding verse of each chapter declares that it is the essence of the Upanishad (i.e., the Gita is the essence of the Absolute and the scripture of yoga, the *Yoga Shastras*). Every verse of the holy Gita explains the secret of spiritual practice, Kriya meditation, and perception of divine qualities like divine illumination, vibration, and holy sound. In the history of explanation of the Bhagavad Gita by different scholars, yogis and realized masters, the yogic explanation of the Gita by Lahiri Mahashaya, Swami Pranavananda, Shriyukteshwarji, Pandit Panchanan Bhattacharya, Mother Suradhuni Devi, Shrimat Bhupendranath Sanyal are landmarks. The Gita is the scripture of yoga and above all Kriya Yoga; one can refer to the book *Bhagavad Gita in the Light of Kriya Yoga* by the author.

In the Gita (18:66) it is written, *māmekaṃ śaraṇam vraja:* "Come to Me alone and surrender thyself," which is the essence of all religions and scriptures. To perceive God and God alone, constantly, continuously is the essence of the practice of Kriya Yoga.

The Bhagavad Gita teaches how to control and even kill all the negative propensities of body, mind, and intellect, and to go to the ultimate reality (the Soul, God) quickly and easily by the scientific technique of Kriya Yoga.

The Brahmasutra

In Indian spiritual traditions, along with all the scriptures, the Upanishads, the Gita, and the Brahmasutra of Vyasa are given supreme importance. These three basic scriptures are known as *prasthana trayi* (the triple canon of spirituality that enables one to return to the source from which one has come). The literal meaning of Brahmasutra is not aphorisms on the Absolute God, like the Yoga Sutra of Patañjali or the Bhakti Sutra of Narada. As the thread holds all the pearls together to make a beautiful garland, similarly the formless God is hiding in all of creation. As people look at the pearls, not at the thread, similarly, ordinary people look to the world, not to God. Brahman (God) + s*utra* (thread).

In this holy book of Brahmasutra is a very subtle description of

Kriya Yoga and its perception. *Guhāṃ praviṣṭāvātmānau hi tad darśanāt:*"By entering into the cave of cranium one is to perceive the union of the individual self and universal Self" (1:2:11).

Kampanāt: "Perception of vibration of *prana*" (1:3:39).

Jyoti darśanāt: "Perception of divine illumination" (1:3:40).

Pranavato śabdāt: "Perception of the divine sound" (2:4:15).

All these perceptions are realized even at the time of initiation into Kriya Yoga.

The Ramayana

The Ramayana is the life story of Rama, a king of Ayodhya and disciple of the great sage Vasishtha. The spiritual life of Rama reveals how he meditated and practiced this marvelous technique of Kriya Yoga. Rama learned the technique of Kriya Yoga from his great Guru Vasishtha. It is described in Adhyatma Ramayana, Kishkindha Kanda (chapter four).

Once Lakshmana saw Rama meditating deeply and enjoying the bliss of *samadhi*. After Rama returned to body sense, Lakshmana approached him and asked politely about this meditation technique, *idāniṃ śrotum icchāmi kriyā mārgeṇa rāghava*: "O Rama! I want to learn the path of Kriya practice, by which the yogis, the householders, saints, and sages got realization."

Hearing such question from his beloved brother Lakshmana, Rama said:

idaṃ rahasyaṃ paramaṃ ca pāvanaṃ
mayaiva sākṣāt kathitaṃ sanātanam
evaṃ parātmā śrī rāmaḥ kriyā yogamanuttamam
pṛṣṭah prāha svabhaktāya śeṣāṃśāya mahātmane

"This secret technique is the sacred and divine. I myself taught it to many."

Being asked and requested by his devotee brother, Rama explains the technique of Kriya Yoga.

The book of Yoga Vasishtha also contains the discussion of yoga practice by Rama and his master Sage Vasishtha.

The Bhagavatam

The Bhagavatam is another holy scripture (Mahapurana) in India, consisting of twelve books; it explains in a subtle sense the essence of Kriya Yoga and spirituality. A few references will clearly explain the secret of Kriya practice.

jitāsano jitaśvāso jitasaṅgo jitendriya (2:1:23)

jitasano: The ordinary meaning is perfection in *asana*, but its real connotation is to be free from body consciousness.

jitasvasa: Thorough mastery over the breath.

jitasango: Getting detached from body, mind, senses, thoughts, and even the external world.

jitendriya: Control over the restless senses.

All these stages are easily achieved by the practice of Kriya Yoga.

It also explains how to meditate:

sthiraṃ sukhaṃ cāsanam āśrita (2:2:15)

> "Physically sitting in a comfortable posture, and metaphorically sitting at the place of concentration (to be learned from the master)."

ruddhvā guhā (2:2:5)

> "By closing the cave, which means controlling all doors of thoughts and emotions arising from the cave of the cranium."

In every book of this scripture there is explanation of this supreme meditation technique, in many ways.

The Yoga Sutra of Patañjali

Patañjali's Yoga Sutra is not the original exposition of philosophy, but a work of compilation and reformulation. Although the practice of yoga in general and Kriya Yoga in particular is the most ancient technique, what Patañjali did was to restore yoga philosophy in a systematic manner.

In the second part of the Yoga Sutra of Patañjali, Sadhana Pada (yoga and its practice), Kriya Yoga is mentioned twice:

tapaḥ svādhyāya īśvarapraṇidhānāni kriyāyogaḥ

samādhi bhāvanārthaḥ

kleśa tanūkaraṇārthaśca (Sutra 1 and 2)

These two aphorisms explain the essence of Kriya Yoga in a nutshell.

The literal meaning of the above two *sutras* (aphorisms) are:

> "Austerity, study and the dedication of the fruits of one's own action to God is Kriya Yoga."

> "That is Kriya Yoga by which one cultivates the power of concentration and removes the obstacles of enlightenment that cause all suffering."

In the first *sutra*, the three words in Sanskrit, *tapah, svadhyaya, ishwara pranidhana,* need more elaborate explanation than just literal translation.

The ordinary meaning of *tapas* is penance or austerity. However, the real meaning of *tapas* is that practice by which *tapas*, the temperature, or heat, that burns all the negative qualities of the body and the mind is maintained in the body. The soul, the power of God, is the cause of breath, which keeps the body alive and regulates body temperature. If one keeps attention on the top, in the soul, then all sins and negative qualities are burned.

The second word is *svadhyaya,* which means study. *Svadhyaya* consists of two words *sva* (self) and *adhyaya* (study): the study of one's own Self. Kriya Yoga enables one to study one's own Self constantly and continuously.

The third word is *ishwara pranidhana,* which means to love God, to perceive God, to realize God as the real actor in every action.

All these three words symbolically explain different aspects of Kriya Yoga. Not only that, through breath control, the disciple, the student, attains concentration and is enabled to remove all the obstacles from the path of meditation and God-realization and becomes constantly engrossed and merged in God consciousness.

Other Yogic Scriptures

Hatha Yoga Pradipika is an important and classical text on yoga. In this book it is mentioned (1:52):

kriyāyuktasya siddhiḥ syād akriyasya kathaṃ bhavet
na śāstrapāṭha matreṇa yogasiddhiḥ prajāyate

"*Kriya yukta* (those who practice Kriya Yoga) get perfection in their life, not others."

One cannot expect realization by only reading scriptures. By changing the outward dress one cannot get God-realization. Kriya is the cause of all-round development, there is no doubt about it.

Another ancient yogic text, Shiva Shamhita (5:270) speaks:

gṛhasthānaṃ bhavet siddhi īśvarāṇām japenavai
yogakriyābhiyuktānāṃ tasmāt samyatate gṛhi

"Even the householder can achieve realization by the practice of Kriya Yoga by thorough control of all sense organs."

It is also said in many scriptures: The fools only read a lot of books, but he is wise who practices Kriya Yoga and gets realization. Even though one gets a prescription from a very good doctor, by chanting the names of the medicine or reading it repeatedly, one cannot expect to be disease-free and healthy.

When people practiced Kriya Yoga in the period of Truth, at that time, there was no religion, no *-ism*, no narrowness, no dogmatic views, nor fanatic ideas. All people were established in Truth. In the course of time, when different religions came, different forms and formalities arose. In spite of all these, Kriya Yoga remained as the essence of all religions, the strong foundation of all spiritual buildings.

If one reads the Torah, the Bible, the Quran, even other holy scriptures of different religions and meditates, it becomes clear that all the saints, sages, and prophets were meditating; they were highly realized. Their teachings carry the essence of spiritual practice and meditation.

The Torah and the Bible repeatedly mention inner transformation through meditation. Although the word "Kriya" is not found there, one can perceive and realize the practical implication of their teachings. Abram, Moses, Noah, Jacob, and Jesus were all meditating, which is evident from their lives and teachings. (For details, one can refer to the book, *The Torah, the Bible and Kriya Yoga*.)

VI

THE HISTORY AND TRADITION OF KRIYA YOGA

Kriya Yoga is a novel technique. It is the essence of Raja Yoga, enunciated by Lord Shri Krishna in the Bhagavad Gita. According to Lord Shri Krishna, he taught this immortal yoga to Vivasvan (the sun god), who conveyed it to his son Manu and Manu imparted it to his son, Iksvaku. Thus, handed down from father to son, this yoga came to the knowledge of the *rajarshis* (royal sages). But, through the long lapse of time, it more or less disappeared. Subsequently, the Lord taught this sacred yoga to Arjuna and the other Pandavas. This yoga was fundamentally meant for householders seeking Self-realization. For ages this was the medium of God-realization. The famous sages, like Vyasa, Vasishtha, Janaka, Valmiki, Parashara, and others practiced this Kriya Yoga in the midst of their family preoccupations and reached the divine goal. This occupied an important place in the Bhagavad Gita and in the philosophical yoga treatise of Patañjali. (Diagram 13; page 179)

In the course of time, the yoga taught by Lord Krishna was neglected and almost disappeared. Chaotic conditions developed in the social life of India, because the people dissociated themselves from the ancient tradition of yoga. A new era was ushered in, during the middle of the nineteenth century when immortal Babaji Maharaj gave a scientific orientation to this yoga and offered it as Kriya Yoga for the spiritual upliftment of the human race. He taught this to Shyamacharan Lahiri Mahashaya, who had been his beloved disciple in a former lifetime, and instructed him to teach this technique to interested divine seekers. Shyamacharan was a householder who worked in the office of the Military Works Department. Babaji Maharaj selected him as the best spiritual representative to spread the technique of Kriya Yoga among the householders of India and abroad.

In the Hindu rituals, several practices — *achamanas,* the external purification of the body; *bhuta-shuddhi,* the internal purification of five elements in the body; *pranayama,* the control of breath or life force; *matrikanyas,* the realization of the existence of God in the different parts of the body — are associated with the practice of yoga. People cannot attain quick realization of God without these practices. Unless God, who is abiding in the body, becomes the charioteer of Arjuna, who represents the wisdom body, and destroys the ignorance in human beings, represented by the Kauravas, a person cannot realize Him. (Diagram 13; page 179)

The science of Kriya Yoga is a wonderful technique. It is very simple, easily practiced, and gives quick results. With the help of the scientific technique of Kriya Yoga, a person can overcome, within a short time, the obstacles of the deep-rooted mental impressions (*samskaras*) of innumerable previous births and can establish himself in the divine consciousness. The spiritual evolution of a common person during one year is equivalent to the spiritual attainment that a Kriya yogi achieves in one inhalation and exhalation in a few moments.

Vedic rituals and sacrifices result only in spiritual development, but Kriya Yoga brings about the simultaneous development of body, mind, intellect, and soul. Kriya Yoga is the essence and synthesis of all yogic techniques taught in the world. Karma Yoga emphasizes service to mankind, which includes public welfare activities, education, health services, and other charitable activities to mitigate human sufferings. But real Karma Yoga lies in the realization that God abides everywhere in the body. God's existence is perceived in every object of the universe. Whatever work is done, it is done by Him. *Prana karma*, or circulating the vital force through the divine channel inside the spine (*sushumna*), is the real activity on which all other outward activity rests. And this, ultimately, fixes the attention of the *sadhaka* (the seeker) in the *sahasrara* and *kutashtha* (in the soul center), and brings about God-realization, leading to internal secretion of some vital juice from the glands. This secretion has an intoxicating effect, helping the mind attain complete absorption in the thought and realization of God.

Unlike Raja Yoga, which is also based upon breath control, Kriya Yoga does not prescribe long retention of breath and closing of nostrils that cause uneasy feelings. Hatha Yoga prescribes many *asanas* and *bandhas,* the physical yogic exercises and postures. From among them Kriya Yoga has adopted some essential yogic postures, which include one type of yogic exercise — *mahamudra* — said by great yogis to be a panacea for all ailments. Thus, Kriya Yoga has not lost sight of all the essential and important features of various types of Indian yogic methods.

At a very critical moment, Shriyukteshwarji came to this world. His birth was well timed for the propagation of Kriya Yoga. He selected Puri, on the seashore in the Odisha state of India, the seat of the temple of Lord Jagannatha (one of the aspects of God worshipped in Hinduism), as the center of his Kriya Yoga *sadhana.* Puri, being the place of Lord Jagannatha, is one of the most suitable places for spiritual practice and quick God-realization. The ashram established by Shriyukteshwarji, known as Karar Ashram, became an active center of Kriya Yoga practice and propagation. It worked as a spiritual laboratory to discover the ultimate Truth. Like scientists endeavouring their utmost to unravel the mystery of nature and its physical laws, the aspirants here devoted themselves to realize the inseparable link between the Self and the Divine. For the last 100 years the tradition has been maintained and innumerable disciples from all parts of the world have made considerable progress in their spiritual quest under the practical guidance of gurus whose teachings are based upon the teachings of Shriyukteshwarji and Paramahamsa Yoganandaji. Shriyukteshwarji had a great love for this ashram and chose this place for his *mahasamadhi.* His beloved disciple, Paramahamsa Yoganandaji, was greatly inspired by him and, with his blessings and guidance, opened several centers of Kriya Yoga in India and abroad. Although he spent most of his time outside India, his spiritual link with his guru and his beloved ashram was inseparable. So, this was virtually the mother center of all Kriya Yoga activities of Shriyukteshwarji and his disciples.

VII

METAPHYSICS OF KRIYA YOGA

Kriya Yoga is a shortcut technique for Self-realization (i.e., God-realization). Kriya may be split into two words: *kri* and *ya*. Any work you are doing is *kri* and that work is done by the power of God (i.e., indwelling Self, *ya*).

Because the power of God is inside your body, constantly inhaling since your birthday, your body remains alive. Because your body is alive, you are able to do some work. So all work you do is really done by the power of God.

It is written in the Bible (Genesis 1:27; 2:7) that God made men and women in His own image and breathed the breath of life into the nostrils of every human being. So every human being is a living image of God. But we ignore Him. We ignore His presence within us. We have to give love to Him. In every breath, to watch Him, to feel that the power of God is activating our every action, is constant liberation.

The Almighty Lord, having created everything, entered into them. In Taittiriya Upanishad (2:6:3) it is written, *tat sṛṣṭvā tadevānuprāviśat*: "The Almighty Lord is hiding in every human being and is constantly inhaling, thus making us alive." So we are able to perform some actions. Through our every action (*kri*), we ought to watch the real doer of the action (*ya*).

The person who thinks he does nothing — although he sees, hears, touches, smells, eats, walks, sleeps, breathes, speaks, answers the calls of nature, grasps, opens and closes the eyes — but instead realizes that the power of God does everything (i.e., everything is done by *ya*), is certainly a better person. (See the Gita 5:8–9.)

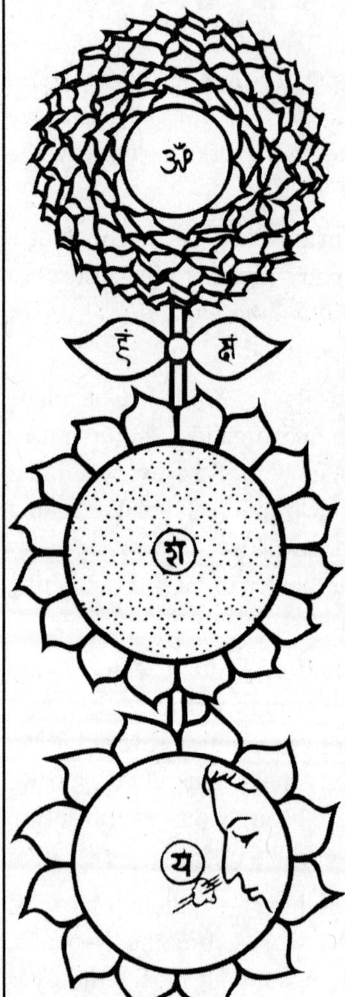

Antasthavarana (1)

The Seat of the Creator, the One Formless Heavenly Father within every human being.

The image of heaven and earth in the human body. *Sa* is the image of heaven within the human body and indicates the soul, the power of God that creates, activates, and conducts all the functions of the gross body. *Ham* indicates the earth and is the seed of the gross body. *In the beginning God created the Heaven and the Earth.* (Genesis 1:1)

Vacuum/*Sam*: The first of the five primary gross elements of God's creation. It is formless, void, and dark. *And the Earth was without form and void and darkness was upon the face of the deep.* (Genesis 1:2)

Air/*Yam*: The second primary gross element of God's creation. The breath of God.
And the spirit of God moved upon the face of the waters. (Genesis 1:2)

Antasthavarana (2)

Fire/*Ram*: The third primary gross element of God's creation: solar light. *And God said, Let there be light; and there was light.* (Genesis 1:3)

Water/*Vam*: The fourth primary gross element of God's creation. *And God said, Let the waters under heaven be gathered unto one place.* (Genesis 1:9)

Earth/*Lam*: The fifth primary gross element of God's creation. *And let the dry land appear; and it was so. And God called the dry land Earth.* (Genesis 1:9-10)

DIAGRAM 11 - *Antasthavarna*. Every human being is a microcosm of the universe. God creates human life according to the same fundamental procedures by which He created heaven and Earth. The five root-syllables or sound vibrations in the five lower lotuses are the first creations of God — vacuum/*sam*; air/*yam*; fire/*ram*, water/*vam*, and earth/*lam* — the primary gross elements from which all life grows. These seed syllables are *antasthavarna*. *Antasthavarna* means, "life giving sound, the generating life-force, which creates and establishes life."

Many people do many types of work. But without the soul, without the breath, one can do nothing. The Almighty Father (*ya*) hides in the fontanel, on the top of the head, and constantly inhales. He allows every human being to do some work (*kri*). This is *kri* and *ya*, so to watch Him in every work is Kriya.

Hinduism has four castes: *brahmin, kshatriya, vaishya,* and *shudra*. If we analyze subtly, we can find in each human being all four of these castes. A Vedic hymn (Purusha Sukta 13) declares:

brāhmanaḥ asya mukhāsit
vāhuḥ rājanyaḥ kṛtaḥ
urutahaḥ asya yat vaiśyaḥ
padvyāṃ śudraḥ ajāyata

Brahmanah asya mukhasit means, above the neck region a person is *brahmin*. The mind, intellect, consciousness which lead to superconsciousness, cosmic consciousness, and wisdom state, remain inside the brain. So the head of each person is represented by *brahmin*.

Brahma janati iti brahmanah: "When one's mind is completely merged with the Absolute wisdom by the practice of meditation, one is a *brahmin*."

Vahuh rajanyah kritah: The hands of a person represent a *kshatriya* because by the help of the two hands one does work.

Urutahah asya yat vaishyah: The thighs enable a person to walk wherever he wants. So the thighs represent *vaishyah*, through which one performs many types of actions, office work, earning money, and so on.

Padvyam shudrah ajayata: *Shudra* represents the feet of a person, as the feet serve the whole body.

It is quite evident from the explanation of the above verse that, in reality, there are not four different types of castes, rather that in each human body there remain the four castes. These are the four types of work being done in a human body: four types of work done by the Almighty Lord (*ya*). A dead person cannot do any work. A person works because the breath is going on constantly. That breath is inhaled by the power of God (*ya*), the indwelling Self who is hiding in every living being.

Every work (*kri*) is done by the indwelling Self (*ya*). You earn money in the coccygeal center, the first or bottom center. That work is done by God who is constantly inhaling and keeping you alive, thus allowing you to earn money. Therefore, you should watch Him while earning money.

In the sex center, He gives you the sex mood. If He does not inhale, then you cannot enjoy sex. So whenever you enjoy sex, you should watch Him, the power of God that allows you to enjoy.

In the navel center, He gives you appetite. You feel it, then you take some food. That food is God. In Taittiriya Upanishad (3:2:1) it is written, *annaṃ brahmeti vyajānāt*. Again, God is the gastric fire that digests the food (Bhagavad Gita 15:14); assimilating the energy from the food, God distributes it to the whole system. It's why your system is able to function accordingly. This is *kri* and *ya.*

In the heart center is a mixture of good and bad propensities: anger, pride, cruelty, insincerity, hypocrisy, debauchery, but also sweetness, kindness, love. Everything that comes from the heart is coming from the Almighty Father (*ya*) in reality. If He does not pull the breath, you have no good or bad qualities; nay, you do not exist at all.

The spiritual development of a person hastens from the cervical or throat center. Here, he reads many books on ethics, philosophy, and religion, and follows many types of spiritual practices. So he possesses a spiritual ego, which becomes the main hindrance to spiritual advancement. If you feel that everything is done by Him, you can overcome the obstacles in the path leading to divinity.

Each human body, inside the spine, has five working centers. We have ten working sense organs, five organs of action, and five organs of perception. So in every work, you have to watch, to see, that it is being done by Him. This is Kriya in practical life.

Now let us come to yoga. The word "yoga" comes from the root Sanskrit word *yuj*, which means to bind or union. So yoga simply means the union of body with the soul. Yoga means to realize that unity.

The divine kingdom in the body is the abode of the soul. It remains in the soul center and above, up to the infinity north. The Almighty Father remains there. He is formless; He is abiding in the body form. But the body is the kingdom of delusion, illusion, and error (i.e., *maya*). So it can be said, the union of *maya* with the conductor of *maya* is called yoga. Oneness of these two is yoga. About yoga it is written in ancient scripture:

parāśakti ātma mithuna
samyogānanda īśvara
ya āste mithunaṃ tat
pareśyāt striṇisebakāḥ

(*Kularnava Tantra 5:109*)

Many people enjoy their sexuality, proclaiming themselves as tantrics and saying this is the *mithuna* (union, joining) through which one can attain God-realization (yoga). But mere physical enjoyment is not the real enjoyment. So it is written, *parashakti atma mithuna*. *Parashakti* means the power of the Almighty Father who is hiding inside the body in the fontanel. It is above the five basic gross elements (*pancha mahabhuta*), that is, *akash* (vacuum) in the cervical center, *vayu* (air) in the heart center, *agni* (fire) in the navel center, *jala* (water) in the sex center, and *prithivi* (earth) in the coccygeal center. In every breath, there is joining, conjugation. This is the real sex enjoyment. This is the *atma mithuna*, which means sex with the Self.

The kingdom of heaven always remains within you; so also the devil kingdom. Kingdom of heaven is called *sa*; and kingdom of delusion, illusion, and error (*maya*) is called *ham*. The whole body is *maya*. In the Guru Gita (74), Lord Shiva declares to Parvati:

piṇḍaṃ kuṇḍalinī śaktim
haṃsa iti udāhṛtam
rūpāṃ binduṃ iti jñeyam
rūpātītaṃ nirañjanaṃ

The meaning of this verse is, the whole body is *pinda* (body). Our flesh body is full of delusion, illusion, and error (*maya*), which is *kundalini shakti*. Contrary to popular misconception, *kundalini* is not a serpent in coiled form lying inert in the coccygeal center. Instead, *kundalini shakti* is *maya*, which is hardly possible to avoid.

Hamsa iti udahritam means, there are two bodies: *ham* body and *sa* body. *Ham* is the *maya* body and *sa* is the conductor of *maya* (i.e., the conductor of *maya* is the Almighty Father who resides in the fontanel and above to infinity).

Rupam binduh means until you go to the atom point in the fontanel you cannot know what is your real form. You see your body form, but inside that the formless is hiding. There is an invisible counterpart in your each body part. So we have to feel these two (*ham* and *sa*) in every step of our life. One has to feel this duality in every moment. Through this duality, one will perceive unity and equanimity. In the Bhagavad Gita (2:48), it is written, *samatvam yoga ucyate*: "That equanimity is yoga."

Parashakti atma mithuna. Parashakti means Shiva, *atma mithuna* is Durga. The Hindus appear to worship the deity, but they do not actually worship the deity. In reality, they worship the formless power of God within the deity. Durga is *prakriti*, mother nature. The formless power of God is inhaling the air.

The air is inhaled by Shiva inside the body of Durga. It is *atma mithuna*. Similarly, in every human body He is inhaling. This is the true sex enjoyment. This is Kriya Yoga:

Breath control is self-control.
Breath mastery is self-mastery.
Breathlessness stage is deathlessness stage.

There are many *-isms* today. In every *-ism* there are some defects. They maintain their own attitudes. They never speak about the defects in their own *-isms*. Some say there is birth and rebirth, and some deny it. There is always a cold fight between the *-isms*. But in Kriya Yoga there is no such *-ism*, no dogmatic viewpoint. Kriya Yoga is the foundation of the spiritual building. Whatever *-ism* it may be — irrespective of cult, creed, sect, religion — all benefit from the practice of the scientific Kriya Yoga technique because it is the highway of the common religions. If one asks, what is the highway of common religions? Then the obvious answer comes, calmness. Kriya Yoga can give you extreme calmness. You will be free from your body, mind, thought, intellect, ego, and worldly sense. If you can attain this state, then your meditation is true meditation.

What is meditation? To go beyond body, mind, intellect, thought, ego, body sense, and worldly sense. In the scriptures it is said, *dhyāna saṃlīna mānasaḥ.* Only Kriya Yoga can achieve this stage. Kriya Yoga is the stepping stone of all religions. So everybody, irrespective of any *-ism,* should practice Kriya Yoga by which he can get complete calmness. He will never feel his body sense and worldly sense while meditating. He can pass beyond *ham*, the *maya* kingdom full of delusion, illusion, and error.

There are two kingdoms in each human body. In the Rig Veda (3:1:3) it is written:

dvā suparṇā sayujā sakhāyā
samānaṃ vṛkṣaṃ parisasvajāte
tayoranyaḥ pippalaṃ svādvatti
anaśnannyo abhicakaśīti

In the body tree there are two birds: one is the body bird and the other is the soul bird. One (body bird) enjoys the fruits of the tree whereas the other (soul bird) does not enjoy, instead it allows the body bird to enjoy. The bird that does not enjoy is your indwelling Self, the formless power of God hiding within each body part. By the practice of Kriya Yoga technique you can feel it practically.

Kriya Yoga is not Ashtanga Yoga (the yogic method with eight limbs). It is Chaturanga Yoga, consisting of the last four limbs of Ashtanga Yoga. These four limbs are *pratyahara* (withdrawing the sense organs), *dharana* (concentration), *dhyana* (meditation), and *samadhi* (complete unity with God, the pulseless stage). The first step is *pratyahara*, which means that when you sit for meditation, first you must withdraw your extrovert sense organs and make them introvert. Then you can proceed further. In the Bhagavad Gita (5:27), it is written, *sparśān kṛtvā bahir bāhyām*: You must forget the thought of the whole universe. But people do not do it. They only chant mantras, sing songs, and repeat names of God. As a result, they get nothing because Brahman is not revealed by the limited sense organs. (See Kena Upanishad 1:3.)

In Vedic scriptures it is written that when you sit for ritualistic meditation, well before that you have to purify your body, then to purify the water, then to purify the whole *asana* (seat). Then you have to purify your fingers, then *kara nyasa, anga nyasa, matrika nyasa,* and so on.

Sanskrit and other ancient Indian languages have fifty letters. In our body system there are fifty body parts associated with the petals in various chakras. These are the two-petalled lotus in the soul center, sixteen in the cervical center, twelve in the heart center, ten in the navel center, six in the sex center, and four in the coccygeal center. (Diagram 1; page 58) All together, there are fifty parts. However, the English language has only twenty-six letters. Whatever we express in writing or speaking, we express through these twenty-six letters. But if you want to know God or want Self-realization, you must go beyond the twenty-six letters or the fifty letters. In many places in the Upanishads, it is written *naiva vacha*, which means God cannot be revealed by speech (i.e., through the letters). If you go beyond the letters, you will be free from everything. Only by the practice of Kriya Yoga can you attain this tranquil state, a state of complete calmness. It is why it is often said that Kriya Yoga is the stepping stone of all religions. Kriya Yoga is the foundation of all spiritual buildings. (Diagrams 5 and 6; pages 110 and 120)

You may remain in any cult, any sect, any tradition, any *-ism*, but you should practice this unique Kriya Yoga technique because it can give you extreme calmness, which is godliness. Your mind will be completely off. You cannot feel where are your legs, where are your thighs, where are your hands, and your whole body. If you add some sugar to a cup of water and stir, then you cannot find any separate existence of sugar. Similarly, by the practice of Kriya Yoga meditation, you cannot feel your physical existence. You will perceive the marvelous power of God within you. You will be as completely merged in God consciousness as sugar in water. It is so unfortunate that you are ignoring Him. But by the practice of Kriya Yoga you can perceive this truth.

A verse in the Bhagavad Gita (2:50) declares, *yogaḥ karmasu kauśalam*: it means there are some techniques in work that help one to be efficient and fruitful. Similarly, in Kriya Yoga there are some techniques if followed through the instruction of a realized master, one can be Self-realized. It is just like a helicopter that takes off from the ground to rise gradually higher and higher. It can also come down from above and finally land on the ground again. As the helicopter moves up and down with some techniques, likewise with the Kriya Yoga technique one can go up the spine, overcome the chakras one by one, and again come down to the base.

In the first center God gives you desire for money, and you earn money. But in reality you are not earning money, rather God is earning money through you. In Kriya Yoga you can feel this while earning money.

In the second center (sex center) God has given you youthful stage. It's why you are getting sex mood. So when you enjoy sexually, you are to watch the marvelous power of God within you, whose presence allows you to enjoy. He allows you to give love to your spouse. So your spouse is the living image of God, that is what you are to feel. Those of you who maintain celibacy should thank God, who allows you to maintain that pure state. In the Bhagavad Gita (14:4) it is written, *tāsāṃ brahma mahād yonir ahaṃ bījapradaḥ pitā*: If your mother does not inhale, she cannot conceive and you could not be born. Again, if God does not inhale through the nostrils of your father, then the seed (sperm) cannot come from him. In this verse the Lord clarifies, "I am the father who plants the seed in the mother's womb who is My divine potency." So in reality father is *purusha* and mother is *prakriti*. Hence the so-called parents, any person male or female in the whole world, are nothing but the living image of God. But nobody wants to realize this truth. They only chant the name of God: God! God! God! Shiva! Shiva! Shiva! Rama! Rama! Rama! They simply chant, feeling nothing internally. They chant the name of Shiva. Lord Shiva represents the sound in the throat, or cervical center (vacuum). But they are ignoring that sound is God. Similarly, in the heart center, Lord Rama represents the touch sensation (air). But they do not feel that air is God.

Likewise, the lord of sight, Surya (sun), resides in the navel center (fire). This fire, *vaishvanara agni*, is God. In the Gita (15:14), God declares Himself as the *vaishvanara* fire. So without His presence, your eyes cannot see anything.

In the sex center, Goddess Kali represents taste. You have to feel this. And, in the bottom center is Lord Ganesh, which is why you can smell.

So by the power of God, you are enjoying life through your five sense organs. While enjoying, you are to feel the presence of God that allows you to enjoy. This is Kriya Yoga. You are fortunate that since your birth, He is constantly inhaling and keeping you alive. He gives constant love to you. So you must express your gratitude of love to Him.

You are born to know thy own Self. That Self-realization can be achieved easily through the practice of Kriya Yoga. Irrespective of any caste, creed, cult, color, race, religion, tradition, any *-ism*, one should come and approach a realized master. Shriyukteshwarji is no longer in this world. As his disciple, I attained *nirvikalpa samadhi* (breathlessness and pulselessness stage), which was observed by many persons on various occasions, even at the request of Sitaram Omkarnath Maharaj in his august presence with his disciples at Varanasi in 1973. If you desire Self-realization, you are to come to my advanced disciples, who are authorized to initiate. They will purify your whole body and can help you feel the three divine qualities (i.e., you can hear divine sound, the talk of God from within; you can see the bright illumination through your third eye; also you can feel the divine vibration, pulsation in your whole body). Then you have to practice the techniques. After that you can get Reality, the absolute Truth, peace, bliss, and joy.

If you touch a bare wire then you feel nothing. But the moment you insert one end of the wire into a socket and touch, then in a moment your whole system will be full of electric charge and it will be magnetized. Similarly, God is remaining in your whole system. If you can be in contact with a good master, then in a moment of that divine touch your whole system will be full of divine charge. You can see divine light, can hear the divine sound, and also can feel the God movement sensation in the whole body.

Before creation there was only white light. The all-pervading Father, the formless, the unseen, was alone. He wanted to be many. Then He contemplated and thereby the whole creation was manifested. By the practice of Kriya Yoga in *paravastha*, one can go beyond all limits, as if consciousness remains in a state like before creation. In this stage, you perceive only milk white light in the whole universe.

In the Mundaka Upanishad (2:2:10) it is written, *tat śubhraṃ jyotiṣāṃ jyotiḥ tat yat ātmavido viduḥ*: In that state the seeker whose mind has gone high up to the infinity perceives only white light, bright illumination like stars and planets. The person who is *atmavid* (knower of the Self) realizes this absolute Truth.

Kriya Yoga is such a simple practical technique that one can practice it 24-hours a day. In every moment, in every breath, in every disposition or mood, the striver feels united with the power of God within. It is written in Bhagavad Gita (2:48), *yogasthaḥ kuru karmāṇi*: Whatever you do should be done being united with the Self.

The whole day and night any work you do is done by the power of God. But everybody forgets God when working. It is written in scriptures that if you remember Him in every step of life, you will get constant God-realization.

In the Kena Upanishad (2:5) it is written:

iha ced avedīd atha satyam asti
na ced ihāvedīn mahatī vinaṣṭiḥ

This means if you know Him just now, then your whole life is fulfilled. If you forget Him, it would be an infinite loss just like death.

Maharshi Patañjali, the author of theYoga Sutra (aphorisms) gives the definition of Kriya Yoga in the first *sutra* of his Sadhana Pada:

tapaḥ svdhyāya īśvarapraṇidhānāni kriyā yogaḥ

Ordinarily *tapas* means austerity, a special type of fire ceremony where ghee (butter oil) is added to the burning flames with the recitation of Vedic mantras. In Kriya Yoga the breath goes inside and touches the soul, thereby making our body alive. The oxygen in the breath is the real fuel to keep the body in contact with the soul. If there was no contact between them, then we would all be dead. This is the real fire ceremony. (Diagram 9; page 127)

Svadhyaya ordinarily means to go through various books on ethics, myths, philosophy, and religion. But its metaphorical meaning is, know thy own Self. So to search your own Self in your whole system is *svadhyaya.* If you remain in the fontanel and practice Kriya, this is real *svadhyaya.*

Lahiri Mahashaya said, Kriya is Veda. One who practices Kriya is like one who reads Veda, so it is *svadhyaya.* Searching your own Self in your whole body and in the body of all human beings is *svadhyaya.*

God planted us in our mothers' wombs and has been constantly inhaling since our birth. He is so kind to us. He loves us so much. But we do not express the gratitude of love towards Him. We should love Him. In every moment, in every breath we should think and say, "O God! You are so kind to us. But we are ignoring You. So please give us alertness so that we can remember Your presence in every breath." To give love in every step of life is *ishwara pranidhana.*

It is written in Vedantasara Upanishad (verse 4), *sa eva enaṃ labhate yah nityam praṇidhānyuktaḥ*: This means that the Self is revealed to those who constantly give love to Him and always remain merged in God consciousness.

In the Mundaka Upanishad (3:1:4) it is written, *ātma-kṛḍaḥ ātma-ratiḥ kriyāvān eṣa brahma-vidāṃ variṣṭhaḥ*: This declares that a person who practices Kriya Yoga (a *kriyavan*) is superior among all realized seekers. In every breath, a *kriyavan* sharply watches the indwelling Self, which is nothing less than the universal Self. It is *atmakridah.* And in every breath, the *kriyavan* watches the breath touching the soul. This is the real sex (i.e., *atmaratih* or *atma mithuna*). So in every breath there is copulation or union.

The Almighty Father, having created human beings and the whole universe, entered into them. This is written in the Taittiriya Upanishad (2:6:3) as *tat sṛṣṭvā tadevānuprāviśat*: There is nothing in the whole universe that is not God. God is all-pervading. He is hiding in every human being.

In the Shvetashvatara Upanishad (6:11) it is written:

eko devaḥ sarva-bhūteṣu gūḍhaḥ
sarva-vyāpī sarva-bhūtāntarātmā
karmādhyakṣaḥ sarva-bhūtādhivāsaḥ
sākṣī cetā kevalo nirguṇaḥ ca

Sarvavyapi sarvabhutantaratma means God is omnipresent, all-pervading and He is the indwelling Self among all. *Karmadhyaksha* means He is doing every work and conducting every action and is allowing every person to perform actions. *Sarvabhutadhivasah* means He is the lone shelter of all living beings, nay, the whole universe.

Sakshi means He is the witness of all. *Cheta* means as the sole Self consciousness, He gives consciousness to every human being, thereby making each rational and discriminatory. Thus by the practice of Kriya Yoga meditation, which is completely transcendental, the *kriyavan* hastens consciousness into superconsciousness, cosmic consciousness, and finally into wisdom, the complete state of tranquility and a state of complete oneness with the supreme Self.

Kevalah means He is pure and is above the three *gunas* (*sattva*, *raja*, *tamas*).

Only by the practice of the original authentic Kriya Yoga technique declared by Babaji Maharaj to Lahiri Mahashaya and then through Shriyukteshwarji, Paramahamsa Yogananda and then to myself (Hariharananda), and so on, can one attain this state with sincere practice.

In Kriya Yoga there is no hardship in breath control, no difficult *pranayama*. One need not control the breath by holding it forcefully by pressing the nostrils with the fingers. However, by the practice of Kriya Yoga technique, the breath is automatically controlled and becomes feeble and very short. There are fifty types of breaths. Out of that, forty-nine give delusion, illusion, and error (*maya*). Only one short breath is utilized in Kriya Yoga to proceed further in meditation. In the Prashna Upanishad (3:7) it is written, *athaikayo urdhva udānaḥ. Udana* is that short breath that leads the *kriyavan* high into the sky, up to infinity. In *paravastha*, a stage in Kriya Yoga, one can realize this Truth.

A *kriyavan* always focuses attention in the fontanel, in the atom point. In the Hatha Yoga Pradipika (4:114) it is written, *yāvad bindur na bhavati dṛḍha.* So long as your mind is not fixed in that atom point, you cannot progress in meditation.

In the same scripture it is again written, *yāvan naiva praviśati caran mārūto madhya mārge*: So long as your breath does not become feeble and short and equally distributed in the two nostrils, allowing the breath to flow in the *sushumna*, you cannot proceed further in meditation. But Kriya Yoga can grant this. It is the simplest, easiest, quickest, surest, and best technique for the simultaneous development of the body, mind, intellect, and soul.

Nowadays, many try to become realized by offering various types of *puja* (e.g., chanting mantras, singing hymns, and repeating the name of God). They are trying to find God with their sense organs. But how can the Unlimited be attained by the limited sense organs?

japāt śānto punaḥ dhyāyet
dhyānāt śānto punaḥ japet

You may do *puja* as you like. You may chant mantras or repeat the name of God as you wish. But after that, you must meditate. Or after meditation you may do your *puja* and repeat the name of God. But still you have to meditate. It is a must and the only passage to go beyond the mundane world and become merged into God consciousness, to be redeemed.

The evolution theory has three aspects: heredity, environment, and culture. You are God in human form. It is your heritage. But you are ignorant of that. This is why you must practice meditation. Before practice, you should come to a realized master. This is your true environment. A student-doctor comes to a teacher-doctor to learn. After homework and thorough practice, the student becomes a doctor. Likewise, after learning the techniques of meditation from a realized master, you are to practice it wholeheartedly. Then evolution comes as a result of Self-realization.

There is always an invisible counterpart abiding in each body part. Wherever you are touching, you are touching the formless power of God. If He does not inhale, then you are merely a dead body. Our breath is His breath and controlled by Him. He is constantly inhaling. It is why our blood is liquid and circulated everywhere inside the body. Through that circulation you have to watch God. You should perceive God, who remains in your whole system.

Kriya Yoga is for all religions. People of any religion should practice Kriya Yoga to get absolute calmness, a state of complete tranquility, and to be free from body sense, mind, ego, and worldly sense. Then meditation can grant you success and all-round development in life. You can feel you are God in human being and human being in God. Only by the practice of Kriya Yoga can you feel it.

Kriya Yoga is the simplest technique, a shortcut technique for God-realization. It also develops body, mind, and intellect simultaneously. It imparts skill and tact in practical day-to-day-life, success in every step of life. You will get the sharpest memory. The receptive and retentive powers of the brain will be increased greatly. You will know how to talk nicely, how to behave politely with others in society. Kriya Yoga can grant you all this. It will give you Reality, Truth, and constant alertness of the inner Self in practical life.

In Kriya Yoga meditation, one focuses attention on the top of the head, in the fontanel. A dead person has no need, as it cannot do anything. God is remaining in the whole system. There are three bodies: gross body, astral body, and causal body. With the gross body, one sees light. With the astral body, one feels divine vibration or God movement sensation. And with the causal body one hears the constant uninterrupted divine sound. Our causal body is above the head up to infinity. This is the father nature. The astral body is within. These two bodies are in constant touch with the Almighty Father. The cerebral cortex, from the pituitary (in between the eyebrows, four inches deep) up to the fontanel. This is your mother nature. According to Hinduism, the father nature is Shiva, and the mother nature is Durga. For other *-isms*, the Almighty Father is the father nature and Moses, Daniel, Jesus, Mohammed, Buddha, Zarathusthra, and others are the mother nature. They are the conductors; they are prophets, teachers, masters. They are in constant touch with the Almighty Father. This is the second body. The third body is our gross body, which is constantly engrossed in delusion, illusion, and error (DIE), so we are livingly dead. If you want to get God-realization, you have to pass beyond the three bodies. You are to go up to infinity, beyond even that. You have to leave your gross body first. Secondly, you have to leave Moses, Jesus, Buddha, Durga, and others, your mother nature. Thirdly, you must go above your head, up to infinity, to merge with the Almighty Father. There is no question of caste, creed, sect, cult; no question of any *-isms* to reach the Absolute Reality, Godhood. Before creation, there existed nothing except milk-white light. So you should remain there. You are to go to the place that is before creation. In Kriya Yoga meditation, one can reach this state of before creation.

If you want God-realization, or the *samadhi* stage, fix your attention in the fontanel and slowly go above infinity north. In *paravastha*, you can feel this state. Your fontanel is not on the top of your head, rather it remains in the infinity north that you can feel. In this state you will have no body sense, no worldly sense. You will feel as if the whole universe is an unmanifested form.

In the Mundaka Upanishad (2:1:2) it is written:

divyo hy amūrtaḥ puruṣah
sa bāhyābhyantaro hi ajaḥ
aprāṇo hyamanāḥ śubhro
akṣarāt parataḥ paraḥ

Paravastha in Kriya Yoga is a state of transcendence. *Divyah amurtah* means in this state you have no body. You are formless. The Almighty Father remains inside your body; also He pervades beyond your body limit infinitely (*sa bahyabhyantare*). *Ajah* means you have no birth, no beginning of life. You have gone before creation. *Apranah* means no life force. When you go deeper and deeper in this state, your breath will be shorter and shorter. The moment the breath ceases to flow inside, you attain the *samadhi* stage. *Amanah* means the complete absence of mind. *Shubhrah* means you have gone before the creation and you are perceiving only milk-white light. In this state you are beyond everything. You are beyond every form and formless:

na sthanam	you cannot feel your existence where you sit.
na manam	you have no mind, body sense, and ego. You cannot feel your body volume.
na rupam	no form, everything is formless.
na ca nadabindu	no sound, nothing else.
na rekha	no feeling of any sign, any limitation.
na ca dhatuvarnam	no color of the society (i.e., no *maya*).

If you feel all these above, then at the very next stage you can attain *samadhi* stage. You will be one with the Almighty Father. You will feel nothing in this stage. Through this "nothing" you may feel "something," which can never be described by any means. It is quite ineffable. It is a state of deadly living. If you are engrossed in delusion, illusion, and error (i.e., *maya*), then you are livingly dead. Only Kriya Yoga can give you this stage of salvation, a life of lively living.

In the Bible (1 Cor. 6:19–20) it is written, "Do you not know your body is the temple of God and God dwells within you?" You are born for God-realization only. It is your birthright. "Know thy Self, presume not God to scan, the proper study of mankind is man" (Alexander Pope). Let not the golden opportunity slip from your hand. Opportunity must not be neglected for it may never return, so practice the scientific technique of Kriya Yoga and be realized.

VIII

UTILITIES OF KRIYA YOGA

Human life is very short, and constantly associated with a multitude of difficulties and obstacles. So, it is the duty of all wise and intelligent people to accept and assimilate the essence of all spiritual practice, like a swan taking away the cheese leaving only water from the milk. Kriya Yoga is the essence of all spiritual practices and it is the common highway of all religions.

Within a very short time, by the practice of the scientific technique of Kriya Yoga, one can get simultaneous development of body, mind, intellect, and soul. By magnetizing the spine by a very simple Kriya practice, one can perceive all-accomplishing divine energy in the body, which in turn hastens physical, mental, and intellectual transformation and, ultimately, gives constant God consciousness.

Like any other science, the meditation of Kriya Yoga has two aspects: theory and practice. The theoretical knowledge of Kriya Yoga, one can inculcate by reading holy books, its metaphorical interpretation by realized masters, or listening to spiritual discourses. An ounce of practice is far better than tons of theories. So reading or listening may create an impetus or desire, but it is not enough. It is highly essential to learn and practice the scientific technique from a realized master or highly advanced *kriyavan acharyas* who are empowered to teach.

Kriya Yoga is a practical science. It does not make attractive promises to be materialized in heaven or the afterlife. It gives immediate result: direct perception of Truth. Kriya Yoga gives payment in cash with immediate utility, not by cheque that needs to be converted. It confers mathematical results. The easiest, surest, simplest, quickest, and best technique of Kriya Yoga is a complete and well-balanced technique that can bring all-round development.

Health is Wealth

The human body is the principal thing and the foundation for a happy and spiritual life. There is a proverb in Sanskrit, *śarīram ādyaṃ khaludharma sādhanam*: "Take care of the body; through good health one can practice and progress in spiritual life."

The body may be compared with a car or a machine. Kept in perfect condition, it gives immense utility. If the body-vehicle is not in good condition, then it is difficult to reach the destination of life, which is God-realization.

The greatest wonder in the universe is the human life (i.e., the soul living in a house, or the body/sense-mind/intellect complex). The human body is the most delicate system with many automatic and powerful organs. Heart and lungs are non-stop pumps, the eyes are automatic camera-*cum*-projectors, which constantly take accurate and perfect images immediately. The nervous system (with its sensory and motor nerves, sympathetic and parasympathetic nerves) is the fastest communication system. The ear, nose, tongue, skin, and genitals are delicate organs in their own fields. The stomach constantly digests varieties of food and the small intestine assimilates the essence of the food. The anus, urinary system, skin, and nose constitute the drainage system of the body. There are many glands with ducts and without ducts like pancreas, spleen, liver, thyroid, parathyroid, pituitary, and so forth, which regulate the human system.

Above all, the human brain, a small part in the human body, has tremendous power; it controls, regulates and systematizes all functions of the body and the mind. It is also known as the divine kingdom because it is the seat of the soul, the source of all spiritual energy. (Diagram 16; page 198)

If any human limb is in disorder, the whole body suffers and life becomes miserable. The human body is the vehicle for peace and happiness, but it may often become a storehouse of diseases. Diseases destroy the blessings of life. Bodily ailment brings physical suffering, mental upset, monetary strain and, above all, loss of precious human energy and time.

By the practice of the scientific technique of Kriya Yoga, the entire human system is magnetized and energized in a very short time. All the internal organs (like the liver, pancreas, spleen, thyroid, pituitary, pineal gland) are activated. They secrete the necessary hormones and enzymes to keep the body fit. There will be sufficient blood circulation in the brain and spine for a balanced supply of oxygen to every remote part of the body. The digestive system, gastro-intestinal system, cardio-vascular system, respiratory system, excretory system, nervous system, genital system, and so on become active and efficient. (Diagram 12; page 178)

The ancient yogis, speaking highly of the technique of Kriya Yoga, wrote:

"Kriya Yoga cures and prevents many unknown and fatal diseases, and increases digestive and assimilating power, which brings a beautiful, lustrous and slim body till death. It prevents premature old age and death, giving a long and healthy life." (Shiva Samhita 4:32–34)

By the practice of this scientific technique, the body and mind remain disease free, enabling one to live a complete life span of hundred years, as declared in the Isha Upanishad (1:2), *jijīviśet satamsamā.* Through a life of moderation and regular practice of Kriya Yoga, one can enjoy the beauty of human life, perceiving peace, bliss, and joy.

Mind Control

Mind is the greatest blessing as well as the greatest human predicament. A regulated, controlled, and channelled mind can give and fulfill all the expectation of human life, but if uncontrolled, it brings hell, miseries, and sufferings. Although humans are endowed with tremendous mental power, it is unused, misused, and even abused. The mind is most powerful and moves faster than anything else.

The Kriya technique highlights the relationship between breath and mind. Breath influences mind and vice-versa. Their mutual relationship answers the mystery of how to control the mind.

Breath control is self-control. Breath mastery is self-mastery. Breathlessness stage is deathlessness stage that brings the state of *samadhi,* the realization of the Absolute.

Kriya Yoga is based on scientific breathing that pacifies, slows the breathing process, and makes the breath flow inside the nostrils, not outside.

By the practice of Kriya Yoga, in a short time the mind becomes calm, quiet, and thoughtless. The blood, absorbing sufficient oxygen and getting de-carbonized, brings better living. We may become free from the stress and strain of life. A number of psychosomatic diseases can be avoided.

Intellectual Development

Man's memory, intelligence, and brainpower bring success in the material and worldly life. Kriya Yoga will make one simple, pure, perfect, humble, and constantly alert. By the practice of the scientific technique of Kriya Yoga, one gets promptness, ready wit, and ability to cope with any situation or circumstance, and positive thinking.

Through more circulation in the brain energizing the brain cells, the working capacity of the brain is enhanced. One will not tire easily. Memory and retentive quality of the brain will increase.

Personality Development

The word personality comes from the Latin word *persona*, which means the mask or the covering. The formless soul is covered with the three bodies: ignorance, thought, and gross body. Man suffers from weak personality because of falsehood, hypocrisy, jealousy, ego, arrogance, malice, duplicity — all negative qualities. All these negative qualities diminish the standard of human personality.

By the practice of Kriya Yoga, one will be free from all negative qualities of human life. Love will flourish. The bond of friendship will be stronger. The body will be beautiful until death. One's appearance will be loving, pleasant, convincing, and divine. One will have sweet and balanced speech. Through avoiding unnecessary godless chatter, one will get immense mental, intellectual, and spiritual energy by the techniques of Kriya Yoga. One's own power of understanding will increase, so also the power to make decisions in a critical moment.

All noble and divine wishes will be fulfilled. One will get thorough control over restless and turbulent senses. Self-content, self-discipline, and God consciousness will bring a change in one's living. Kriya Yoga brings change in the entire personality, making one free from falsehood and the negative, and constantly absorbed in Truth.

Spiritual Growth

Self-realization is our birthright and the highest objective of human life. The power of God is ever present, constant in every moment; one is not able to perceive it due to delusion, illusion, and error. Kriya Yoga enables constant soul awareness, in every breath, every thought, and every moment. It quickens spiritual evolution and takes one to the door of spiritual realization in a short time.

Free from unnecessary hardship of other so-called yogas that call for extreme body gymnastics, with a little effort and endeavor, one gets ample spiritual harvest. However, the necessary precondition is to practice the technique with love, daily, regularly, and sincerely with implicit faith in God and guru. Kriya Yoga meditation enables one to feel that God and His creation are one. Constant happiness, peace, bliss, and joy will be the constant companions of one who practices Kriya Yoga.

These few words cannot explain or highlight the immense benefits of the marvelous technique of Kriya Yoga. The real path is perceived by the one who follows, practices, and realizes.

IX

ANTASTHAVARNA

Inside the spinal canal, from the cervical center down to the coccygeal center, there are five centers. Associated with these five centers are five letters. (Diagrams 10 and 11; pages 148 and 149) In the cervical center there is *sam,* which means vacuum. In the heart center the letter is *yam,* which means air. In the navel center there is *ram,* which means fire. This is also called *vaishvanara* fire, which is the fire that digests your food. The food is transformed and from it you are getting chyme, which is the power of God. In the sacral center is the letter *vam,* which means water. This is the water center. Finally, the coccygeal center is the earth, which is *lam.* Everything is grown in the ground.

These five letters are *antasthavarna. Antasthavarna* means to establish life, to create life. *Antastha* means to create life from the five gross elements (vacuum, air, fire, water, and earth). If you cultivate the ground and sow seeds in it, life will come from the seeds. Plant the seed in the ground and give it water. The sunlight shines on the ground and the air and vacuum are also there. Then the seed will germinate. The seed is germinating with the five gross elements.

The power of God is remaining in the seed. The seed is the life of God (i.e., *sa*). *Sa* is in the pituitary, which is the sixth center, the soul or Christ center. The letter for this center is *ham,* which means life or life energy. *Ham* means "I am." It is the seed of God.

Before a baby is born, the father placed his seed into the mother's womb. The seed germinated and after nine months the baby emerged in the full shape of a human being. That seed has become the living power of God. Your entire gross body is *ham,* which is your life energy. *Ham* is remaining in the pituitary. There you see light and feel that you are the living power of God — you are formed from the seed of God.

From one seed placed in the ground, the plant sprouts. From the many types of seeds we get all the different trees and plants. Everything comes from a seed, so the seed is the principal thing. The seed of God is above, in the sixth center.

In many diagrams of the centers in the spine there are mistakes. The main mistake is that *ham* is placed in the cervical center at the base of the neck. There are not two *hams.* The only *ham* is in the two-petalled lotus in the pituitary. *Sa* is the seed of the vacuum, so *sam* is in the cervical center. Then *yam* is in the heart center, *ram* is in the navel, *vam* is in the sex center, and *lam* is in the coccyx. Through these five gross elements, God gives life to each human being. The life of God remains inside the sixth center (i.e., *sa*).

The seed of God is covered by twenty-four gross elements. The deadly electric current in the wire is covered by the insulator surrounding the conductor. Similarly, the marvelous living power of God is covered with the twenty-four gross elements, the body insulator. *Panca-maha-bhuta* means the five gross elements (earth, water, fire, air, and vacuum) and *jnanendriya* are the five sense organs (eye, ear, nose, tongue, and skin). The five senses are the essence of *panca-tan-matra*; sight, sound, smell, taste, and touch sensation. The five work organs are *karmendriya*: *vak* is the work of talking; *pani*, work of hands; *pada*, work with legs; *upastha*, work with the genital center; and *payu*, by the rectum. These elements total twenty. The remaining four elements are *manas* (mind), *buddhi* (intellect), *ahamkara* (ego), and *chitta* (thoughts and restlessness).

These twenty-four gross elements cannot do anything without

the soul. Along with these elements, the soul, *sa*, is remaining on the top in the pituitary. We should purify these twenty-four gross elements and feel that God is within them. We should feel that *sa* is pulling breath.

In the soul center, in the Christ center, there is *ham* and *sa*. This is why it is said that *ham* means life; we have life. The body is *ham* and the soul is *sa*. The Soul is pulling breath; this is why we are alive. So our inhalation is *sa*. After your exhalation, if you cannot again inhale, you are a dead body. Your gross body, your *ham* body, will be a dead body. Your *sa* body infuses life into the dead body. Life is given by God, the power of God. This is the multiplicity of divine being. You are only the power of God — you are to perceive that you are That.

The more a person goes toward spirituality, the more he will experience calmness. Through breath control the person can attain a very feeble breath and reach the introvert stage by withdrawing attention from the lower centers. Then by offering himself with love, the person can see that God is doing the work.

In the coccygeal center, there are four *varnas*: *vaṃ*, *śaṃ*, *ṣaṃ*, and *saṃ*. *Sa* means God. These three *sa*(s) are activated from the vacuum center (throat) up to the fontanel. But we are in the extrovert stage, which is why the four *varnas* are engrossed in money, sex, and food. By the Kriya Yoga technique, you can withdraw your senses from the lower centers and come up to the top, in the soul center.

Some people have the wrong impression that the space (*akasha*) is only in the sixteen-petalled lotus, which is in the cervical (throat) center, the vacuum center. Undoubtedly, it is in the vacuum center, but there are five vacuums. In the scriptures it is written that *akasha* is in the cervical and *chidakasha* is in the pituitary. Then comes *parakasha*, which is one-half inch above the pituitary. Above that is *daharakasha*. *Parakasha* means superconscious state. *Daharakasha* means you have no sense of the body, everything is burnt. *Dahara* means burnt; in *daharakasha* you have no worldly sense, you have no body sense. Then comes *atmakasha* — the soul, the power of God, the Son of God, the children of God. That is your life, *sa.* That is *atmaksha.* (Diagram 7; page 121)

In *hamsa*, we say *sa.* This is the soul. And above the soul, there is *mahakasha.* That is the one almighty, formless Father of all religions. God is remaining in the fontanel, even above it. In the Bible (1 Cor. 3:16) it is written, "Do you not know your body is the temple of God and God dwells within you?" This means the power of God is abiding in the fontanel. So these are the five vacuums where the sixteen-petalled lotus is remaining. From the forehead, from the top, it is moving in counterclockwise direction.

The Bhagavad Gita (6:25) says:

śanaiḥ-śanair uparamed
buddhyā dhṛtigṛhītayā
ātmsaṃsthaṃ manaḥ kṛtvā
na kiñcid api cintayet

"Gradually you are to come up from the lower centers
and merge in the soul center."

Jesus said that you are to be born again from above through water and spirit. This author and his authorized disciples teach the original Kriya Yoga technique of Lahiri Mahashaya and Shriyukteshwarji. They can purify the whole body within five minutes' time and raise the whole energy from the lower centers to the two-petalled lotus, to the soul.

In the English language there are twenty-six letters, five vowels and twenty-one consonants. Similarly, in Sanskrit there are fifty letters, of which sixteen are vowels and the rest are consonants. From the letters we make words and from the words we make sentences. Through our speech we express our mind, our thoughts. Since we constantly remain in the extrovert stage, we always express our money thoughts, our sex thoughts, and our food thoughts with the fifty letters. (Diagrams 5 and 6; pages 110 and 120)

The first vowel of Sanskrit is *am*, which also can be pronounced as *ham*. The first consonant is *ka*, and the last is *sa*. When the two consonants are combined, they form *ksha*. In the pituitary the two-petalled lotus has two letters, one for each petal. One letter is *ham* and the other is *ksham*. By the practice of Kriya Yoga, within five minutes' time a person can withdraw all fifty letters into the two-petalled lotus and lock them in the mid-brain.

When the two-petalled lotus has not unfolded, it is just like a bud. This is why Shriyukteshwarji created the symbol for Kriya Yoga that is shown on the front page of this book. The central bud represents the third eye and below are the eyebrows. We are always engaged in matter and memory, so the lotus bud — the third eye — has not bloomed. The lotus bud looks just like the palms of our two hands pressed together. When we open our two hands side by side, the two-petal lotus opens — one is *ham* (our gross body) and the other is *sa* (soul). *Sa* means He who is constantly pulling our breath. The *ham* body is a dead body, if *sa* (soul) does not pull breath and take oxygen.

If you take all the fifty letters and put them inside a box and lock it, you cannot speak. So put all your fifty letters inside the cranium and calmly remain there. Do not allow any thought. Watch the sound: God, God, God; Lord, Lord, Lord; *om, om, om*. Then you will be free from all thoughts. All thoughts come from God. If you remain only in God (*sa*), human thoughts (*ham*) cannot come. This is *hamsa sadhana*.

If you chant *hamsa, hamsa, hamsa* 1,000 times, you are a human being. If you watch your breath, you are a human being. If you go beyond thoughts, then you are not in breath. Your

Human Physiology

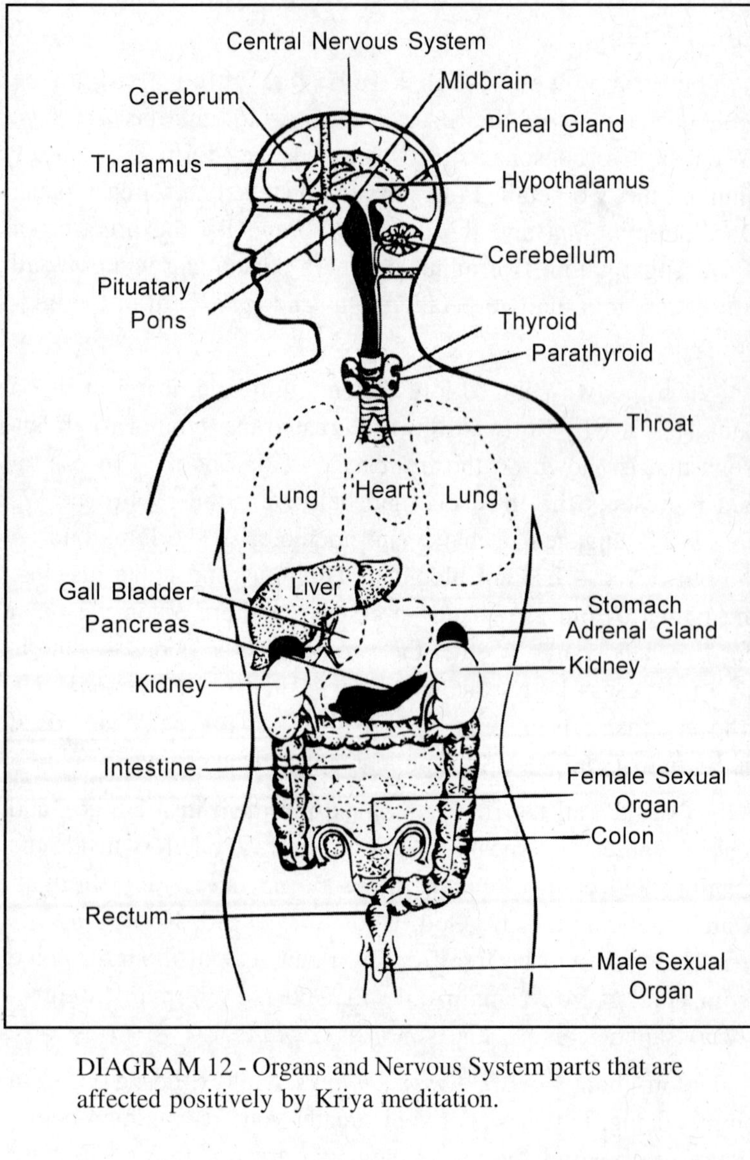

DIAGRAM 12 - Organs and Nervous System parts that are affected positively by Kriya meditation.

Each Human Body is a Bhagavad Gita

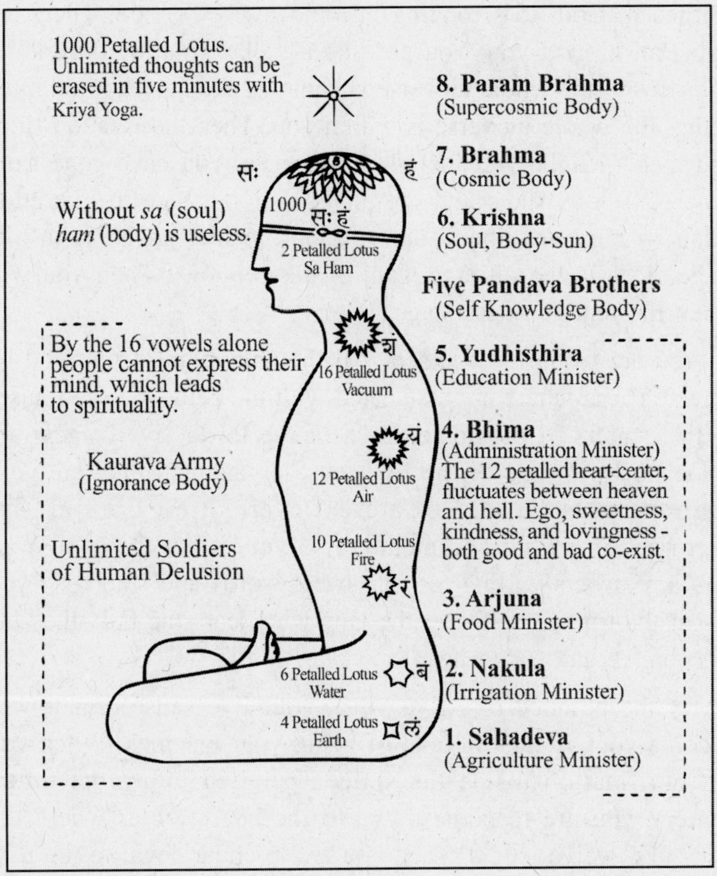

DIAGRAM 13 - Each human body is a Bhagavad Gita. Human beings exchange feelings and thoughts through these 50 sacred letters, one for each lotus petal. If they do not go beyond thoughts and worldly sense, their meditation is useless. With the first technique of Kriya Yoga, people can go beyond mind, thought, intellect, ego, body sense, and worldly sense.

breath is very feeble. *Ksha* is on the right side of the brain. All the consonants are there: *ka* to *sa.* Then they dissolve; *ham-ksha* becomes *ham-sa.* Then you are in the soul; you are almost merged in God. It is rotating in a clockwise fashion. There are lights all around you. You are like a globe, rotating. You are a microcosm; the whole universe is spinning. You are not a limited being; the whole universe is within you. Then the rotation stops and there is light over the whole universe. You have gone from superconscious stage and cosmic conscious stage to liberation stage — constant liberation. You can go into *samadhi* in this stage. This is the ultimate goal of all religions. Then you will reach the real formless stage.

You are to purify yourself. All thoughts come from God by letters. These letters are associated with the petals on the lotuses in the centers of the spine. Each of the lower five centers are associated with one of the five sense organs and they are your main enemies. Your eyes are extroverted; they are always engrossed in matter and memory, so you forget the soul. Your ears are always willing to hear sweet words and songs, so you forget the truth. You forget the One who hears the talk, the One who directs the ear to hear.

By the practice of Kriya Yoga, your five sense organs will become your friends instead of being your enemies. When you get purification inside the sixteen-petalled lotus (the throat center), you are to come down to the heart center where the lotus has twelve letters. Then you are to come down to the next center, and the next. In this way, you are to purify all the centers of the spine.

All the centers are activated from the top by the power of God. That is *ya,* soul. But until you purify all your centers, you will not feel it. Any work you do in the coccygeal center; to earn money is done by God. God is earning the money. You are enjoying sexually, but a dead man cannot enjoy sexually; so, you should feel that it is the power of God who is remaining detached and allowing you to enjoy. We should keep fifty percent attention on God and fifty percent on our activity. God has made nine holes, nine doors — two ears, two eyes, two nostrils, mouth, sex organ, and rectum — only for divine joy. God has given nine holes to the animal beings also, but they cannot perceive the power of God. They cannot get that divine joy.

Kriya Yoga is not inaction. It is God in human being, human being in God — static in dynamic, dynamic in static. You are to feel that everything is conducted by the indwelling Self. Watch your food center and see that this center is also conducted by the soul, that is, *kri* and *ya.* While getting the food, tasting the food, your work is to watch that you are not eating. A dead man cannot eat, even a human being cannot eat. You are feeding the power of God who has given you appetite. You are giving Him satisfaction. God is getting satisfaction within you. So love Him. This is Kriya Yoga. This is not religion; it is a sound technique by which you will get purity and perfection. You will feel that you are God in human being.

Any person, whoever one may be, of any religion, should cultivate his land by the ancient technique that is brought by God. That is Kriya Yoga. This means you should do your work the whole day and night. It is nature's law that you will work. But you should perceive that it is the power of God who is doing the work. Kriya Yoga is not inaction, it is not religion.

When devotees, true spiritual seekers for God-realization, come to a realized master, the master will purify their bodies and raise the power of the devotees. At that time they will immediately feel they are super-human beings. They will feel the divine sound, divine light, and divine vibration. At the same time they will be released from body sense, mind, thoughts, and ego. They will get knowledge, consciousness, superconsciousness, and cosmic consciousness. At that time the extrovert gross body (*ham*) is completely merged with the introvert invisible body (*sa*). With the practice of this *antasthavarna,* they can easily perceive calmness and get liberation. Their body will be completely charged with the divine current. The more they practice it daily, regularly, sincerely — for five to ten minutes' time — and apply it in their daily life in every step of their work, the more they will feel that they are God in human being. That is *kri* and that work is done by *ya.*

Everyone — poor, middle class, or millionaire; doctor, engineer, or scientist — does work by the soul. If they practice this technique, they can feel the power of God is doing work through their body in every activity. They will get constant alertness in the soul. This is Kriya Yoga in practical life. This is Veda in practical life. This is Bible in practical life. In the Bible it is written that your eyes should seek God. If not, pluck out your eyes. If your arms and legs are not seeking God, cut off your arms and legs. (Matthew 5:29–30)

We do not feel the teachings of the Bible and apply them in our daily life. God is the sole doer. In the Bible (Matthew 4:4) it is written that your mouth is not made for bread only, but the words that proceed from your mouth are the talk of God. Also in the Kena Upanishad (1:7), it is written that God directs the eye to see, allows the mouth to speak, and activates all the sense organs. The same teachings are given in the Vedas.

Many people want God-realization. They spend many hours in their church, mosque, temple, synagogue, and even in their house for their spiritual upliftment, for their divine change. That is good, because half a loaf is better than no loaf. But if they ask their conscience, they can easily say they have not changed their habits. They don't feel that God is activating them. They still have the same anger, pride, cruelty, selfishness, and extroverted stage. They have no calmness.

Kriya Yoga is the ancient technique. God brought the supreme mystery of Kriya Yoga with His creation. At that time there were no *-isms*, no religion, no scriptures. In the period of the Satya Yuga (era of Truth) 23,300 years ago, people were only practicing breath control. In the Bible (Genesis 1:27 and 2:7), it is written that God made men and women in His own image and He breathed into their nostrils the breath of His life and He became the living Soul in the whole universe. So He is pulling His own breath — this is *ya.*

Now there are many religions, emotions, hallucinations, speculations, imaginings, and suggestions. When all these disappear, you will get God-realization.

From the moment we get up until we go to bed, we are doing work. That work is *kri* and it is done by *ya*. This is an easy, simple technique. A person that attains the superconscious and cosmic conscious stage can easily avoid drugs and intoxicants and can do work for the nation. At the same time, they can feel that they are God in human being, human being in God.

This is not mere talk. The author is a world teacher. He travels nine months of the year in foreign countries, because these countries have everything except peace. The people are in frustration, sorrow, and trouble. The author is moving from one place to another and changing the people's bad habits. He is helping people to get calmness, which is godliness.

You should read books — the Bhagavad Gita, the Upanishads, the Vedas, Patañjali's Yoga Sutra, the Bible, the Quran, and the Torah. Along with this you should meditate practically for five to ten minutes each day. A person cannot be a doctor, engineer, or scientist only by reading books. They must also do practical experiments. Through such experiments they invent many things.

Take time by the forelock; seek the realized master, and taste the truth. Purify your extroverted stage — your sins, animality, and ego — within a short period. During the whole day and night, remain in the material world and feel that you are human being in God and God in human being. This is your constant liberation — alertness in your inner Self. He is the sole doer; that is your constant liberation. Every moment you are the power of God, but every moment you are forgetting Him. It is a rare opportunity to conceive God, perceive God, and realize God because you all are the children of God.

X

HAMSA

The creation of God consists of five gross elements, which are: vacuum, air, fire, water, and earth. Human beings are part and parcel of this creation of God and have in them these five gross elements.

In the human body, inside the spinal canal, there are six main work centers. The coccygeal is the money center, the sacral is the sex center, the lumbar is the food center, the dorsal is the animality and attachment center, the cervical is the center for beginning spirituality (emptiness), and the pituitary is the God-realization center. (Diagram 9; page 128)

In the pituitary there is a two-petalled lotus; one petal is *ham* and the other is *sa*. Although *ham* and *sa* appear to be different, in fact they are one. *Ham* is the gross body and *sa* is the soul. The lotus flowers in the remaining five centers (cervical, dorsal, lumbar, sacral, and coccygeal) have a varying number of petals. Each center represents one of the five gross elements (vacuum, air, fire, water, and earth), with the help of which life is grown and sustained. (Diagrams 1, 10, 11; pages 58, 148, and 149)

Ham (our gross body, "I am") always feels, "I am the monarch or master of my entire being." But the real "I" is our soul, which is *sa*. *Sa* remains in our whole system. *Sa* means our soul and is the sole doer of the body; without the soul a human body is a dead body.

When we are under the influence of biological force and ignorance, we feel, "I am the monarch of all I survey." But when people get Self-realization, they perceive that there are two bodies. One is the ignorant body, which is "I am." The other is

Human Physiology

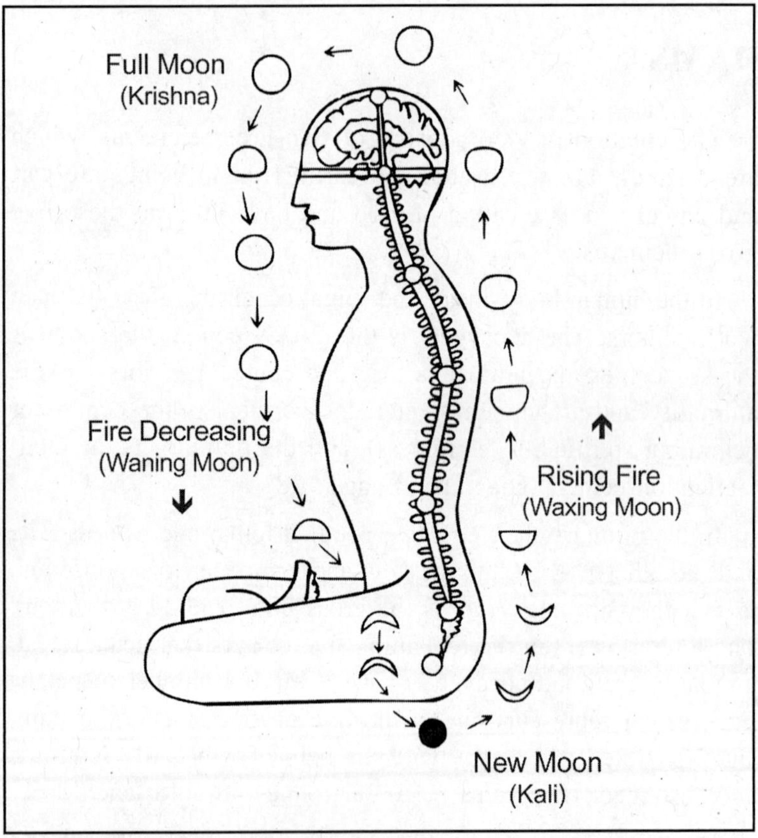

DIAGRAM 14 - All-Pervading Fire of God. The moon cycle represents the changing desires of the human mind. Kriya Yoga spiritualizes the desire for money, sex, love, or food by drawing their elemental essence up the spine into the crown and back down into the coccyx. The 14 phases or "lights" of the moon symbolize the life force in the 14 centers (7 centers downward in front and 7 centers upward in the back). The 15th, or new moon, recalls the spontaneous moment of creation by mahakāl. Kali is time, i.e., Isha the great Soul (Kali) who is the conductor of time.

the real body, "He," who is our indwelling Self, and the sole doer of all activities of the gross body.

When people get Self-realization, then the feeling becomes "I am He" (*hamsa*). This is the time when the two words *ham* and *sa* merge together and become *hamsa* — similarly *so'ham*. The apparently separate words *ham* and *sa* are in reality one word, *hamsa*, which is to be realized by *sadhana*.

The matter can be further explained as follows: Our gross body and dead body are both *ham*. Each human body is just like a motorcar standing on the street. Without the soul, the driver of the body motorcar, our body cannot move. So our body is *ham* body, which means "I am." And who is pulling inhalation through the nose? He is the real "I," *sa*, the soul.

A dead body cannot inhale. So inhalation cannot be *ham*, because the power of God is inhaling. So *sa* is inhaling; *sa* is the power of God, who is pulling inhalation through our nose.

In Gheranda Samhita (5:83), *kevala kumbhaka*, it is written: *haṃkāreṇa bahir-yāti-sakāreṇa viśet punaḥ*: it means the outgoing breath is *ham* and the incoming breath is *sa*, because *sa* means soul, who is pulling inhalation.

In the Shiva Svarodaya scripture (verse 51) it is written, *haṃkāro nirgame proktaḥ sakārastu praveśane*, which means when the air is going out through the nose it is *ham* and when the air is entering through the nose it is *sa* because *sa* is the soul and only the soul is pulling inhalation.

Now I am explaining the higher philosophy of *hamsa*. In Kriya Yoga, when a devotee goes beyond mind, thought, intellect, ego, body, and worldly sense, at that time he gets *paravastha*, the superconscious stage. At that time the devotee only feels divine sound, vibration, and light. Only then he really feels the real love for God. This is called mother nature. During that time the devotee really perceives *sa* (soul only) and merges in the cosmic conscious stage. This is real *yoga nidra*. In that stage the devotee gets extreme divine peace, bliss, and joy. This is really *sa sadhana*. Just after this type of meditation, when the devotee opens the eyes and keeps attention inside the pituitary he perceives the triple divine qualities and real love for God. And as he keeps his attention in the lower center with open eyes, although he remains in the body sense (*ham*), yet he perceives the living presence of the soul (*sa*) in the whole system and visualizes the material world and gross body plus the living presence of the soul everywhere. This is real *hamsa sadhana*.

But those who are like a machine, exhaling *sa* and inhaling *ham* and mentally chanting *ham* and *sa*, are undoubtedly doing lower grade meditation.

In the Mahanirvana Tantra it is said, *uttama brahma sadbhāva dhyāna-bhavastu madhyamā stutir japa-adhama bhāva bāhya pūjā adhamādhama*: which means the first grade meditation is *brahma sadbhava*, the perception of the soul in the gross body and in the universe. Second grade are those who only imagine form constantly, which is not possible without soul culture. Third grade are those who are mentally chanting or praying or through inhalation chanting *so'ham hamsa*. Fourth grade are those who offer flowers and worship forms with mantras and waste precious time, but perceive nothing. Those who are inhaling *sa* and exhaling *ham* are in lower grade meditation.

But after Self-realization, when the devotee remains in the material world and constantly perceives *sa*, the soul, as the sole doer of the gross body, that stage of perception is the real *hamsa sadhana*. Wisdom cannot be perceived by the five sense organs; it can only be perceived by the atom.

Rabinarayan Brahmachari in 1941 at Karar Ashram, Puri.

In the year 1947

In the year 1958

Hariharanandaji at Habibpur, Nadia District

Paramahamsa Hariharananda being installed as President of Sadhu Mandali and President of Karar Ashram 1972

Worshipping the Divine Mother

Looking at infinity

At Karar Ashram

In Karar Ashram's garden

His journey to Yuktashram in Bhisindipur, Bengal

While teaching.

His blessing hand

His Divine Smile

At Rourkela, 1984

1986 Birthday in Paris

Gurudev in Vienna

Humble Hariharananda

At Kolkata:
near a coconut tree

In a moment of deep thinking

At Yuktashram near a jackfruit tree

In a relaxed state

In Europe

Overlooking gaze

His Divine Look

1995 Birthday in Chicago

His blissful smile

1997

XI

OM

Kriya Yoga is a science of correct breath. By proper inhalation when calmness descends, the devotee remains in complete bliss and perceives three divine qualities: divine sound, divine light, and divine vibration.

In the Bible (John 1:1) it is written, "In the beginning was the Word, and the Word was with God, and the Word was God." Here the Word means the divine sound.

When a devotee is in deep meditation he hears sounds. The sound may be a humming sound, buzzing sound, rumbling sound, roaring sound, church bell sound, and varieties of other sounds. When a devotee hears any of these absorbing sounds, it is called *om* sound.

The human body is a microcosm and the sound of the cosmos motor is *om*: *shabda-brahma*. *Om* is God. In the Gita (10:25), God says, *girām asmyekam akṣaram*: which means that "amongst sound I am manifested in *om*."

The causal body of a human being is "A," the astral body is "U," and the gross body is "M." In the scriptures it is written, *oṃkārasya-brahma-ṛṣi-gāyatrī chanda-agni-devatāḥ sarva-karma ārambhe viniyogaḥ*: which means *om* is coming and expressing before we think anything, talk anything, or do any work. Before we get hunger, the formless "A" gives inspiration of hunger from the vacuum. Then in our brain, astral body, "U," we perceive our hunger. Through the brain, in the stomach, we perceive and feel that hunger. But our hunger cannot be satisfied until our gross body, "M," speaks through the mouth that — I am hungry. So our causal body is "A," our astral body is "U," and our gross body is "M." The aggregation of these three bodies is A + U + M — *om.* (Diagram 15; page 192)

So, any work or thought, good or bad, that comes through our mind and is expressed — that is *om.* Any verbal sound or worldly sound is the aggregation of *om.* But we cannot perceive that until we come to a real realized person and get the technique to hear *om* sound from him. By the power of a realized Kriya Yoga master, any person can perceive that divine *om* sound within a short period.

The aggregation of the whole world is *om.* The more a person meditates deeply, the more he will be able to hear the sound constantly, even in diversity.

When the devotee withdraws his senses from the coccygeal center and through a gradual process comes to the pituitary, the kingdom of God, then he merges in the superconscious stage. In that stage he rises above the gross body and automatically hears *om* sound in all the spinal centers.

According to many yogis, you are to chant *om* in each of the six spinal centers from top to bottom. But when you constantly hear the sound in each center without pressing your ears, you are merged in God and it is then not required to chant *om* in each center, as you are already in the midst of the sound.

When God created the universe, the creative power was sound — *om* — and His first creation was vacuum. It is in the vacuum that the sound *om* is clearly heard.

There are five vacuums in the head above the cervical center. From the cervical center the vacuum centers are: *chidakasha, parakasha, daharakasha, atmakasha*, and *mahakasha.* (Diagram 7; page 121)

In the medulla oblongata, the devotee only feels the sound. The sound comes from the vacuum. In the scriptures it is said, *indriyānāṃ mananāthaḥ mananāthāstu maruta maruta-stu laya-nāthaḥ sa laya-nā dam āśritaḥ.*

Mind is the master of the five sense telephones and the master of the mind is breath. Breath control is mind control. By breath control and breath mastery, you can get calmness. Calmness is godliness. In that state, you can hear constant *om* sound.

In the *akasha*, the vacuum, you are feeling divine vibration and seeing divine light and hearing divine sound. It is flowing down from the top to the bottom. You are in joy, peace, and bliss. (Diagrams 10 and 11; pages 148 and 149)

In the formless stage — vacuum stage — you hear extreme divine *om* sound. At this stage your limited body is transformed and you are in your unlimited body in the superconscious stage, *paravastha*, and you hear divine melodious sound, see divine light, feel divine vibration, and enjoy the divine nectar. In the Mundaka Upanishad (3:2:9) it says, *brahma veda brahmaiva bhavati*: "The knower of Brahman becomes Brahman." That which is all-pervading is Brahman. Any talk or sound you hear is the talk of God, which is the aggregation of *om*.

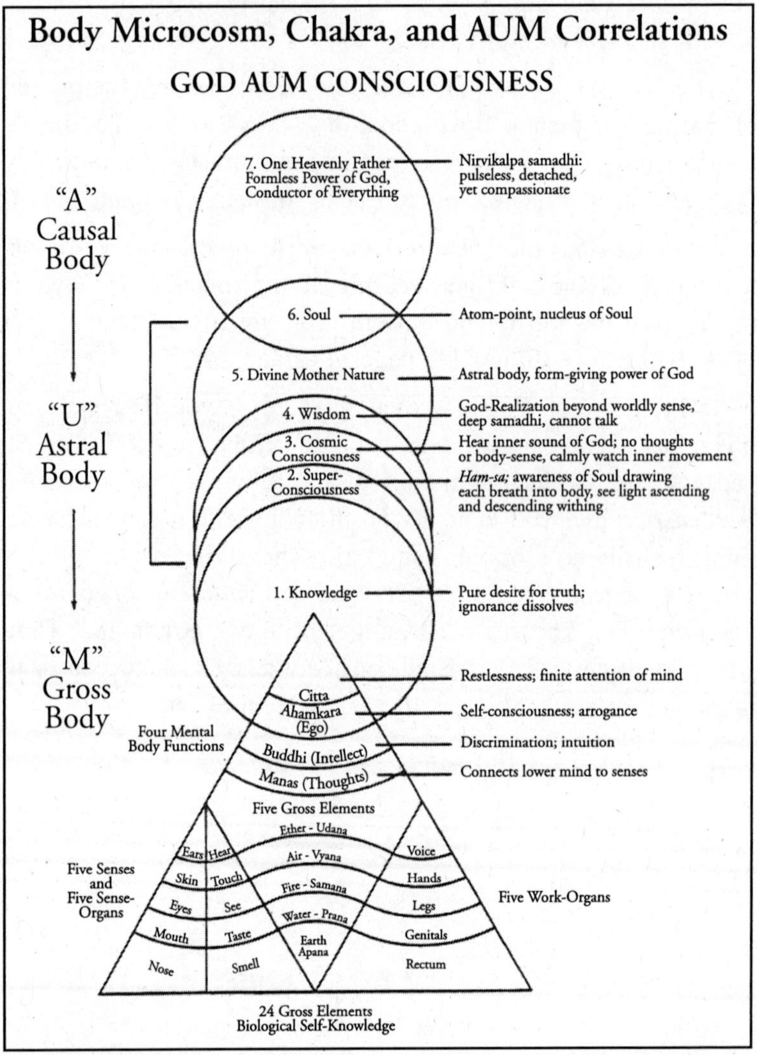

Diagram 15 - Body microcosm, chakra, and AUM correlations. The human system, which includes the physical, astral, and causal bodies, is the prototype of the whole universe (creation) with the Creator (God) and various entities of human beings, spiritual and material.

XII

BEING WITH THE TWO GREAT MASTERS

AS I SAW THEM

There was no train communication to Puri in those days, yet Shriyukteshwarji had already paid a number of visits to Puri to see Lord Jagannatha. Shriyukteshwarji was the direct disciple of Shri Shyamacharan Lahiri Mahashaya, who was one of the very great yogis of India, as described in *Bharatera Sadhaka* and *Autobiography of a Yogi.* As a *sadhaka* (practitioner of yoga), Shriyukteshwarji was highly advanced. He achieved the supreme spiritual state in the midst of a common earthly existence as a householder. He was a versatile genius and had tremendous knowledge of astrology, palmistry, ancient Indian scriptures, and also Western philosophy.

Having devotional and spiritual propensities in abundance, Shriyukteshwarji attracted many great *panditas* in Puri and discussed with them the physical, mental, and spiritual development of the people of Odisha through the practice of yoga. He selected Puri for its rich spiritual climate to be the suitable place to establish an institute of yoga. Accordingly, on the auspicious day of *Mahavisuva Samkranti* (Spring equinox, March 22) in the year 1903, he established an ashram near the sea beach in Puri and named it Karar Ashram. He chose the occasion of *Mahavisuva Samkranti*, because on this day the sun rises and sets equally, dividing the day and night into two. This type of equal division, the equinox, occurs twice in a year, once on March 22 and the other on September 22. On these days heat and cold are evenly balanced. In human lives, sorrows, suffering, and frustration symbolize the cold; whereas pride, insolence, and egoism stand for the heat. Man achieves Godhood only by harmonizing the two states. *Mahavisuva Samkranti* thus stands for this equilibrium and so Shriyukteshwarji would arrange religious meetings on this day every year.

The Karar Ashram in Puri, in the course of time, has become a primary center in the world for the culture and propagation of Kriya Yoga. Getting inspiration from here, Yoganandaji, the great disciple of Shriyukteshwarji, traveled throughout the world to teach Kriya Yoga. Shriyukteshwarji entered *mahasamadhi* at this place in 1936. For a long time before his *mahasamadhi*, Shriyukteshwarji worried about to whom to entrust the responsibility of running the ashram. Discovering Yoganandaji's interest in the West, Shriyukteshwarji had sent him there in 1920.

In 1932, I came in contact with Shriyukteshwarji for the first time and was initiated into Kriya Yoga by him. He read something from the lines on my palm and, as it happened, my appearance as a young *brahmin brahmachari* and my knowledge of scriptures fascinated him very much. He seemed to entertain a desire to place me as the steward of the ashram. This was confirmed in 1934, when I met him in his Serampore ashram in West Bengal. Studying my horoscope, he predicted that I was destined to be a *sannyasi*, not a *samsari*. He told me again, "You see I have grown old; I have some access to astrology from which I come to know that my body can no longer survive. Puri is a sacred place; you are the son of a *brahmin.* Your body looks godly and you have abundant treasure of spiritual wealth. I sincerely desire you to remain in charge of that ashram. I have a strong conviction that only you can inherit the spiritual energy within me and can spread it throughout Odisha." I replied, "You are the embodiment of knowledge, farsightedness, and a great master in spiritual practice. Your wish can never remain unfulfilled, but I am only 27 and have yet to achieve a lot of things in *sadhana*."

Shriyukteshwarji left his body in the year 1936, but many people are reported to have seen him in his gross body even two years after his death. I was also fortunate to see him in his gross appearance once toward the end of 1938. On that very night, I saw him in my dream and was directed to settle down in the ashram. Previously, in 1935, I had been again initiated into Second Kriya Yoga by Yoganandaji on Shriyukteshwarji's advice. In the year 1949, Paramahamsa Yoganandaji authorized me to impart the technique of Kriya Yoga to interested disciples.

Paramahamsa Yoganandaji was born at a very crucial moment. The Indian political scene was turbulent and religion had lost much of its meaning to the people. The great Indian yogi Shyamacharan Lahiri, popularly known as Lahiri Mahashaya, predicted to his beloved disciple, Bhagavati Charan Ghosh, that a divine child would be born to him in the form of an incarnation. The divine child was born on Indian soil on the 5th of January 1893, with an unusually handsome look. Unlike most of the spiritual practitioners of India, Yoganandaji was born into a rich family and spent his whole life in the midst of plenty. But this did not deter him from the ideal of selfless sacrifice. A superhuman light was emanating from him.

He was absorbed in the worship of God and practice of yoga from his very childhood. At a young age, he took initiation in Kriya Yoga from Shriyukteshwarji. In his college days, all his co-students were astonished at his unique power of spiritual practice and his guru, Shriyukteshwarji himself, developed a great fondness for him. Through the direction of his guru, he came out successfully in the B.A. examination after only four months of study and proceeded the next year to the West to propagate the principles of Kriya Yoga.

Swami Vivekananda, the highly accomplished spiritualist of India, said that he had come to the Western world and had laid the foundation of spiritualism and that after him another great yogi would come who would bring about a reconciliation among all religions and would popularize in the West the Indian Vedantic culture and yogic practices. This prediction came true. As ordained by God, that supreme yogi, the great Indian spiritual leader, Paramahamsa Yoganandaji, came as the preceptor of the whole world. He was a precious soul. Combined in him were the action of Swami Vivekananda, the wisdom of Shri Shankara, and the divine love of Mahaprabhu Shri Chaitanya. He established ashrams at several places in the world and made them all self-sufficient. About 100,000 people had the opportunity of being initiated by him into Kriya Yoga. All the other high-ranking spiritual practitioners of India, except Swami Vivekananda, confined themselves to India. But Yoganandaji taught the yogic principles that are the essence of Hindu culture to everybody with whom he came into contact in different parts of the world, irrespective of social position and religion; he established a common tie of spiritual fraternity. It will be no exaggeration, therefore, if we call him one of the most spiritually accomplished souls of the world.

The significance of the technique of Kriya Yoga, as we know from him and this line of gurus, is that it brings about simultaneous development of body, mind, and soul. This is also the real meaning of *sarvodaya* or the welfare of all as envisaged by Mahatma Gandhi. In 1935, Mahatma Gandhi, the greatest political leader of India, met Paramahamsa Yogananda in Wardha and was so impressed with him that he was initiated by Yogananda into Kriya Yoga. Gandhiji realized the significance of *sarvodaya* and accepted it as the wellspring of all his efforts in life.

As regards my acquaintance and meeting with Paramahamsa Yoganandaji, I had heard that Yoganandaji could transport himself into the *samadhi* state at any moment at will. This filled me with curiosity and I met him in 1935 during his stay in

Kolkata. I was initiated into Kriya Yoga before this meeting by Shriyukteshwarji, the guru of Yoganandaji and had been regularly practicing. Paramahamsaji told me that by only seeing, neither could I gain that power nor would I fulfill my life's desire. I replied that I wanted to experience the power of his spiritual practices and to learn from him the advanced techniques of the higher forms of Kriya Yoga. Paramahamsaji asked me how many hours I could devote for spiritual practice. I replied that it was not a matter of hours, days, or years. In order to gain the contact of such a great power, I was prepared to sacrifice my whole life in spiritual practice in a hermitage and that I had taken a vow of lifelong service and dedication for this purpose.

Paramahamsaji, being satisfied, took me with him to a separate room and sat in meditation and within a short time reached the *samadhi* state. I was overwhelmed with astonishment to behold his body luminous with divine light, without any heartbeat or pulse. When, after half an hour, his normal physical condition was gradually restored, I bowed to him with all devotion and love. I wanted spiritual initiation from him and he fulfilled my desire with all kindness and sympathy. When I asked him what were the things to be collected for the initiation ceremony, he smilingly replied that the offering of full-hearted love is the best offering to the guru.

The next day, after the initiation, he embraced me. At his loving and superhuman touch, I experienced a divine vibration and blissful sensation in me. On another occasion, he touched my head and said that one day I would awaken the Supreme Power in me through spiritual practice and I would attain the superhuman state. I now realize the truth of his profound prophecy. The inspiring words and godly behavior of Paramahamsaji are still alive in my memory and will remain an ever fresh and permanent treasure for me.

The Human Brain - Kingdom of God

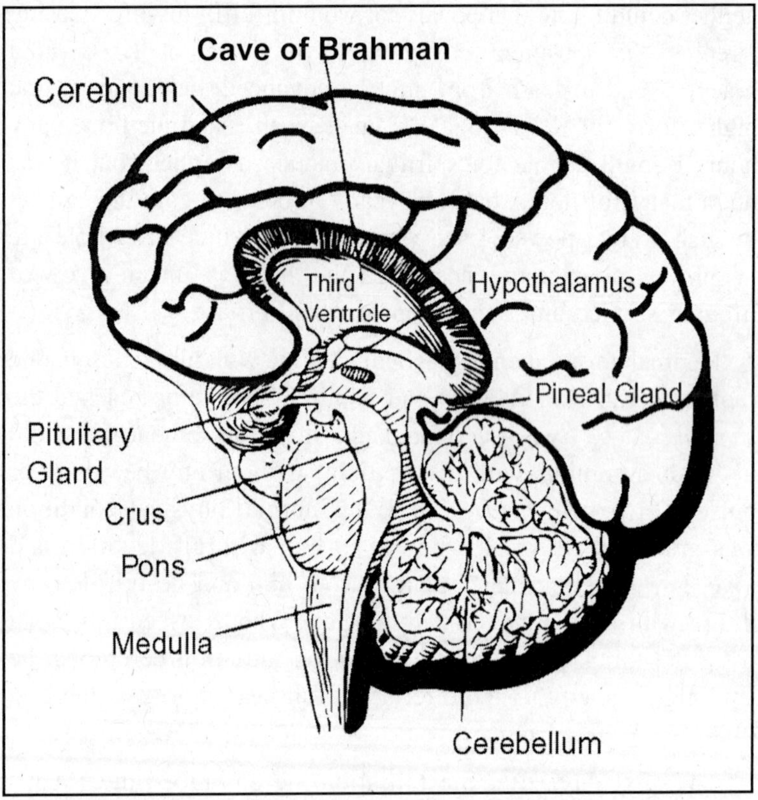

Diagram 16 – The human brain – The Kingdom of God. The living human brain is the mightiest power in the creation. The life and world of every being is dependent on it and controlled by it. It has the power to reach beyond its own existence. The "Cave of Brahman" is an etheric chamber where Brahman, the creative essence of universal spirit, manifests in man's altar of the individual soul's fire (Krishna). It burns and radiates pranic life force to the 24 gross body elements via the medulla, cerebellum, etc. The pituitary and pineal glands, at opposite ends of the cave, are positive – negative poles of Self-knowledge: solar/lunar, male/female, Krishna/Radha, etc.

XIII

TRANSCRIPTS OF TALKS

"Know What You Can Gain"

A radio broadcast at Washington, D.C., in July 1975

I pray to God and gurus to speak through my mouth and I shall try to give clear answers to your questions.

First, I want to bow to God the Father, God the Son, God the Holy Ghost, to Moses, Allah, Mohammed, Krishna, and Shiva. All are only one God. I bow also to my four gurus: Paramahamsa Yoganandaji, Shriyukteshwarji, Lahiri Mahashaya, and Babaji Maharaj, because he, Babaji Maharaj, has brought the message of Kriya Yoga and in the whole world, has given this technique only to Lahiri Baba, with the purpose that it be further spread only through his true disciples.

You all know the definition of God. He is all-penetrating, omnipresent, omniscient, omnipotent. He is everywhere. So, I want to bow also to all the people who are in the conference room because I revere the invisible soul, which is residing in them and to all the radio listeners and even to those who are not listening because the Omnipresent abides in everyone.

You know that many monks and saints come from different places and you have to study them profoundly and receive from them all the good you can obtain that is applicable to your lives. In the *shastras* (sacred Hindu scriptures), it is said, "There are millions of religious books, millions of yogic books, millions of monks in the world, but our longevity of life is very short." We do not know when we shall expire. We have many difficulties, problems, anxieties, ups and downs, and limitations in life.

"Nevertheless," the scriptures say, "that which is the essence of religion, the attainment of superconsciousness, the divinity felt in the whole body, the invisible in each one, that must be gained." That is Kriya Yoga.

Do not give importance to what others say and think about me, but you should know what you can gain from Hariharananda. It is that you can perceive the essence, the Truth, the invisible God who is always in you, in your family life all of the time, through all of your activities.

In the Bhagavad Gita (4:7–8), Lord Krishna says to Arjuna, "I incarnate always when the *dharma* is forgotten and injustice is triumphing. I incarnate to liberate the good, to destroy the evil, and to establish the kingdom of justice." So, every 400 to 500 years, you will be able to see that great masters will come to this universe and give something new. At this auspicious moment in the scientific age in this materialistic world amidst the satisfaction of greed and transitory joy, what will be your inspiration, your realization of God? That is why Babaji and Lahiri Baba appeared.

Babaji was in the high mountains of Ranikhet and Lahiri Baba by his own desire went to the high mountains through the jungle. As he walked, he heard someone calling in a loud voice, "Shyamacharan!" He sharpened his hearing. He was astonished. "Who is calling me in this jungle?" Lahiri Baba went forward in the direction of the voice and he saw a monk. Approaching the monk, Lahiri Baba then bowed before him and the monk asked, "Do you recognize me?" The monk touched his head. "Yes, I have recognized you." He touched his feet and added, "You were my guru in a distant life." The monk said to him, "I was waiting for you. Please come. You have practiced for many years this Kriya Yoga technique and you will have to propagate it in the world. I have brought you here, but you will not remain here. Within a few days you must return."

All the techniques were given to him. And Babaji said to him, "Propagate this scientific technique all over India. Your disciples will go throughout the world and they will carry this message to be known by all."

That is why I shall talk to you now about Kriya Yoga. It has two words. *Kri*, which means action. Do all your duties from morning to evening. Do your work. *Ya* means God, the invisible who resides in the visible body. He is the one who does the work, not you. He is inspiring you. He is impelling you. You act through the power of God, the invisible, without form. Everything that people do from morning to evening is done by the power of God. Without the power plant that generates the energy no electricity can be obtained, in the same way we cannot talk nor see nor hear nor work without God. This is Kriya. It is not just for the monk, but it is also for the family man and all humanity. Finally, what is yoga? Yoga is union, immersion, communion. The unity between the gross body and the invisible body can be obtained through the practice of Kriya Yoga and the consequent consciousness of Being.

This Kriya Yoga technique is based on deep inhalation. It is the easiest, the simplest, and the best, because you are constantly inhaling. In the night when you are sleeping you have deep inhalation and your mind is refreshed. Retain the respiration for a short period, according to your capacity; if you fix your attention to any point, guided by a realized guru, you will be able to verify that, automatically, you can attain calmness. Our lack of tranquility originates from our senses, our mind, our thoughts directed outward. That is why in the sacred Hindu scriptures it is said, "The master of the five senses is the mind, and the master of the mind is the deep inhalation." The control of the respiration is the way to the control of the mind. Who is inhaling? Perhaps the human being? No! That unknown invisible, not seen, not manifested, resides in the visible body.

He is the one who is breathing. He is the one who is giving breath to you all. As long as you do not attain calmness, coolness, you cannot realize God.

In all religions — Christianity, Hinduism, Islam, Buddhism, even in Kriya Yoga — they say that you must direct your five senses inward and go deep within until you reach the point where He is seeing and hearing, where He is inhaling, where He is talking. The Kriya Yoga technique, based on deep inhalation, attains this.

You do not have to dedicate much time to it. Fifteen minutes is sufficient. Inhale deeply and fix your attention on the top of your head, between the fontanel and the pituitary. If you practice daily, you will attain calmness, but not only that, the deep inhalation also awakens all the energy of the spinal column, from the coccyx to the top of the brain. The spinal column will become an empty tube through which the energy that circulates freely will purify and overcome all the lower tendencies, instincts, and desires. By magnetizing the spinal column, you can change your vital power into radiant, all-consuming divine power.

Our body is like a ball; the people of the world are very busy with this body ball. They want wealth, power to rule over others, pleasures of the senses; but they ignore the reality that this body ball is illuminated by divine light. Without that light you would not be able to see the body. When you go to the cinema, the first thing you see on the screen is light. In the light you see images and you enjoy yourself with that play. But you do not think that upstairs there is an operator who projects the light, without whom you would not be able to see the picture. Similarly, in each human body there is light. That is why Jesus said, "If thine eye be single, thy whole body will be full of light." He is the light of the body; everywhere there is light. We do not feel it. To feel it, we need the Kriya Yoga technique. With its practice you will be able to verify that there is an invisible counterpart for all the parts of the body and you will be able to perceive that it is the invisible that is the doer of everything. When this stage is reached, it is possible to have calmness, joy, bliss. It is our birthright, our real nature, which we have to realize; because the divine, God, the treasure of bliss, resides within.

If you practice with perseverance, you will attain good health, efficiency, and creativity in work and you will be able to attain the experience of God as much in worldly life as in spiritual activity, because you will remain in the third circuit in the superior part of the brain. I do not disregard nor deny other types of yoga. All are good. With Hatha Yoga through *asanas*, you can attain good health, physical balance — but not spiritual realization. Formerly, the *rishis* taught people to inhale from the center of the heart to the pituitary; so, automatically, it was possible to reach the superior center where the invisible soul resides. This is the authentic Hatha Yoga, which has disappeared. Today, they are doing something that improves the health and gives relaxation.

There is also Japa Yoga. Many people repeat mantras — Rama, Rama, Rama; Jesus, Jesus, Jesus; Allah, Allah, Allah — and they obtain something. I do not say they obtain everything, because it is written in the Upanishads, "What the talk cannot reveal but what reveals the talk, know that, that alone is God." Through mantras, many people got salvation, but the process takes much time. I shall tell you about two such great Hindu yogis.

Valmiki repeated mantras and by means of this, he obtained external calmness. He forgot the universe and attained realization.

Shri Chaitanya Mahaprabhu used to sing. He sang the name of Lord Krishna and disseminated it everywhere. After much practice of repetition, he felt that he had to sit down, to stop singing, no dissemination, to look for Lord Krishna in the whole universe, in his whole body. Each body is a kingdom and in each kingdom, there is the king. He knew that Lord Krishna, the king, was residing in his body, his divine kingdom. He felt it, he experienced it. Thereafter, he maintained silence. He forgot everything; he got extreme calmness, extreme bliss. Transformed, he did not talk anymore. He remained sitting in the joy of unity. The chanting, as well as the mantra, was transformed into quietness.

Raja Yoga consists of the control of the mind, so that you can reach complete calmness and Self can be manifested. It is a difficult method. It requires continuous struggle with the thoughts and repetitions of the mind. In all religions everywhere you will see the religious game, dogmatic points of view, fanaticism — in Hinduism, as well as in Christianity, Islam, and Buddhism. This is because they remain in rituals, in external forms. If you do not remain in forms, but look for the essence, you will attain success in the realization of God. The body of the human being is a field without cultivation and, therefore, you cannot expect a harvest. Each day we must cultivate, fertilize, irrigate the fertile ground, so that the seed develops, the seed of God. We are eternal. Why not always seek that immortality? Why not shorten the way to Self-realization?

Regularity is needed in the practice — a short time each day with devotion and concentrated attention. Remain in your family, fulfill your daily tasks, but practice Kriya Yoga every day. You will attain balance of mind, peace in the family, true friendship. Vanity will disappear and the mind will remain directed within. It does not matter what you do, but you should feel God acting in everything. You remain in the Christ center, completely detached.

Desires for money? You would not have them without God. Sexual desire? God is in sex. Use sex without losing your freedom, knowing that in every vital manifestation, the invisible is acting. Do you have appetite? Thank God you are healthy and strong. It is He who preserves life and who gives food. Do you feel vanity? All human beings have it. God is also the impulse to power and expansion. Through deep inhalation, established in the Christ consciousness, you will be able to complete in one practice of Kriya Yoga the evolution of one year.

The technique has until recently remained in India. The monks, disciples of Lahiri Baba, knew it. Those who have received initiation from Hariharananda will soon be able to testify to what they have attained: divine light, sensation of the touch of God, and perception of God.

Lecture delivered at the Kosmos Club in Amsterdam, The Netherlands

This mantra is quoted from the Vedas. "O Lord, so long as I am alive, I will remain constantly conscious that You are hearing through my ears. O Lord, You are the seer in my gross human eye. Without You, my eye cannot see; so, I will remember this. Whenever I am seeing anything, I will feel that You are the seer in me." This is also written in the Bible.

"O Lord, my body is very restless, but You are abiding in my body. You are remaining there calmly, so please give me extreme calmness by which I can feel that the restlessness and calmness come from You. You and I are always one in me. O Lord, so long as I am alive, I will seek Thee. So please give me such power by which my gross body, my knowledge body, my astral body, and my soul will remain very nice and perfect, and I can see Thee through my every activity."

In the end of the mantra it is said, "For the gross body you want peace. Because your gross body is full of diseases and your activity is excessive, you are also getting some nervousness and other trouble in the gross body. So, please give me calmness by which I can feel peace in my gross body. In my knowledge body I want peace and in my causal body, my soul, I can seek peace."

My reverend souls, you all know the definition of God is all-pervading, omnipresent. So, He is abiding in every human being. I am seeing many living souls here. I want to give my due love, regard, and respect and I want to bow to you all. There are even many people, those who are not here, to whom I want to give my deep love and regard, and I want to bow to them for my salvation.

My reverend souls, you have come to the touch of many monks and many yogis in Holland and you have learned so many things from them. In the scriptures, in Vedanta, it is written, "There are many books, spiritual books, yogic books, and also there are many lessons for soul culture, but life is very short. So, within the short span of your life, you should learn the truth of all religions." What is the essence of all religions? What is the truth that you should seek? Because the gross body is not fit, your mind is covered with so many thoughts, sensations, passion, anger, anxiety, avarice, office work, industry work, with your friends, and also with your frictions; so, your mind is not free. You should cool down your mind. If you meditate, then you can do it. One ounce of practice is far better than tons of theories. This Kriya Yoga technique is a shortcut technique. This is the essence of all religions. It gives the quickest means of success. I want to give an example. You come here quickly from America by plane. Similarly, if you practice the Kriya Yoga technique, you can perceive, you can feel, the development of body, development of mind, and development of soul.

Now I am getting to my point of discourse here: the simultaneous development of body, mind, intellect, and soul by the scientific technique of Kriya Yoga. In every religion they preach about our salvation, but in Kriya Yoga they preach how to get salvation. Also, they preach how to get sound health. If you get sound health, you will get sound mind. With sound health and sound mind, you can earn more money. Also, through this you can get peace, joy, and bliss.

Now I am telling what is Kriya Yoga. In the words "Kriya Yoga" there are two words. The first is "Kriya" and the second is "yoga." In the word "Kriya" there are two syllables. One is *kri*, the other is *ya*. *Kri* means you do your work from morning until you go to bed. You are always doing work. A dead body cannot do any work. *Ya* means soul. *Kri* and *ya* mean body and soul. The soul is abiding in every human body. So, the body can move, the body can work. The body is like a motorcar standing on the street and the soul is the driver of the body car. This is Kriya Yoga. So, through your every activity feel that any type of work you are doing is done by Him. In the Brahmasutra it is said that there are forty-nine types of work.

There is a center in the spine at the bottom of the spinal canal. It is called the coccygeal center and it is also the money center. So, the mind is always engrossed in money, but we do not feel that we are earning money by the help of *ya*, soul. Second is the sex sense in the sacral center. Soul is there. Without the soul you cannot feel sex sense in your body. So, through your every activity you will seek the soul. Even when you feel the sex sense, you will keep awareness both of body and soul. This is Kriya Yoga. Next is the lumbar, the center behind the navel. This is the food center. Mind is coming from food; so, whenever you eat anything, you should feel that the soul is there. It is why you get hunger and you call for food. After that, you see food in front of you. The food is also the power of God. God is remaining in the smell of food, in the food, in everything. Without that matter, that food, you cannot get energy. If you do not get energy, then you cannot get strength, memory, and a healthy brain. If you have no memory, you cannot seek God. So, whenever you are getting the taste of any fruit, you are not getting it by the taste of your tongue. A dead person cannot get the taste. The taste that you are getting is from the soul only.

If you practice the Kriya Yoga technique, then you will get this *kri* and *ya*. Work is there and also the worker, the soul; so, through your every activity you can seek Him. It is why you require calmness. That is in the heart center. The heart center is controlled by the air. For your every disposition there are different types of air. Our natural inhalation is eighteen times per minute. When you get passion, you have from twenty-four to thirty inhalations per minute. Then your heart beats more and more, and your arteries become very stiff. You get nervousness in the whole body. If you get more passion and if you enjoy more and more, then you will get nervousness in the body, nervousness in the mind, even nervousness in the brain. Also, when you are angry, you get rapid pulse and inhalation from thirty to thirty-six per minute. But, even through your anger you can seek the soul.

The senses are the enemies. We are to make friendship with that enemy. How to make friendship? Kriya Yoga can give you that friendship through your inhalation. Your five sense telephones are functioning. They are absorbed in the world. But, without the soul your five sense telephones cannot function. So, the body and soul are always there. The union of body and soul is called yoga. That yoga is always with you, but you don't feel the living presence of the soul in you. You cannot separate your soul from the body. You cannot separate your soul from the five sense telephones.

Kriya Yoga means that you will control your breath. The power to inhale is coming through the medulla oblongata from the soul. How to control your breath? Generally, our five sense telephones are engrossed in the world. Through this we are getting anger and passion. If you practice Kriya Yoga, you can switch off your external restlessness and cool down your brain very nicely. When you sleep, you take only eight to ten inhalations per minute. At that time you get extreme calmness of the body and mind, and you forget the whole universe and sleep. Kriya Yoga is based on such inhalation, but you are not to hold your breath. There is no rigorous practice by which you are to give strain or do so many exercises. You can do this Kriya Yoga very easily. It is a shortcut technique, simple technique, and sure technique. You are not to lock your nostrils and hold your breath for a long period.

Now I am telling how to bring that sensation into the brain. You have seen tap water in a house. If you open the hot water tap, you will feel it is very hot. You cannot touch it immediately; but if you open the cold water tap also, then you can adjust the temperature. There is one cord through which the life force in the body is going to the brain; that is our spine. The life force from the air that you are inhaling is passing through the spine. We are getting restlessness, because this life force is going directly to the five sense telephones. You can switch on, switch off, and adjust this flow of life force, just as you can adjust the hot and cold water. Controlling the inhalation will bring such balance. Inhalation when balanced brings balance of mind. That inhalation is coming from the medulla oblongata at the base of the brain. If you fix your attention in a point and take the type of inhalation that is taught in Kriya Yoga, then automatically the oxygen will go in great quantity to the brain. Oxygen is the food of your brain. By breathing in this manner, gradually all the evil thoughts will pass off.

To get this balance of mind, you require two things. First is environment. This means a guide who will teach you the technique and guide you. After that you require the technique itself, which you are to practice nicely. Generally, you will see in every human being there are many varieties of thoughts in the brain. People are busy in their industry, in their wealth, in their pleasures of senses, so they are getting many thoughts and sensations in the brain. Even past thoughts are remaining in the brain. Also, in human life, there is so much friction between friends. This is why people are getting extreme anxiety and sorrow. They are getting constant nervousness in the body, in the mind, in the brain. So, they cannot do their daily duty, office duty, or any work with a cool brain. This Kriya Yoga technique will enable them to remove all thoughts and anxieties, and they will get the finest mind. That mind they can convert into intellect. Intellect is a higher thing than mind. The more they get intelligence, the more they can judge, "What am I doing?" Then, from intelligence, they can acquire knowledge, the higher state of mind. From knowledge you can go to consciousness, superconsciousness, and cosmic consciousness. If a person goes there, then he can do his office work, housework, and worldly work very nicely with a cool brain. He can even perceive that a human being cannot do any work and that in the whole universe only the soul, the power of God, is remaining.

People should practice this technique for a short time; then they will get divine sensation in them. The restlessness and nervousness of the body will disappear and they will get a divine sensation in the whole body. This is called the power of God. We say this is one of the trinities of inner perceptions: touch sensation of God, divine sound, and divine light.

Our physical body and mind are engrossed in the world. When they are withdrawn from the world, we can judge nicely what is good and what is bad. Then we are getting superconsciousness and the perception of the soul in the whole body. We can introvert our mind. We can withdraw our mind in consciousness and, if we calmly watch, we can see that the soul is functioning in the body.

By the practice of Kriya Yoga, we can hear the divine sound:

om sound, *Amen* sound. This is the second part of the trinity. If you seek within your body and practice, control your five sense telephones in the centers of the spine where the soul is abiding, then you will see the divine light. Jesus said, "If thine eye be single, thy whole body will be full of light." Jesus repeatedly said that you should seek God through your eyes. But you are not doing that. You should seek God through your ear, through your hearing. He repeatedly requested and told everybody, but we are not doing this. If we introvert and seek the soul within, then we will get our spiritual light. By the practice of the Kriya Yoga technique, automatically we can get real wisdom in us. With the help of Kriya Yoga, we can feel the living soul is there in the flesh, in the bone, and that our five sense telephones are always seeking the soul. The Kriya Yoga technique can change your life force into radiant all-accomplishing divine force. The power of the inhalation is passed through the spinal column and automatically you can feel that when you are earning money, the soul is there and that is why you earn money.

When the spiritual current is coming, you are getting this radiant all-accomplishing divine force that hastens your physical, mental, intellectual, and spiritual regeneration and rejuvenation. Then you will get balance of mind. As I said, the hot water is there and you open the tap. Also, you open the cold water tap and feel it and balance the temperature, by which you can use the water in your daily life. Similarly, Kriya Yoga gives balance of mind, amity, friendship, everything — the inner peace that everyone wants. This inner peace is the birthright of every human being, but we are not getting such peace because we are engrossed in delusion, illusion, and error. If you remove your illusion, delusion, and error by the practice of this simple technique of Kriya Yoga, then you can feel inner peace.

You require wealth, you require industry, you require pleasures of the senses, you require power, you require a motorcar, you require a big house in the Holland town. You should get it, you should be very rich people, trillionaries. But without meditation, without the practice of Kriya Yoga, you cannot get inner peace. Rich people think, "Where can I hide my gold?" People are constantly seeking for more money, more sex. More sex, more nervousness in the body. Endless sex, endless nervousness in the body, endless nervousness in the mind. A person feels weakness, he knows his capacity, but still he is endlessly engrossed in the pursuit of sense pleasure. With the practice of this Kriya Yoga technique, he can balance his mind. Kriya Yoga is a mystery. By the help of Kriya Yoga, you can evaluate worldly and spiritual matters equally. When you are doing any work, through this work you can watch your soul. The moment you will seek the soul, you will get inner peace.

Any man or woman, boy or girl, intellectual or illiterate, employer or employee can practice this Kriya Yoga technique and get inner peace and repose. It is the desire of every human being to get peace, joy, and bliss. If you practice Kriya Yoga, your friendships will increase. There will be no friction and your bond with your friends will become strong. Also, you can do your work nicely. So, the Kriya Yoga technique can bring peace to every human being.

In Vedanta scriptures it is said that Kriya Yoga is the applied part of Vedanta, Upanishads, and Gita. Kriya Yoga is the combination of three yogas: Karma Yoga, Jñana Yoga, and Bhakti Yoga. Karma Yoga does not mean that monks are doing missionary work or someone is doing volunteer work in schools, colleges, and hospitals. Karma Yoga means that the life force is going from the coccygeal center up to the fontanel and again coming from the fontanel back through the spinal column down to the coccygeal center. In this way, every moment you are giving charge to the used-up body battery.

There are two lights in the coccygeal center. One is the work you are doing, the other is the soul. He is remaining there. In the Book of Revelations in the Bible, St. John referred to seven churches. These are the seven churches in the human body. You keep two lights in each church and in every action, you watch the soul, the real doer, functioning in the appropriate center. If the battery of the motorcar is used up, you have to recharge it; then, in darkness, you can drive your car. In our whole body there is ignorance, which is darkness. By the Kriya Yoga technique, you can charge your used-up body battery. In the sacral center, the sex center, you will get sex and soul jointly. In the food center you will get light, food, and soul jointly. In the heart there is negative and positive jointly. You can get consciousness, superconsciousness, and God consciousness there. If there is no light, there is darkness. The knowledge is light. By the help of the Kriya Yoga technique, you can get constant awareness of the Self. This is also taught in the Bible. The latter says that, if your hands and legs do not seek God, you should cut them off. You do not require them, because they are not seeking God. If your eyes do not seek God, you pluck them out. So, constantly you should seek Him in all your body parts. (Diagram 14; page 186)

If you practice this Kriya Yoga technique, you will get triple divine qualities in the gross body: light, sound, and touch sensations. There are three bodies. In the gross body, you will feel the living presence of the soul as a particular type of blissful sensation in the whole body. If you practice this exercise and technique properly, then within a short period you will feel this sensation. If you do not get that sensation, you should not practice it. Of course, if you are a true seeker, following one guru and one technique, you should not be coming to get another. That is bad. You should not make your journey by placing your legs in two motorcars.

The Kriya Yoga technique will give you power, immediate

power. Your nervousness will disappear. Your body wants something. You can feel supersensation in the whole body. You can feel the sensation of the blissful hand of God in your whole body. You will also see your third eye, if you seek within. This is the spiritual eye, the eye of God. It will not take a long time. You can have that perception because your mind — your knowledge body — is there; through the knowledge body, you can see the spiritual eye. Also, by the power of the soul that is abiding within you, you can hear the divine sound, the whispering sound of God within.

One thing I have forgotten to tell you. I should add that Kriya Yoga is the combination of Karma Yoga, Jñana Yoga, and Bhakti Yoga. I have said that Karma Yoga is to circulate the life force up and down through the spine to charge the spinal column and brain. By the help of that Karma Yoga, you get some supersensation in the body. You will get the touch sensation of the soul in the whole body, which will give you extreme calmness. You will get more love for Him. Also, if you introvert your five sense telephones and go into the center, you will hear the divine sound and perceive illumination inside the cranium and all over the universe. Generally, people think Jñana Yoga means to read some good books, such as the Bible or the Quran or any spiritual book. But that is not Jñana Yoga. Jñana Yoga means the knowledge that comes with superconscious inner perceptions. When we work, we get the result of the work; from karma we get *jñana*. So, in meditation we "work" by charging our spinal canal by the Kriya Yoga technique and we get triple divine qualities. Through calmness, we feel that triple *jñana*: sound, light, and vibration.

From this *jñana*, we get love. Love is a very precious thing. It is said in Hindu scriptures that it is very difficult to get God-perception without divine love. You are going in the church; there with folded hands you send Him prayers, because your girlfriend is ill or your mother is ill or your son is ill. So, you are shedding tears. That is love, but that is not the real love. You are going in the church, or in the temple, or in the mosque, and you are crying and shedding tears and with fullest emotion are chanting something. This is not Bhakti Yoga. In *bhakti-kanda* it is said that real love for God dawns when you follow the teachings of the scriptures and feel the practical sensation of the soul in your body, see the inner light throughout the body and hear the divine talk, the whispering talk of the soul in your body. That is a very precious thing. By the Kriya Yoga technique you will get constant love for God, because every moment you are getting the real karma and *jñana*. I am doing something; I am not doing something. I am getting a result; this is not my result. I am earning money; this is not my money. On the street I may die at any moment. The soul that is in my body, by His help I am earning this money. So, in that way, you will feel the deepest love and indebtedness and humility for God.

In the *shastras* it is said, "This machine is a non-stopping machine." In Vedanta it is said, "What is Kriya Yoga? *Tapas*." Offering of oblation to the fire, but not the fire that you light with wood. That is external *tapas*. The real fire is remaining in the body (i.e., the soul) and oxygen is constantly inhaled and offered as the oblation. So, you should constantly inhale and feel, "I am not inhaling; I am offering oblation to the soul." That is Kriya Yoga. The light is there; but if I cover the light with a bowl, surely the light will be extinguished. Similarly, the divine power, the spiritual fire, is remaining in the whole body. So, you should remain inside the cranium. That is the real place for God-realization. You can only seek God inside the cranium, not by the mouth. In the Upanishads it is said, "You are speaking, but speech cannot reveal the soul. The soul, who is revealing this speech, knows that, that alone is God. If you only shout God, God, God, you cannot get God."

The definition of God is all-pervading. So, where is He not? He is abiding everywhere, He is abiding nowhere. He is very far, He is very near. He is abiding inside the body, He is abiding outside the body. "I am abiding everywhere. If you cannot seek Me everywhere in the body, you cannot seek the soul." You cannot find the soul, but the soul is there. By *tapas* you can feel that, if you do not inhale for five minutes time, you will die. Everything is finished. So, He is inhaling, not a dead body. Constant awareness of the inhalation is going and touching the soul. The communication is there, because God and I are one and always have been one. This is *tapas*.

Svadhyaya means to read scriptures, read so many spiritual books: Vedas, Upanishads, Bible, Quran. Is that *svadhyaya*? No, *sa* means soul, *dhyaya* means to seek the soul. The soul is everywhere. You seek the soul in the hand, in the finger, in the arm, in the leg. Jesus used to wash the feet of his disciples with his own hands. Why? Because he felt the soul everywhere. The soul is everywhere. Similarly, if you constantly practice Kriya Yoga and follow Kriya Yoga in your daily life, then in your every work, whether it is worldly work or spiritual work, you will get perfection. You will get inspiration from God, from God the Son. He will say, "Do you want peace? You will get it."

Then what is *ishwara pranidhana* of Kriya Yoga? It means scrutinizing and seeking God everywhere. Scrutinizingly, I am watching whether He is here, how He is remaining here through my inhalation. If I go to the top of my head, I can seek Him. I can catch Him. So, the more you will seek, the more you will calmly hear where He is. You will hear the talk of God: *om* sound, *Amen* sound. This is *ishwara pranidhana.* If you calmly seek, then you can feel the blissful sensation of the soul in your whole body and have love for God and can express it through your mouth. You can feel joy, bliss, and peace. This is *ishwara pranidhana.* Hearing sound and seeing illumination, you are sitting and seeking God calmly. Your restlessness will disappear and you will see illumination all over the universe. Even in every human being you can see the divine illumination. You can see the light of the soul. Then, while living in the world you can remain free from chaos, ups and downs, shortcomings, worries, anxieties. If you practice Kriya Yoga, you will feel that you are the prototype of God's thought. You are the immortal soul. You cannot die. You are the imperishable soul and automatically you will get liberation, constant liberation. Anything you are doing will get you liberation. When your hands are moving, you will feel, "They are not my hands, but the hands of the soul. My lips are moving; these are not my lips, but the soul only." Anything you are doing, you will see the real doer. This is Kriya Yoga.

In the scriptures it is said, "If you have thirst and I give you a little water — if you only take a sip — your thirst will not disappear." So, if you practice Kriya Yoga, then you will see that Kriya Yoga is an ocean. As there is a tree in the seed and seed in the tree, similarly, the soul is in the world and the world is in the soul. So, through Kriya Yoga, if you meditate, meditate, and meditate, then surely you will behold the divine goal.

Hari om tat sat om.

"Kriya Yoga Is the Base and Unity of All Religions"

Lecture delivered at the Washington Ethical Society, Washington, D.C.

The Self is free from ignorance and delusion. From the Self you will get immortality, peace, bliss, and joy. Without knowing the Self, you have no escape. *Om santih, om santih, om santih.* I bow to my guru, *param-guru*, *para-paraguru*, *parameshti-guru*.

Today our point of discourse in this meeting is, "Kriya Yoga is the base and unity of all religion." What is the goal of all religion? The goal of all religion is calmness; calmness is divinity. But what do we get in all religions? Only chaos. In the church we shout, in the temple we shout, in the mosque we shout. We chant mantras and we fast, but calmness is not taught in religion. Only Kriya Yoga teaches how to get calmness. Calmness is godliness. Seclusion is the price of greatness. If you practice this Kriya Yoga technique, within a short period you will feel calmness, even within five minutes time. The Kriya Yoga technique can give you divine sensation, can give you divine light within a short time. Many people have taken initiation here in Kriya Yoga.

The dormant spiritual energy of every human being is remaining in the body, in the form of illusion, delusion, and error. Until and unless you can remove the delusion, illusion, and error by Kriya Yoga practice, you cannot conceive the soul, you cannot perceive the soul, you cannot realize the soul. Kriya Yoga gives the power to accomplish this. The minds of human beings are restless. Throughout the day they are getting so many sensations, so many thoughts, so many worries, so many anxieties, activities, friendships. Through this they are absorbed in worldly things. Their hearts will become very weak. They will get nervousness. Only Kriya Yoga can remove this nervousness and heartsickness and can give the single-minded state. If you want Self-realization or not, no matter. Through meditation every human being can get calmness, balance of mind, amity, and solve the problems in the family, in the office, in the industry.

Indriyāṇām mananātha. Yoga scriptures say that the mind is the master of the five sense telephones. Our five sense telephones are engrossed with matter. We are absorbed in the material world, so we cannot perceive the calmness and divinity that remain in every human being. *Mananāthastu marutaḥ*. You should control your breath by deep inhalation, then you can get extreme calmness. Otherwise, you cannot get calmness. In the night when you go to bed, you take deep inhalation: at that time, you get calmness. People are always busy with the worldly sense. Their mind, intellect, and five sense telephones are their enemy. Until and unless they introvert and go in the center, they cannot get calmness.

In the practice of Kriya Yoga you take deep inhalation, by which you get sufficient oxygen, which is the nutrition of the brain. So, your brainpower increases and the brain becomes free. *Maruta-sthu layanātha*. If a person practices Kriya Yoga with deep inhalation, he can control his breathing. Through our every disposition our inhalation varies. During the time of passion, we take more inhalation. During the time of anger, our heartbeat increases. With fear inhalation changes. But when we sleep, we get calmness. At that time our inhalation varies. In the Kriya Yoga technique we take the type of deep inhalation that we take during the time of our sleep. But only a Kriya Yoga teacher can teach this technique by which, within a short period, you can get calmness. Within a short time you can withdraw your mind from the body, from the room, from the universe, and you can get the single-minded state. From mind we go to intelligence, from intelligence to talent, from talent to knowledge, from knowledge we go to consciousness, from consciousness to superconsciousness, from superconsciousness to cosmic consciousness, and, finally, wisdom. We can perceive wisdom, and wisdom is the level of God-realization. In scriptures it is said, *prajñānaṃ brahma*.

When you take deep inhalation by the practice of Kriya Yoga, at that time you hear divine sound. *Sa laya nādaṃ āśritaḥ*. The Kriya Yoga technique can give calmness and divinity within a short time. You will forget the world. You will get supersensation in your body. You will hear virulent sound. You will also see inner illumination. The divine kingdom is remaining in every human body. It is written in the Bible that the Kingdom of Heaven is within you. By the Kriya Yoga technique, you can reach that Heaven.

First, I am telling the technique. In *Yoga Shastras* it is said, *mūlapadme kuṇḍalinī yāvat nidrāyate prabhuḥ tāvat kiṇcid na sidhyate tantra-maṇtra-arcanādikam*. The *kundalini shakti* is remaining in our coccygeal center in a coiled form. If you cannot withdraw that power, that divine power, from the coccygeal center to the fontanel, you cannot get perception of God, conception of God, realization of God. How to do this is not taught in the church, not taught in the temple. So, instead, the people shout.

In the Upanishads it is said, *yad vācā nubhyuditam yena vāk abhyudyate tadeva brahma tvaṃ viddhi nedaṃ yad idam upāsate*: "What the speech cannot reveal, but what reveals the speech, know that alone is God and not what people worship here." Until and unless you cultivate the land and sow seeds on the ground, you cannot expect any harvest. Everywhere in the present day you will see there is adulteration. It is why in the Bhagavad Gita (4:7) it is said:

yadā yadā hi dharmasya
glānir bhavati bhārat
abhyutthānaṃ adharmasya
tad ātmānaṃ sṛjāmyaham

God Himself has said, “Whenever I find falsehood in humanity, even about truth and religion, I bring Myself forth.” So, every five or six hundred years a preceptor comes to the earth. It is why Babaji has come. He came and taught his disciple Lahiri Baba, Shriyukteshwarji, and Yoganandaji this Kriya Yoga technique, which can give the calmness and unity in all religions. No question of person, caste, creed. The question is only receptivity. If anyone desires, he can get this calmness.

Prāṇāyamāt-rite anyat tārakaṃ narakād eva saṃsāra-sāgaramajjānāṃ tārkaṃ prāna-saṃyama: You have the natural ability to control your breath, but you have no natural ability to control your heart. By controlling your breath, you can control your heart. If you hold your breath for a short time, you can feel that your whole system is affected. Your brain, tissues, diaphragm, and everything are changed. Also, your heartbeat is changed. It will be reduced and, if you practice this regularly, you will get a strong heart. Generally, people are very busy with worldly things, in the mundane theater. They are getting heart trouble, because they do not know how to control their mind. Kriya Yoga technique can teach them how to get balance of mind, how to get amity, how to get friendship, how to work nicely, how to speak nicely. Their life in this universe will be happy. Kriya Yoga says that, until and unless you control your breath, you have no rescue from the sin in which you are engrossed. This world is an ocean of sins. You must introvert your five sense telephones and make a friendship with them. If your eye is your friend, then through your sight you can perceive that the soul is abiding in the body. Also, you can perceive how the soul is functioning in the body. Also, you can perceive how the soul is functioning through you by which you can immediately make friendship with the five sense telephones. This Kriya Yoga technique can grant and promote peace and all-around development. This Kriya Yoga technique is a noble technique, simple technique, easy technique, sure technique, and the best technique. Those who have taken it, they have felt it. On the day of their initiation, they have received the super-sensation, divinity, calmness, and the triple divine qualities in them. So, this Kriya Yoga technique will grant everything in every human being.

Kriya Yoga gives simultaneous development of body, mind, intellect, material existence, and soul. If you practice this technique, then your body will be sound and healthy. You are giving pressure on your colon to aid in normal elimination and massage the liver by which the bile secretion and other factors are stimulated that aid in digesting your food nicely. If you give pressure over the pancreas, insulin comes out and keeps your blood sugar level normal. The secretion of salts from the adrenal gland is also stimulated. All endocrine glands become more balanced in their functioning, leading to health, strength, and happiness. Your brain will be fertile. You will get prompt understanding and ready wit by the Kriya Yoga technique. At the same time you are getting God-realization, because you are getting calmness. Oxygen is the nutrition of the heart, so your heart will remain sound. You will get the breathless stage by Kriya Yoga. Your longevity will increase and you will work nicely and enjoy the world for a longer period.

You are taking food, so you are getting a body. From the body you are getting mind. Food gives us two qualities: one for hell, the other for heaven. One gives animality and the other gives divinity. In the scriptures it is said that from food we are getting mind.

Mana eva manuṣyāṇāṃ kāranaṃ bandha mokṣayoḥ: From mind we get bondage. For example, our mind is always running in sex feeling. Of course, it is essential; but, if you practice Kriya Yoga, even through your sex sense you can perceive God. In your money sense, you can perceive God. In your hunger for food, you can perceive God. When you are getting sex sense, the soul is there. You can perceive that the soul is remaining detached during the time of sexual pleasure. So, the Kriya Yoga technique will give you constant divine perception. Throughout the day and night, if you can transform the mind you can get divinity, peace, bliss, and joy. You can judge what is right and what is wrong. Our psychology is determined inside the brain. From here we get reason; we can think deeply. Accordingly, we can do work. The Kriya Yoga technique gives good mind and intellect.

Any person above thirteen years old can practice this Kriya Yoga technique. This technique is helpful for students, because by taking sufficient oxygen their brains will be healthy so they can prepare their lessons nicely within a short period. They will be well educated and creative in the future and be able to earn much money. Kriya Yoga also promotes this — that a person can earn sufficient wealth in the universe. The Kriya Yoga technique gives salvation. Accepting this technique, people of any religion will get balance of mind. They will get divinity. Every religion speaks ill of other religions. "My religion is the best religion. My religion is the best religion." But they do not know what their religion truly is. If they practice this technique, they will feel the unity behind every religion. They will feel what God is. There are not many Gods or a separate God for every religion. God is one. Soul is one. They can perceive it.

Piṇḍaṃ kuṇḍalinī śaktim: God has created the whole gross body in such a way that people are always keeping their attention below the eyebrows. Physiological senses are there, so they are engrossed with delusion, illusion, and error. The truth is remaining far off. It is remaining in the psychological jurisdiction inside the cranium. A person can judge everything from that place.

The Kriya Yoga technique is the quickest means of success. You can go to foreign countries by plane very quickly. Similarly, the Kriya Yoga technique can give you divine sensation within a short period. Many ladies and gentlemen present here are practicing Kriya Yoga. They are feeling the real effect and utility of Kriya Yoga. Worries and anxieties disappear. They are meditating nicely, by which they can get God-realization throughout their lives. Kriya Yoga is the highway of common religions. It gives mathematical results. Kriya Yoga is the applied part of Vedanta, Darsana Shastra, Samkhya, Upanishads, Bhagavad Gita, and the Bible. It is the combination of *jñana*, *karma*, and *bhakti*. Until and unless you get *bhakti*, you cannot get God perception. Karma is going on through the spine, which by the Kriya Yoga technique you can spiritually magnetize.

Danger remains in your coccygeal center, money center. You require money. You require wealth, house, industry, car, good husband, good wife, undoubtedly; but you also require sound health, sound mind, long life. If you don't practice Kriya Yoga, you cannot enjoy your wealth. You may be a trillionaire, but who will enjoy the wealth if you die at the age of thirty or forty? Who will enjoy if you get heart trouble? But Kriya Yoga can give you the power by which you can have a healthy heart and lungs.

The sacral center is where people get sex sense all the time. They cannot withdraw their minds. By the practice of magnetizing your spine, you can change your life force into all-accomplishing divine force, which in turn hastens your physical, mental, and spiritual regeneration and rejuvenation. Every moment through your every activity and in your every thought, you can perceive *kri* and *ya*. *Kri* means the work that you are doing from morning to evening. What is *ya*? Soul. Without the soul you cannot do anything, you are a dead body. So, anything you are doing, is done by Him, not by you. The soul is remaining everywhere. The human being has two bodies: the visible body and invisible body. The visible body is your delusion. It is always remaining in the jungle of matter. Your invisible body is real. Cultivate your invisible body through the visible body, then you will get awareness of the inner Self and you can perceive the soul, you can conceive the soul, you can realize the soul. Through your every activity you can feel the oneness of the body and the soul. This is called yoga — Kriya Yoga.

Today I will not speak more. I will only chant one mantra. I will finish my discourse and then you can pose questions if you like.

oṃ saha nāvavatu
saha nau bhunaktu
saha vīryaṃ karavāvahai
tejasvi nāvadhitaṃ astu mā vidviṣāvahai
oṃ śāntiḥ oṃ śāntiḥ oṃ śāntiḥ

Does anyone want to pose any question about Self-realization, about God-realization, or about Kriya Yoga, which is the basis of all religions? It can bring unity in all religions. Anyone who likes can pose a question.

Q: If I practice Kriya Yoga, will it hamper my family life?

A: At every moment our thought changes, so we are changing our mood. When you practice Kriya Yoga, at that time you will only feel that your soul is doing Kriya. This will not hamper your work in the family, because you are not working in the family — soul is working. Anything that you are doing is done by the soul. This perception does not clash with family life. Suppose you have desire for food. You are not off from the soul then. Desire for food is given to you by the soul. You can perceive this, because you are practicing Kriya Yoga; practice will make you perfect. Through your every activity you can feel that He is functioning. When you will practice Kriya, your other moods will, undoubtedly, disappear. Similarly, when passion comes, anger cannot come at the same time; only passion remains in the body. When anger remains in the body, then passion cannot enter. When I laugh, I cannot shed tears. Only one mood will remain and that mood is given by the soul.

Q: Is it essential to read scriptures to get knowledge of Kriya Yoga or God-realization?

A: Surely. But when you practice Kriya Yoga, you do not require scriptures. Suppose in the scriptures it is written that you meditate and you will get God. If you only read that you will get God, it is not possible. One ounce of practice is far better than tons of theories. If you only chant, "God, God, God," you cannot realize God. If you chant, "food, food, food," and read about food in a book, your appetite will not disappear. If you meditate deeply, then you can get the truth. Should you read the scriptures or should you seek God through your daily life, through your activity? Through your every activity you should seek Him.

Q: What is the Kriya Yoga technique?

A: If you want to know how to be a doctor, then you have to go to a medical college. You will have to take admission there. But, if you stand outside of the medical college and ask, "How can I operate on the patient, doctor?" you cannot learn. If you want to know the Kriya Yoga technique, you come in the ashram, sit with me and tell me that you are willing to learn. Then you will surely get the technique. And you will perceive the triple qualities by the divine touch of the realized master.

Q: Is it essential to go to a guru? What is the relation between guru and disciple?

A: *Gu* is the invisible body, abiding within your physical

body by which you can speak; *ru* is your luster, your gross body. The gross body is remaining by the power of your invisible body. So guru does not mean anything negative to which you should have a mental allergy. When you go to school, you learn something from the teacher. When two people join in family life, they get something from each other — is it not? What is the relation between them? If they establish the relation of husband and wife, they can share their lives. They can proceed forward together. They can get love. Suppose a man makes your acquaintance. Will he give all his dollars to you? But, if you make friendship with him or take him into your family, surely he can give many things to you. Similarly, if you take the technique from me, then surely there will be a relation between us. I will feel that you are my child. Toward me you will have humbleness. If you have no humbleness, if you have no receptivity, then you are not a true seeker and there will be no relation between us. The relation between one who is giving the technique and one who is receiving the technique is the relation of guru and disciple. In India, the teachers are called gurus. The boss is called guru. So guru is used in a wider sense in India. In the Western countries, many people have a mistaken impression of the meaning of guru. The moment they hear guru, they will get a headache. Is it clear? Such a person will surely say, "Swamiji, thank you very much. I cannot give you abode. I cannot give you food. You please go back." But, if I go to my disciple's house and say, "Baba, I want to stay in your house and I want to take my food here," then my disciple will say, "Oh, Baba! I am very happy. Come to me, take my food and my bed. You enjoy!" Why? Because he has earned something from me: more money, more spirituality, divine money. So there is a relationship. That relationship is called guru and *chela*. But, if you have a mental allergy to guru, you should not proceed.

Q: What is the difference between calmness and divinity?

A: Until and unless you get calmness, you cannot get divinity. So, calmness and divinity are one. You are to get calmness. You will have to do some work and from the work you will get some knowledge. When you have learned something by your study, you work in the office; the result of your knowledge is money, which is entering into your pocket. Then you will get love, peace, bliss, and joy. By practicing Kriya Yoga, you are getting knowledge, superconsciousness, and supersensation in your body. That sensation will give you love. Until and unless you are getting perception of God, conception of God, realization of God — you cannot get love for God. If you go to the office and do not get money, you have no love, no peace, no joy. So, love is possible only when a person is deriving something by his action. If you know superconsciousness, then you can perceive the super-stage (i.e., divine light, divine sound, and divine vibration in your whole body). By getting the taste of it, you can feel that He is taking inhalation through your nose. That inhalation is the base of all religions. That inhalation is the life force of all religions. Then you will feel indebtedness to God and love for God.

Q: What is the Trinity?

A: The Creator has created some senses in me. You ask a question. Accordingly, in my brain something appears and I am giving answer. This is supplier and preserver. When you are satisfied with my answer, I will not say more. In every moment, you will get three things: the creator, the preserver, and the destroyer. The wish of appetite is given by the soul. You feel it by your brain, then you express through your mouth that you are hungry. Food comes. You take your food and your appetite is destroyed. It is a triple process: creator, preserver, and destroyer. Similarly, in your every thought and in your every inhalation there is the creator, the preserver of the body, and the destroyer. *Tredhā medhate padaṃ samura paśyatāṃ śule.* It is said, "I am coming with three steps." These three steps are creator, protector, and destroyer.

Q: What is the cause of the visions seen by many sages, saints, and gurus? In many scriptures, it is said they have seen angels or incidents that have occurred long before.

A: The snake has never bitten me, but I have learned that it is poisonous, deadly, and painful. I have only heard it. Even in my dream, I can get terror. That is hallucination. So, people have only heard about angels and so many things. That is hallucination. That is imagination. You are to go above it, above thought, above emotion, above hallucination. Then you can only get perception of the Self. You can feel that the soul in you is so great and all-pervading. You are getting sensation from the high heaven to the earth, so you are not an insignificant, limited person. The gross body is limited, but the invisible body is great. We meditate only to perceive this invisible, all-pervading body. If we can get this, then we will be the Son of God. *śṛvantu viśve amṛtasya putrāḥ ā ye dhāmāni*: The formless God, the Creator, is telling, "Whatever you are seeing in the universe, it is I. I am abiding in every human being." *Āye dhāmāni*: Know thy Self, know thy Self. You can know that you are that invisible soul, that all-pervading power. *Āditya varṇaṃ tamasaṇ parastāt*: Your ignorance will disappear and you will see the light. Your darkness will disappear, you will perceive divinity. *Tam eva viditvā atimṛtyum iti*: If you know that the powerful soul is abiding in you, then it is surely your greatest achievement. You will be immortal. Why don't you seek your immortality just now? Hallucinations will disappear and you will merge with your soul in peace, in bliss, and in joy. Many of you are getting a little taste, but you have not enjoyed the full flavor. Only a little honey is given on the lips and you all are licking it.

Q: Is there any existence of angels?

A: I am angel, I am devil, I am monk, I am debauched. In

this universe everyone is an angel, if he prepares his field like an angel. Have you seen that any angel has come to you? We have only heard about angels, is it not? So, you forget this. Act only to perceive the living presence of God within. You meditate, meditate, and meditate. One day you will behold the divine goal. Don't receive any visions. They are useless. If any vision is coming, remove it. Perceive that you are the prototype of God's thought. You are the immortal soul. The power of God is there. The invisible counterpart is in this body and the real part is remaining in the soul. If you meditate, you will perceive it. Then you will get the truth. You require this. Every religion wants calmness. Every religion wants that people will perceive divineness. Calmness is divineness.

Love is God, undoubtedly, but it is very difficult to have love for God. You know the love for your girlfriend or boyfriend, but you do not know love for God. For this, you will have to meditate. In the scriptures it is said, *kāmahi nārī pyāri jimi lobhi pyāri jimi dam timi hi raghunātha nirantara*. As the boyfriend keeps his mind on the girlfriend and the girlfriend keeps her mind on the boyfriend, similarly, if you can constantly keep your mind on God, because He is inhaling through your nose, you will perceive that sexual desire and girlfriend and boyfriend are given by the soul only. If you can cherish this type of disposition, then you can get real love for God (i.e., *maha bhakti*). The love that you feel is given by soul. But love for God is too great. You are to earn it by the practice of Kriya Yoga. You are to go to the coccygeal center. You are to charge your spine. Then you will get *jñana*, knowledge. This is the result of your karma, supersensation. By churning milk, the cream is coming up. You cannot mix the cream with the milk again. The cream is your superconscious perception that has come up to the cranium. When you will get the cream above, then you will get love. My activity has given me cream. Only when you will feel the superconscious stage, divine stage, then you will get love for God. Otherwise, not. The *karma, jñana, bhakti* are correlated and causally connected.

Q: Yogananda has written in "Autobiography of a Yogi" that other masters had materialized and had appeared before him. Is that imagination? Or may this happen?

A: A scientist can invent one telephone or one airplane. It is imagination to me. I am a foolish man in this matter. A scientist has given us the opportunity to talk from his place to another place. Is it imagination? Paramahamsa Yoganandaji was extremely charged with divinity. Power was there. Shriyukteshwarji came to him several times. It is a fact. If you hear this, then you will tell me that I am a fool. I have seen Shriyukteshwarji in the Puri Ashram after his demise. Not only I, but many persons. Those who were his neighbors saw Shriyukteshwarji roaming inside the ashram. He called me. He brought me. I have seen him not once, but several times. It is also written in *Autobiography of a Yogi*. Even I have met Babaji. You can believe or you can disbelieve, as you like.

Q: What is the difference between atma and paramatma?

A: The multiplicity of divine being is *atma* and the unity of divine being is *paramatma.*

Q: Why is Jñana Yoga higher than Karma Yoga?

A: Without Karma Yoga there will be no Jñana Yoga. Who is posing this question? You are posing this question. Have you seen me before? No. So you have come here, you have done some karma. You are seeing me here. I am giving answer, so you are recognizing me. This is your karma. Then you are posing this question. If you do not know me and you see me in the street, you will not pose the question to me. So, your karma is giving you *jñana*. You are posing the question to me to get *jñana.* You are reading — that is your karma. You are getting education, then you are getting a job. Without karma, there is no *jñana.*

Without *jñana*, there is no *bhakti*. They are correlated and causally connected. Don't think that for Karma Yoga you will go to work in the hospital or start one nursing home or library or press or you will help somebody. This is not Karma Yoga. Karma Yoga means to seek God through the spine. In your spine there are many vertebrae and the subtle channels, *ida*, *pingala*, and *sushumna*. Because of these three powers, you do not know who you are. Your spine is locked, so you cannot perceive God. By the practice of Kriya Yoga, you can open the passage inside the spinal canal. After that the *pingala* will go to the right side and *ida* will come to the left side and your spine will be just like a tube. That is Karma Yoga. Your mind is in matter and memory, so you are puzzled. If you come above this, up to the pituitary and fontanel, you can judge, you can realize who you are. You will get the real sense of God. That is *jñana*. Unless you churn the milk, you cannot get the cream. Kriya Yoga is the karma and *jñana* is the cream. When I see the cream, I become very happy.

Q: Is it dangerous if the kundalini shakti comes up?

A: So far as my conscience goes, those who are practicing this are not getting any trouble. Many people have come to me for initiation and during the time of initiation, the *kundalini shakti* has come up inside their spines. Inside their every limb is the sensation of the soul. If you only hear this from a long distance, then you may think that I am a fool and you will be deprived. That is your wrong idea. If you only pose a question, you will only get an answer. If you taste it for yourself, then you can feel. "Oh! The mango is very sweet!"

Q: Why does the Indian monk put on ochre-colored cloth?

A: Generally, at a sight you can realize that he is a monk. If you see a military man in the street putting on olive green color, immediately you can understand that he is a military man. Similarly, this dress signifies that we are monks. We are pure.

Perception of God is there. Realization of God is there. Have you seen fire? The color of the fire? The color of the fire is like this ochre-color cloth. So, if anger, passion, avarice, greediness, or any evil thought comes from the mind, immediately it will be burnt by the power of this color. Thank you very much.

Q: Yoganandaji came here long before, but why have you come here so late? Why have you not started an ashram?

A: Paramahamsa Yoganandaji came in 1920. I started moving throughout India from 1960 to 1975. Having received the divine commandments from Babaji Maharaj to spread Kriya Yoga to the ardent seekers of the world, I accordingly started.

If you are not going to join, then how will there be an ashram? You please call thousands, thousands, and thousands of your friends, relatives, workers, then I will start thousands and thousands of ashrams here.

Q: How much time will it take to get divine sensations?

A: It will take a very short period. The day you will take this Kriya Yoga, you can feel divine sensations in the same moment. Your body will be charged. All the viciousness of the five sense telephones will disappear. By the power of Kriya Yoga we remove it. We say, as Jesus said, that inside the eye there is another eye. You will feel in your every activity that He is the actor in you. Through your hearing, through your sight, through all your works you will feel that the soul is functioning. This practice depends on your desire. If you have receptivity and you follow the master, you will feel this inner power on the day of your initiation. You will hear the divine sound. You will see the illumination, inner light. Also, you will feel divine sensation in your whole body. Within a few days, you can get supersensation in your whole body. In your every activity, you will feel joy that He is acting through you.

Q: What do you mean by receptivity?

A: Suppose I have a pot. If there are many holes in the pot and I carry milk in it, then when I reach home I will see that all the milk has leaked out on the street. If you come with single-minded state (i.e., if you repair the holes of your "pot" and try to receive everything as you are trained at the time of initiation), that is called receptivity. Even before that, when you came to me, you got supersensation and from the day you took initiation until today, you are proceeding towards the goal. The more you will come to Hariharananda, the more you will get the taste of the Vedas, Upanishads, Brahmasutra, Bhagavad Gita, and meditation. Every day it is new as the sun. Every day you are getting new sensations. Yesterday you felt that the sensations are coming from high heaven to the earth — is it not? This is called receptivity. The truth which is given by guru — that is, the power of guru. If you touch the living electrical wire, you will be electrified. Similarly, if you have desire to take initiation, you will get power — because you are not a dead body, you are a living soul.

Guru means friend. *Tvam eva mātā ca pitā tvam eva, tvam eva bandhuś ca śakhā tvam eva; tvam eva vidyā draviṇaṃ tvam eva, tvam eva sarvaṃ mama deva-deva*: "You are my mother. You are my father. You are my friend. You are my intimate. You are my knowledge. I am merged with you." If you come with this attitude, then you will get the treasure of guru within you. It is not a terror that you are taking initiation. You will not be the slave of guru. Don't fear. When a person goes to his friend, what relation do they have? Friendship. It is also friendship with guru. If we don't have friendship, how can I give my treasure to you? You are meditating. You are a spiritual person. If you go to your church now, you will feel that you are a better self because of your meditation. All the people will pray, you will hear the prayer and you will feel a powerful vibration. This is the power of God within you. You will perceive the living presence of God among all the people. By practicing Kriya Yoga, you can continuously proceed forward.

Q: How will the practice of Kriya Yoga affect my worldly life?

A: Every moment you will perceive unity in diversity, diversity in unity. Whatever you do, you will remain always in seclusion. In your every attachment, you will be able to remain compassionately detached. For instance, passion is there, but without the soul passion cannot come. You can feel that the soul is there and it is always free. Without the body, the soul cannot function. Without the soul, the body cannot function. So, the body is your best friend by which to get Self-realization. The soul is floating in the vacuum. He cannot talk. He cannot see the flower. So, when he wants to enjoy, he comes in the body.

Q: Is it true that St. John practiced this Kriya Yoga?

A: If I will go to Jesus, surely I will ask Him. I should not say anything that I do not know. Because Jesus is Jesus. In the Bible I have not seen that He has practiced Kriya Yoga. Is it not?

Q: You have said that St. John mentioned keeping seven lights in your seven chakras, is it not?

A: Yes, it is written in Revelations. Accordingly, I have referred to it.

Thank you all for hearing my talk patiently. I am very happy to meet you all. Good night.

Hari om tat sat.

Lecture delivered at the Curacao Rotary Club, Antilles, The Netherlands

Kriya Yoga is not a religion, but a spiritual stimulant. Kriya Yoga is a technique. It is based on theory, but I never teach that you should carry this theory in your pocket to get Self-realization. You are to come, then see, feel, and judge whether it is true or not. Within five minutes time, you will get marvelous power. Your gross body is *kundalini shakti*. Your whole awareness is engrossed in matter. This is called *kundalini shakti*. You are to withdraw this material sense. You are not matter. Only the soul is here. Without the soul, you are a dead body. After ten hours, after twenty-four hours, the bad smell will come and nobody will go to your room. The husband will not touch the wife, though he had deepest attachment for the wife. The wife will not touch the husband. You know everything. You are conscious and educated, but you have not yet tasted the fruit of meditation. The Kriya yogi tests people by sight, whether they can get calmness or not, then teaches the technique. Within a few minutes' time, it is possible to get absolute calmness. You can forget that you are in the body or you are sitting in the room. But, normally, when you go for meditation, you see thousands and thousands of thoughts are coming to you. Memories of all the work and activity that you have done properly or not done properly will come. The credit that you have forgotten, the thanks that you have forgotten, that will also come: "I did the work nicely and they spoke highly of me."

What is meditation? Meditation means to go beyond mind. When there is no existence of mind, then meditation starts. In the church you do not see calmness. You go with tiptop dress and after prayer you gossip and leave, but you learn very little spiritually. If you concentrate, if you introvert your five sense telephones, you can go in the center. Then, surely, you can get some perception of the soul (i.e., your invisible body, your real body, that is always abiding in your gross body). This Kriya Yoga technique can give you the awareness of the Self. Also, the power of *kundalini* will come up. Divine consciousness, God consciousness, will constantly remain in you.

Anything we are doing, is not done by us. You are hungry, so you are asking for food. Before asking you thank God, because you are fortunate to get hunger. Constantly, you should feel this, in your practical life that you will work nicely and think, "I am not working. The soul is the sole doer in me. How nicely He is finishing the work." You will get energy, agility. You will get joy. You will know that you are not the doer, so you won't get any hallucination. You won't get any vanity.

When you take deep inhalation, you get millions of oxygenated red corpuscles in your body. Oxygen replaces the carbon dioxide waste bound with the hemoglobin carried in the blood. Oxygen is the nutrition of the brain. Oxygen is the nutrition of your heart and lungs. Your heart is pumping so much blood daily. People are getting more strain in the heart through more passion, more anger, more money sense — so, the heart must pump more and more blood. Through the practice of Kriya Yoga, the heart gets rest. We are giving pressure on the liver. Bile comes and it helps to digest food. Pressure is given over the pancreas, stimulating the secretion of insulin, which helps to keep your blood sugar level normal. There are hormones from the testes and ovaries that directly affect the nervous system and aid in its refinement. You will come to know how, when you learn the technique. Balanced secretion of estrogen and progesterone help to increase the beauty and luster of the body. Most importantly, you will get secretion from the pituitary, which is the master gland.

We go to the temple, we chant mantras there. We carry flowers and we remain in emotion. Emotion is not God-realization. When the emotion finishes, then the God-realization starts. Your wife is ill. You go to the church and pray deeply. You shed tears for your wife, but you do not shed tears for God. God knows that your wife is ill, you need not tell Him. He feels it constantly. But if you can go near Him, then He can help you. I am staying in the Kriya Yoga ashram and you are here. If I do not come, you cannot hear my talk. Either I am to come to you or you are to go to me. This gross body is a dangerous body. The visible body creates delusion, illusion, and error. If you cultivate your invisible body (i.e., your soul), then you will become aware of the soul. That soul is constantly with you. You should love Him. In your every movement, you cannot move without His grace. If your soul does not remain in your body, immediately you will be removed. But the soul is so kind to you. You are walking, He is walking through you. You are seeing, He is seeing through you. You are hearing, He is hearing through you. But we all feel that we are the doer, not the soul. This Kriya Yoga will give the power by which you will get Self-realization. In the scriptures it is said, *iha cet avedit atha satyaṃ asti iha cet nāvedit mahati vinasti*: "If you seek the soul just now, it is a profit to you. If you do not seek the soul, you are not a rational being. Your life is wasted."

Bhūteṣu bhūteṣu vicitya dhīrāḥ pretyāsmāllokād amṛtā bhavanti: "If you practice this Kriya Yoga in your every thought, then when you are mixing with people you will perceive that you are mixing with the soul." Talking with you all, I am talking with the living soul. You can perceive it. The gross power is remaining in the coccygeal center. Kriya Yoga can enable you to draw up your power from the coccygeal center to the cranium. You know there is cream in milk. If you churn it, then the cream will come up. That cream cannot be mixed again with the milk. Similarly, our gross power that is given by the soul is remaining below. Your sex power is given by the soul. You will have to seek the soul even through your sex sense. If you are dead, you cannot enjoy sex. If you cannot inhale, you cannot enjoy sex.

Without the soul you have no power there. Kriya Yoga technique can assist you in every sphere of your life, every disposition of your life. (Diagram 13; page 179)

Food center is there. You are taking food and thinking that the food will give you energy. No. If you take a full belly of food and after that do not inhale, the food will not be digested. It will not be consumed. Energy will not come from the food, energy that is converted into life. Life can be converted into the spiritual life or the devil's life after taking food. If our attention remains below the navel center, we get animal quality. If our attention remains above this center, we get divine qualities — because the divine qualities are remaining completely above. You will have to seek God above your dorsal and cervical centers. It is said in the scriptures that if you seek God in the heart center, your mind will be restless — because the heart wants to mix with another heart. So, the real power is remaining inside the cranium. Here you are to seek God. Pituitary is here. You must go above this, because our five sense telephones cannot go there. Here you can convert your mind into knowledge, consciousness, cosmic consciousness. Here you perceive the movement sensation in the whole body.

You should know where the light switch for the room is. If you turn the switch on, immediately the darkness of the room will disappear. If you touch anywhere else on the whole wall, it has no effect. So, you are to seek the proper place to touch. Similarly, it is possible to withdraw all thoughts and anxieties and to perceive the Self in the cranium. Now I am going to finish my discourse with one prayer and after that, if you have any question, you can ask me. But, the questions must be about Self-realization.

oṃ saha nāvavatu
saha nau bhunaktu
saha vīryaṃ karavāvahai

tejasvi nāvadhitaṃ astu mā vidviṛṣāvahai
oṃ śāntiḥ oṃ śāntiḥ oṃ śāntiḥ

It is said that the soul and body — that is, the teacher and student, the master and disciple — should remain together. They will love each other. If the student does not give attention to the teacher, he cannot receive anything. If the disciple does not follow the master, he cannot receive anything. We require amity and love between the student and teacher. The gross body is the student and the invisible body is the teacher. We eat jointly. I do not feel that I am eating. I feel that I am feeding and also I am eating; body is there, soul is there. When you feel you have some disorder in the stomach, God will not permit you to take food. So, you should thank God and feel that you are feeding God. The power of God is there. If the student obeys the teacher, then in the future the student will be the teacher. Why are the disciples taking initiation? So, in the future, they will be good teachers. I was a student in the beginning. At present, I am a teacher. So, if you follow the lessons, then you will get Self-realization. You will get immense power. You will feel, "I am not a body. This is not flesh. The power of God is there. I am fortunate that I can walk, I can see, I can hear." I am relating this from the scriptures, the Bhagavad Gita. I am not just saying my own thoughts.

The whole human life is for Self-realization and the Self is not far. One day the door of the brain will be opened and you can get the truth and treasure. So, if you keep amity between the soul and body, you will get quickest Self-realization.

Then the mantra, *oṃ śāntiḥ, oṃ śāntiḥ oṃ śāntiḥ.* I have no physical peace. My health is not good. I should follow my guru, soul. Guru is the invisible body. *Gu* means invisible and *ru* means visible. If you add *gu* and *ru*, it means soul and body. I am to keep my body sound. Kriya Yoga will give three-fold development: sound body, sound mind, and sound culture. You can earn sound money if you get sound health. If you take more food, you will suffer from indigestion. You will lie down on the bed. You will not work. You will not go to the office. You will go to the lavatory fifteen times, sixteen times. There will be no energy for work. So, it is said that if you keep amity with the soul, then your physical body will remain fit and your intellectual body will remain fit. Kriya Yoga technique will keep your knowledge body fit, your cosmic body fit, and also you will get Self-realization. This is said in the mantra.

Piṇḍaṃ kuṇḍalinī śaktim. This means that our gross body is covered with delusion, illusion, and error. If you close your eyes, you cannot see anybody. If you open your eyes, immediately you can see everything. In your brain you are seeing so many persons, so you are engrossed in the mob. Similarly, all of the sensations from your sensory motor and nerves are engrossing you in delusion, illusion, and error. *Rūpaṃ bindum.* If you follow the master, then the master will tell you how you can keep pinpointed attention in the proper place.

Rūpaṃ binduṃ iti jñeyaṃ rūpātitaṃ niranjanaṃ haṃsa ity udāhritam. You are to withdraw your senses up to the third circuit, above the pituitary. This is the real place for God-realization. The *kundalini shakti* will come up. The milk is churned and the cream has come up. Similarly, the whole body is churned. The coccygeal center has entered into the sacral center, the sacral into the lumbar, the lumbar into the dorsal, the dorsal into the cervical, the cervical into the medulla oblongata — then it is called *hamsa. Hamsa* means you are in real seclusion, you are not talking with anybody. In Sanskrit, the first letter is *ham* and the last one is *sa.* You take all the letters and lock them inside the brain, so you cannot talk. You can only sit calmly. *Haṃsa ity udahritam rūpaṃ bindum.* Following the guidance of a realized master, if you firmly fix your attention for five minutes' time, you will feel that your spiritual current has come up and all your thoughts have disappeared. *Rūpatītam nirañjanam.* Then you do not feel your body sense. You do not know where you are sitting. Then the power of God will come up inside the brain. You will perceive God, you will conceive God, you will realize God. If you come and sit for a short time, then you will feel that your power has come up and your mind is no longer running in the market — your mind is not running various places, it is completely locked.

Madhu lubdhā yathā bhṛiñga puṣpa-puṣpāntaram vrajet jñāna lubdhā tathā śiṣyaḥ guru gurvāntaram vrajet. When the bee is seeking honey from one flower and it does not get honey, it goes to the next flower. Similarly, each person will seek the truth, not dogmatic views or fanatic ideas. I have taken shelter under a big banyan tree. So I should not move. If a big branch of the banyan tree falls upon me and I die in the storm, still I will sit under the tree and I will die peacefully. You require salvation, you require peace, you require constant awareness of the Self. If you feel it, then you need not learn Kriya Yoga.

Q: What is the difference between knowledge and mind?

A: Between knowledge and mind there is a gulf of difference. Is it not? Mind is functioning through the five sense telephones and knowledge is functioning through philosophical and psychological forces inside the brain. Mind is giving us ignorance. Discriminative knowledge is giving us light. The sense of whether I should do something or not is given by the cerebrum and cerebellum. If you control the mind and keep attention on cerebrum and cerebellum, all sensations will come up. Automatically, you will get consciousness. After that, you will get extreme illumination on each side of the brain. The more you practice, the more you will see light in the whole brain. Gradually, you see light inside the thalamus and hypothalamus. If you have desire for Self-realization and you go deeper and deeper, then you can reach near the thalamus and pineal gland.

After that, if you get the chance to enter in, you will see brilliant illumination and powerful rotation of the light. It is easy. Don't think that it will take a long time. You are thinking Swamiji has kept a bushy beard. He is meditating from his infancy so he is saying, "Very easy, very easy." If there were no airplanes and I said that it is very easy to go from Kolkata to Curacao within twenty-four hours, people would laugh at me. They would say it was impossible.

I have said much today. Now I am going to finish my discourse.

Q: Swamiji, please repeat the shloka which you chanted in the beginning. I like this shloka very much.

A: Thank you very much. I also like this mantra. Listen:

oṃ saha nāvavatu
saha nau bhunaktu
saha vīryaṃ karavāvahai
tejasvi nāvadhitaṃ astu mā vidviṣāvahai
oṃ śāntiḥ oṃ śāntiḥ oṃ śāntiḥ
hari om tat sat

XIV

TETE-A-TETE WITH DEVOTEES

Q: Can a person be too old or too young to practice Kriya Yoga?

A: God-realization is our birthright. The moment you are born, the living power of God is within you. So, in India, all the children of four and five, even they try to practice this technique a little. They are always after God. So, it is our birthright. Your whole system is the system of God. There is no question of age. Now is the time to earn God. Shriyukteshwarji said, "Don't think it is too late and don't think it is too early." The child of thirteen can receive initiation. Even the elderly, if they can practice it, their brainpower will be fertile because the technique is so effective. The frontal lobe of the brain will become energized. Kriya Yoga is the energizing technique for body, mind, intellect, and, ultimately, bringing God-realization.

Q: Is it necessary to read scriptures to get knowledge of Kriya Yoga or God-realization?

A: One may read scriptures but when you practice Kriya Yoga, you do not require scriptures. In all the scriptures it is written that you should seek within, meditate, and you will find God. If you only read that, you will not get God, you will not perceive Him. One ounce of practice is far better than tons of theories. If you say, "food, food, food," or read food in a book, your hunger will not disappear. If you only chant, "God, God, God," or read about God in a book, your desire to realize God will not be fulfilled. You will remain in the extroverted stage. God dwells within you. If you meditate deeply, then you can get Truth. Should you seek God through your daily life, through your activity or should you only read the scriptures? In your every activity, you should seek Him. This is practical spirituality.

Q: Swamiji, am I to sit for meditation for one or two hours at a time?

A: No! You should not. You should practice 20 minutes each day, morning and evening. By the practice of Kriya Yoga, you will get single-minded meditation, in a very short period, through which you will get divine knowledge and peace of mind. Many are sitting for hours and only getting so many thoughts. So it is not fruitful. This is adulterated meditation. You require quality of meditation, not sitting with eyes closed and thinking of the whole world.

Q: Swamiji, you have said that at the time of Kriya Yoga initiation you awaken the kundalini shakti. Many people say the kundalini is a snake that is coiled two and a half times at the base of the spine and that we should not arouse it or attempt to raise it, because it will bite us. Many teachers are telling this to their students. Is it truly dangerous?

A: Not at all! This idea is completely false. In scriptures it is said, *piṇḍaṃ kuṇḍalinī śaktiṃ haṃsa iti udāhritaṃ rūpaṃ bindum iti jñeyaṃ rūpatītam nirañjanam. Pindam* means your gross body — our flesh and blood body. *Kundalini shakti* means your divine power. *Pindam kundalini shakti* means that your divine power is remaining latent in the gross body and this is giving you illusion, delusion, and error. *Hamsa iti udahritam* means that by the proper technique you are to magnetize your spine. When you magnetize your spine, then the divine power that is remaining below, in the gross body, will come to the top, at the soul, and you will experience liberation. Your *ham* body, gross body, is your illusion and delusion, but the *sa* body is for dis-illusion. The *sa* body, soul, is remaining in between your eyebrows in the Kingdom of Heaven. If you keep your attention fixed in that point, in the vacuum four inches inside the brain between the eyebrows, then according to the direction of the realized Kriya Yoga master, you magnetize your spine, then automatically your divine power, *kundalini shaktim,* will come up to the top and all delusion, illusion, and error, all mind, thought, intellect, ego, and body sense, will disappear and you will get the *samadhi* stage. If you have a little portion of water in the bottom of a bottle and you bend the bottle over, automatically the water will come up to the top. This is why in the first exercise of Kriya Yoga you are to bow several times and touch your head on the ground.

Money, food, and sex are three principal things that people need. The creative center is therefore essential, because you require money, sex and sex control, and you also require food. The *brahma-granthi* is the creative center. So gradually, if you magnetize your spine, automatically the *kundalini shakti* will come up to the top. Then you will only perceive the atom point and you will perceive the divine light and movement (vibration) sensation in the soul. Then you will get the real formless, liberation stage. You will perceive the living power of God activating all the functions of your body.

What is the real form of the body? *Rupam bindum* — the atom point, in the soul, remaining in the cranium. *Iti jñeyam rupam bindum*. You should know this is your real body, your formless body. Your invisible body is your real life. *Iti jñeyam rupatitam niranjanam. Rupatitam* means formless. *Niranjanam* also means formless. Beyond form, only the formless is pervading all over the universe.

This formless power of God is the *kundalini shakti.* If a snake remains inside the lower center, then the present day doctors, who can perform miraculous surgery on deadly diseases, even brain surgery, heart and kidney transplants, would simply remove the *kundalini* snake, the dangerous cobra at the base of the spine. With this, everyone, at a young age, could become highly realized. But all these notions about the *kundalini shakti* are completely false. It is not that a dangerous snake is remaining inside of you. The danger inside you is your delusion and illusion, your five sense organs, your twenty-four gross elements and your nine doors. They lead one to be extrovert. So, to transform all of this you require the practice of Kriya Yoga, which will raise the *kundalini shakti* to the top. This is how your evil qualities can be removed. Then you will be divine. These are the real facts concerning *kundalini shakti*.

Countless people have come to me for initiation and during the time of initiation the divine power has come up inside their spines. Inside their every limb, they have felt this divine sensation of the soul. If you only put forth a question, you will only get an answer. If you come and taste the divine nectar for yourself, then you will surely say, "Oh! The mango is very sweet!"

Q: Swamiji, why are people bowing and touching the feet of the guru? It is a new thing here!

A: If you touch a living electric wire, then your whole body will be electrified. Similarly, the marvelous power of God is remaining within the highly realized yogi — the guru. Vast spiritual power is remaining in their whole body, but it radiates strongly from their feet. This is why others are touching their feet. These yogis never touch their feet on the bare ground, they do not walk with bare foot, they put on wooden sandals or plastic shoes, which are insulators. So in this way, the divine current coming down into their body remains in their body. They are storing their current in their body. So whenever someone touches the feet of the guru, the divine current remaining in guru immediately enters into his body. In the scriptures it is written, *draṣṭum śrotuṃ jñātuṃ vaktuṃ tattvena anuprāvistum*: If you see, you will be, if you touch, you will be, if you hear, you will be.

So, those persons who have little divine power in their body, by touching the feet of the guru they are getting divinity within them. The youthful boy is touching the youthful girl and they are getting the youthful sexual sensation in their whole body. This is a fact. Similarly, it is also a fact that if you go and touch the feet of a realized yogi, then you will surely get divine current in your body. In India, it is the ancient tradition that they should touch the feet of the yogi from the core of their heart. Most seek to touch the realized person. Through that, they are getting more power in their body. It is a divine blessing to those who do.

Q: Many teachers say they are enlightened or realized. How can we distinguish who is truly the realized guru?

A: In the Holy Bible, Jesus said to be beware of false prophets who come to you in sheep's clothing, but inwardly they are ravening wolves. We shall know them by their fruits. The tree that cannot give forth good fruits should be cut down and burned to fire.

This means that you should avoid those who have no divine fruits. The real spiritual teacher, the spiritual master, will give you evidence of his divine power, just as Jesus and his apostles did. Jesus said: "You will know them by their fruits." Divine power is the real fruit. If you come to the touch of the true guru, then you can quickly come to know whether he is advanced or not. The true guru is a person who will immediately infuse divine power into the disciple. Not tomorrow, not after one month, but at the time of initiation. That person is the real guru.

Q: I am born Christian and I have a very deep love and loyalty towards Jesus, so I am a little confused about meditation. Since Jesus does not speak of meditation in the Holy Bible, is meditation in conflict with being a Christian? If I meditate, am I being unfaithful to Jesus and Christianity?

A: You say that Jesus does not speak about meditation. In the Holy Bible, does not Jesus say that the Kingdom of God dwells within you? And does he not also say that you are to seek first the Kingdom of God? Surely he does. It is a fact. So how can you seek the Kingdom of God, within you, if you do not seek within? Kriya Yoga meditation means to look within yourself and seek God and His Kingdom. Therefore, if you do not follow the words of your master, Jesus, and seek the Kingdom of God that is within you, it is then that you should feel that you are being unfaithful to Jesus and Christianity. Without meditation, a person cannot get God-realization. So, maybe you are a Christian and you should read the Holy Bible, but you must also seek within, meditate, to find God.

If you only hear the lecture of the professor and you do not do your homework, then you will never succeed. You cannot become like the teacher. So, to get God-realization you require study plus meditation. But less study. One ounce of practice is worth far more than tons of theories. I am saying that if you meditate very deeply, then Jesus, or some other ascended master, may appear near you and will hear Him speaking to you.

So, I want to say that we are all very busy with little things, insignificant things, and what is passing before us, that we do not perceive. But without God we are doing nothing. We cannot do anything. We cannot talk. We cannot move our head. We cannot see. He is activating everything and we are to constantly perceive this. *Kri* means whatever activities you are doing, it is done by the power of God, soul (i.e., *ya*), and you are to perceive it. Through the practice of Kriya Yoga you can perceive it.

Shriyukteshwarji was a great Kriya yogi and he had marvelous power. What type of power? One day I was asleep in the ashram and at about 12 o'clock he began to shout, "Narayan, Narayan, Narayan, please get up." At that time, there were three other persons staying there with us at the ashram and we all jumped up from our beds. Shriyukteshwarji told us, "There are 14 persons coming to the ashram from a long distance and they have yet to take food. You should immediately begin preparing some food. In big pots, you make dal, rice, and vegetables." We began preparing the food and when it was almost finished, I thought to myself, "He is such a marvelous master that he can foresee all this." Then, just five or six minutes after we finished preparing the food, there was a knock at the ashram door. There stood fourteen hungry disciples and they were all so happy to see the preparations we had made for them.

Shriyukteshwarji was a saint of tremendous spiritual power, foresight, and many other marvelous qualities. Divine power! One touch from his hand, and immediately you would get divine sensation throughout your whole body. He gained all of his powers through meditation and he has made great contributions for the upliftment of mankind.

Q: So, I can worship Jesus as I am meditating?

A: Yes. You can worship Jesus. You can worship Moses. You can worship Daniel. No matter. You should have extreme love for them all — as one should love their own wife or husband or their boyfriend or girlfriend, extremely, because they too are the living power of God. Jesus was manifested and he is the living power of God. He ascended. Moses was highly realized. He left everything and he went to the desert and meditated very deeply. He became a topmost spiritual person and in his technique, there are so many forms and formalities and his people worship just like the Indian people. They are observing silence, they are fasting, they are chanting, singing, and doing so many other things. So you should think of Him. You should keep His photo in your house. Many Jewish people, they keep the picture of Moses in their home and those who are the followers of Jesus should keep His photo, but they should also see that Jesus, who is the living power of God, is activating their whole system.

Q: Swamiji, if I am born Christian or Jewish, do I have to give up my religion to practice Kriya Yoga?

A: No! You have a wrong impression. Religion in Sanskrit is *dharma. Dharma* means the power which upholds your body. What is upholding your body? Your breath only. But who is pulling the breath? The power of God is pulling the breath. It is why you are alive. And this is *dharma*. If you watch your breath and feel that He is pulling breath, if you perceive this, then it is *dharma*. This is religion. In the Bhagavad Gita, it is said that it is better to remain in one's own religion than to follow the religion of another, which is no doubt dreadful. Kriya Yoga is non-sectarian and for the people of all religions. There is no question of any cult, creed, sect, color, or country. The answer is to practice Kriya Yoga for fifteen to twenty minutes and you will get divine sensation in the whole body and God-realization.

Q: Swamiji, I see that you often quote Jesus when speaking about Kriya Yoga. If the teachings are related, why doesn't Jesus speak about Kriya Yoga in the Bible?

A: In the Bible, Jesus said, "Believest ye not that I am in my Father and the Father in me? The words that I speak unto you I speak not for myself: but the Father that dwelleth in me, He doeth the works." This verse contains the exact same literal meaning as the words Kriya and yoga. *Kri* means whatever activity you are doing — word and deed — and *ya* means it is done by Him, the Almighty Father. Likewise, in that verse, Jesus says, "The Father that dwelleth in me, He doeth the works." This is Jesus' explanation of Kriya in his way. The word yoga is used to express the ever-present union of body and soul — the human being with God. Likewise, in that Bible verse, Jesus declares this same thing by saying, "I am in my Father and the Father is in me." Jesus also has stated that the Almighty Father is dwelling in every person and every person in the Almighty Father. So, every person should understand that the meaning of the word yoga is simply, "the ever-present union of man and God." The practice of Kriya Yoga aims at bringing people to a state of constant realization of this union, whereby one can know and follow the will of God. That spiritual practice which brings one to a constant realization of one's unity with God is called Kriya Yoga.

Jesus' life purpose was to help mankind realize its unity with God, to bring salvation to the world. This conscious uniting, this oneness with God, is called yoga. The word yoga comes from the Sanskrit root *yuj,* which means "to join" or "unite." The word yoga literally means "the act of uniting." In the Book of Matthew (11:29), Jesus said, "Take my yoke upon you, and learn from me; for I am meek and lowly in heart, and ye shall find rest unto your souls." In this verse, the Greek word which has been translated to the word "yoke" is derived from that very same Sanskrit word, *yuj*, from which the word yoga comes and like the word yoga, it literally means, "the act of uniting" or "joining together." In the Holy Bible, what was that "yoke" which Jesus wished every person to take upon themselves? It is that process through which one attains conscious union with His Heavenly Father. The Biblical "yoke" and the Sanskrit word "yoga" have exactly the same literal meaning, "the act of uniting" and both words signify the human being's conscious union with God.

Q: If I have received a mantra from another guru and I take initiation from you, can I still practice my mantra?

A: Yes! That mantra will remain your same mantra. However, when you use it to hear the inner divine sound after a short period of chanting, then there is no need to continue chanting. Anyone who is not hearing the divine sound of their mantra should come for Kriya Yoga initiation. Their mantra will be infused in them and they will get continuous divine sound.

Q: Swamiji, is there any non-God in the universe?

A: No. There is no non-God in the universe. One of the

definitions of God is "all-pervading." It is only by His all-pervading power that all creations come into being, are sustained, and evolve. So, if He is all-pervading, then there is no question of non-God anywhere.

Q: Do you mean to say that God is even in wicked people?

A: Yes. He is abiding even in the wicked person. He is in the stone. He is in the clay. He is in the plant. He is in the trees. He is in the wall. Where is He not? All-pervading, omnipresent, omniscient means everything is His presence. He is remaining everywhere. But people are remaining in delusion and illusion. It is why they do not perceive Him. Nevertheless, He is activating the body of each person and they are the living power of God.

Q: You mean that the living power of God is within every human being?

A: Yes, that is what I am saying. He is abiding in every human being, in our whole system. Not only in the fifty body parts, even in the fingernail, even in the toes, even in the skin, even in the flesh. Everywhere. So when you see any person, you are seeing the living power of God in the material world.

Q: But when I become angry, Swamiji, it is not so easy to perceive that God is in the other person.

A: You are in delusion, illusion, and error. It is why you are getting anger. But God has no anger. So, to be godly, you should offer that negative feeling back to God, with love. Then it will surely be removed. Then you will be free from anger, pride, ego, body sense, and worldly sense.

Q: God has no anger?

A: Yes, God has no anger, no pride. God has no skin, no flesh, no bone, no marrow, no pain, no boil, no knot, no vein. This is written in the Isha Upanishad (mantra 8). So, He is remaining in the whole body system and remaining detached, but He is activating everything in the body. It is why we are alive.

Q: Swamiji, is there a heaven and a hell?

A: Yes, there is heaven and hell. It is not very far, it is within you. If you do something wrong, that is your hell, and if you do something good, it is your heaven.

Q: Swamiji, can an extremely evil person leave his bad qualities and be divine? Even a murderer or a robber?

A: Yes. It is possible. But only by perceiving the power of God within him. So you are in darkness. If you turn on the switch, immediately you will see the light. The darkness will immediately disappear. So, the murderer, he is doing wrong because the soul is not known to him. But the moment he realizes it, then immediately he will leave his evils and he can become highly realized.

This has been told in many stories of the ancient scriptures. Ratnakar was a murderer, Takshavil, he was a murderer. And in a moment's time they were changed and they became highly realized persons. Then they were worshipped by the whole world. Their names are recorded in history saying that they are topmost spiritual persons. So even devils, those who are devilish, they also have the supreme good within them.

Mary Magdalena was a very naughty lady. In a moment's time she took a turn. So, how was this possible? Many people, they posed that question to me, whether a bad person can become good? I always say, "Yes. In a moment's time." It doesn't take five minutes. You all know of St. Paul. Before he was St. Paul he was Saul. Saul persecuted Jesus' disciples. If anybody spoke good about Jesus, he persecuted him. Then Saul saw the light of Jesus and took a turn in a moment's time. He became St. Paul. St. Peter was a wild and ferocious man, yet he took a turn, In India's scriptures, there are many such examples. The evils within you are to be removed. One eye should remain on the soul, the other eye on your activity. Whatever you are doing, you are not doing. God is doing. The more you perceive it, the more you will advance. This can be accomplished quickly by the practice of Kriya Yoga. This Kriya Yoga is so easy, so simple.

Q: Swamiji, can one become realized in this birth?

A: Every person is the living power of God. But it is covered by delusion, illusion, and error. If you practice Kriya Yoga ten minutes on the bed when you arise in the morning bowing a few times, then in the whole day you will feel that the living power of God is activating. He is breathing in and out. He is doing your work throughout the day and night, and as He is doing the work you should perceive that the work is being done by Him. This is *kri* and *ya*. Whatever activity you are doing, that is *kri*. A dead man cannot do anything. The living power of God within you is doing the work, is *ya*. If at every moment you feel that you are not the doer, that only God is the doer, then you will get constant liberation and God-realization. Then you will avoid trouble and have all-around success.

Q: Swamiji, why are some people born rich, some people born poor and some people born normal, some deformed?

A: It is their destiny.

Q: Can we change our destiny?

A: Yes, you can change your destiny. Only by environment and culture.

Q: Will Kriya Yoga change our destiny?

A: Yes, with Kriya Yoga meditation you can change your destiny. At every moment, God is trying to change you. He is constantly changing your whole system. If you can perceive Him and you follow His guidance 100%, then you can change your destiny. Any person can change his destiny if he truly wishes it. In a moment's time however busy he may be he can change his destiny. At every moment, God is changing the age of every

Haripada Bhattacharjee,
Father of the Author

Nabin Kali Debi,
Mother of the Author

Shri Yukteshwar's Samadhi Mandir nearing completion.
Back row fifth from left Sananda Lal Ghosh (Yogananda's Brother)
Sixth from left Rabinarayan Brahmachari.

Shriyukteshwar's Samadhi Temple, Karar Ashram, Puri

The Author's last Residence in Homestead, Florida

Cuttack Ashram

Hariharananda Gurukulam, Balighai, Orissa

Yuktashram, Bhisindhipur, Bengal

New Meditation Hall in Homestead, USA

Kriya Yoga Zentrum, Austria

Holland's Ashram

person. Similarly, you can change your habits and become divine. Then you will feel that, "Thou art That." At every moment, you are only the living power of God. Kriya Yoga teaches you how to revolve divine life force currents around your spine and this evolves you at an amazing rate. This also will change your destiny. There is nothing that can be compared to the transforming effects of Kriya Yoga.

Q: Swamiji, do you ever read astrological charts to help people know about and avoid the negative influence of stars and planets?

A: Yes, but not in the usual sense. I do not do predictive astrology. In the scriptures it is said that even the Father of astrology, Parasara Muni, a highly realized sage, made mistakes in his predictions. So how can any person today hope to accurately perceive coming events and tell others what to do? Shriyukteshwarji taught that it is a human frailty to want to know the future. So, I do not encourage it.

All of the good and bad influences of the stars and planets are remaining in the spinal centers of the human being. When, through the practice of Kriya Yoga, we learn to revolve the divine life force current around our spine, in each center, it begins to remove the bad influences of the stars and planets from our body. In one breath, one can accomplish the meditation of one year. So, to practice Kriya Yoga, a traditional astrological reading is useless because each day he is changing his destiny.

In other words, at birth we have certain influences, which are present in our astrological chart. The traditional idea is that as the stars and planets revolve, day-by-day, we encounter those influences, which are indicative of the present evolution of our chart, whether they are good or bad. So, the traditional astrologer will reflect upon the ancient astrological scriptures or some other revised versions, to see what they say about the present planetary positions within our chart. Then some prediction is made and some advice is given. Traditional astrology cannot remove the negative influences within your chart. At best, it can give you some advice to try and prepare you for what may come.

If you practice Kriya Yoga throughout the whole day, you will constantly remain in the divine *om* sound and you will hear the voice of God directing you in every matter. This is your liberation and constant God-realization. You must admit, this is far better than the work of predictive astrology. However, in Kriya Yoga we do use a system of astrology, which was established by my guru, Shriyukteshwarji, which is called Cosmic Astrology. It is not predictive astrology in the usual sense. However, we do look to the chart for the existence of bad influences during whatever time period a person is in. Then we give some special planetary mantras and roots, which were given by Shriyukteshwarji, to minimize and even to eliminate the negative influences of those particular planets. These mantras are used in coordination with special Kriya Yoga techniques, which infuse the power of the mantra into whatever center the negative influences are remaining and thus neutralize the influence. This holy science is truly the most marvelous and effective astrology.

Just as a medical doctor is working practically to cure illness and prevent disease in the human body, I work on the subtle body to eliminate the root causes of disease, as well as worldly problems, through Kriya Yoga and Cosmic Astrology.

Q: Swamiji, there are many people in this world who do not meditate, who do not even believe in God or respect priests and monks. They do not go to any church, yet they seem to be leading a peaceful life. Many of them have attained great wealth and they are always in sense enjoyments. Yet they do not seem to be coming to any harm. Will they meet with difficulty if they don't seek God?

A: God is all-pervading, omniscient, and omnipotent. His power is giving life to every human being. Realizing Him gives only true joy. It makes all sense pleasures and worldly gain to be insignificant. God-realization is our birthright. We are born for it. If we don't meditate, then we cannot get the greatest peace, bliss, and joy. They may earn huge amount of money. They may enjoy sexually. They can eat, drink, and be merry. No matter. But they are not getting true peace, bliss, and joy. They have many ups and downs, unpleasantness, anger, pride, greed, insincerity, and hypocrisy. There are many people gaining wealth who promote killing other human beings. This is not good. We are born for God-realization. It is a must. In scriptures it is said:

āhāra-nidrā-bhaya maithunaṃ ca
samānaṃ etat paśubhir narāṇāṃ
dharmo hi tesām adhiko viśeṣaḥ
dharmeṇa hināḥ paśubhiḥ samānāḥ

Āhāra-nidrā-bhaya maithunaṃ ca samānam etat paśubhir narānām: means that eating, sleeping, fearing, and enjoying sexually are equal, common, in both human beings and animal beings. *Dharmo hi tesām adhiko viśeṣah dharmena hināh paśubhiḥ samānāḥ*: means that there is one special thing in a human being, which is divinity. Those who do not meditate, do not feel their divinity, and so they remain in the same qualities as all other animals.

Everyone should meditate. Through meditation, every person will get divine peace and calmness. That is godliness. When they practice Kriya Yoga, their divine power will come up from the lower centers to the top and this will increase their rationality and divinity. Just as an illiterate person has a different state of mind than those who are educated and are highly honored, similarly, if people practice this technique, then within a few minutes' time they will get that calmness, which is godliness.

They will remain in the material world and they may earn money and enjoy sexually, but they will feel that the living power of God is earning the money and enjoying sexually. You will eat food, but you will feel that by the living power of God you are eating the food. Your heart will remain in that divine state.

You will get no anger, pride, ego, or cruelty. You will get peace, bliss, joy, and you will watch the formless power of God, which is remaining in the vacuum stage. You are to watch God in the vacuum. So you will remain in the material world and you will also remain in the divine stage. You will feel the living power of God and see that He is activating everything. He is inhaling the breath. It is why we are alive. If He doesn't pull the breath, then the human body is a dead body. So, as He is giving us everything — peace, bliss, and joy — we should meditate to know God and we should give Him extreme love and devotion. It is only right.

There are two things in each human being. One is He, your soul, and the other is the physical body. The union of these two bodies is your life. So if you meditate, then you will feel that the soul is doing everything, not the gross body. Without the soul, you cannot do anything. In the electric wire, there are two wires. It is why you are getting light. Similarly, if you do not see body and soul as one, then you cannot get light, you will remain in darkness and ignorance, you will commit many mistakes and you will get so many troubles in your life. So you should know God. Know thyself. Presume not God to scan. The proper study of mankind is man. What is the proper study of mankind? To know thyself. This is God-realization. So, each human being should meditate and feel the living power of God within him.

Each human being has two bodies. One is *ham,* the other is *sa. Ham* is your gross body and *sa* is your soul, who is inhaling and exhaling from within. So, if He is pulling the breath from within, why should you not know Him? Any work you are doing, that is He. So at all times, you are to watch two bodies. This is yoga, union with God. *Gu* and *ru*. *Gu* is the invisible body hiding in every human being. *Ru* is the visible gross body. The *ham* body, the gross body, is full of delusion, illusion, and error. Therefore, every human being should meditate and perceive God in his gross body, the *ham* body. This is why meditation is essential and Kriya Yoga will grant you this divine power and perception.

Q: Swamiji, many people are taking drugs, some pills to calm themselves. If you say that calmness is godliness, then why do you say that people should not take any drugs?

A: Drugs give numbness in the brain. Your brain becomes bewildered. You are getting drowsiness. This is not spiritual calmness. You can only doze and sleep mindlessly. If you take heroin or marijuana, you can forget the world only because the drug has made you mindless of it. Many are taking so many tablets or cocaine. This is not good. This is extremely harmful for your health and brain. Your brain should always be made fertile. Until your brain becomes fertile you cannot know God. If you magnetize your spine, by the practice of the scientific technique of Kriya Yoga then your brain would be fertile. So, if you practice Kriya Yoga, if you bow once, then immediately you will get sufficient circulation in the brain, rejuvenating power and many new cells. Divine power will rejuvenate and regenerate in your brain and you will be far from all restless thoughts. You should never take any drug. In the Holy Bible, in Corinthians, St. Paul says that you should not defile your body because it is the temple of God. You should get calmness by a practical method, that calmness is godliness. You will get no sense of the world. You are not feeling drowsy or sleepy like people who are taking drugs. You are feeling peace and joy. This is the calmness achieved through the practice of Kriya Yoga. It is a very marvelous and precious technique.

Q: Swamiji, would you please explain the spiritual significance of the relationship between Radha and Krishna?

A: The word *radha,* comes from two words, *dha* and *ra*. *Dhara* means to flow. The water is flowing down from the mountaintop. This is the meaning of *dhara.* So all thoughts of the human being, which are coming into the mind, are coming from the top, from the north from His presence. This is the *dhara* of Krishna. The word *krishna* comes from *krishi* and *na*. *Kṛṣi bhuvācaka śabdah naṃ ca nirguṇa vācakaḥ tāyor ekair paraṃbrahma kṛṣṇa iti avidhīyate. Krishi bhuvachaka sabdah* means that each human body is the cultivated land. *Nacha nirguna vachakah* means that in that cultivated land one cultivator is remaining there. He is the formless power of God abiding inside the body. He is Krishna. *Nacha nirguna vachakah.* It is the formless power of God abiding and hiding on the top of every human being.

The divine flow is coming constantly from the north, from *dhara* — *Radha* — and through this we are alive. Breath is coming down and breath is going inside. The power of God, Krishna, is inhaling and exhaling breath from the top. It is why our blood becomes liquid and the blood is flowing throughout our whole body. It is why Radha is alive. Radha-Krishna. Radha is not the beloved of Krishna nor Krishna is the lover. Each human body is Radha, the female or mother nature. Nature is feminine by gender and in each aspect of nature abides the living power of God. The human body, Radha is the receptive counterpart of Krishna, the soul.

So this flow is constantly coming from God. If you constantly remain on the top, then you will perceive the reality — the Truth. In the ancient paintings of Radha and Krishna, they are clasping each other. That means in your whole system, everywhere, the living power of God is clasping you. So, by the practice of Kriya Yoga, when you magnetize your spine, immediately you feel the vibration of God in your whole body. This is the union of Radha and Krishna.

In the scriptures, Radha, who was a village girl, was extremely attracted to Krishna, who was the Supreme Lord. She had extreme love for Him. She was always leaving her family and worldly life to go and be with Him. She was completely absorbed in His beauty and His love and was always wanted to serve Him. In His presence, she felt His divinity and was ecstatically happy. But one day she got some pride and vanity because of her own beauty and service to Him and because He would not submit to her wishes she became arrogant towards Him and told Him that He should go and she would remain without Him. So He left her. She soon began to long for Him and could not stop thinking about Him, always thinking He would return to her, but He did not return.

She became dejected and sat under a tree and she could only think about Him, thinking He would soon return to her. She remained sitting for a very long period, constantly thinking of Him, expecting that He would return to her at any moment. But He did not return. Months passed. Some villagers came to see her and saw that she was not breathing. They went and told Lord Krishna that she had died, that she was not breathing. But He only laughed and said, "Radha can't die. She is completely transformed into Krishna. If you go to her and chant the name 'Krishna' in her ear, then you would find the real Radha." They did it and found that Radha slowly rose and stood in that very pose. So you see, Radha was completely transformed into Krishna.

From this, we learned that when we seek the Lord, place Him before our worldly attachments and we love Him and seek to serve Him, we can go to His abode and remain with Him and we will feel His divinity within us and have all the joys of knowing Him. But when we cherish some pride, ego, or vanity, then by our own fault and strong will we isolate Him. As long as we remain in these moods He will not come to us. But then we get a feeling of dejection and we begin to long for Him and want Him to come back to us. But we will get no result until we go and sit and meditate only on Him. If we sit longer, meditate, meditate, and meditate, only on Him, then, just like Radha, we will eventually get the pulseless-breathless state of *nirvikalpa samadhi* and we will be transformed into His divine being. This is how Radha, a human village girl, became a goddess.

Q: Swamiji, many scriptures say that you should seek God in the heart center. Is this correct?

A: In the Bhagavad Gita, 18th Chapter, 61st verse, it is written, *īśvaraḥ sarva-bhutānāṃ hṛddeśe 'rjuna tiṣṭhati bhrāmayan sarva bhutāni yantrārūdhāni māyayā*: God is remaining in the heart and is activating the human being. This scriptural reference to the heart does not mean that you are to remain in and seek God in the heart center. Your heart is completely dependent on the breath. The breath is inhaled by the soul, the power of God, Who is remaining in your pituitary. This is where you are to go, four inches deep in the pituitary. The soul is abiding there or even you can go to the fontanel. If the power of God does not pull the breath, then your heart cannot continue pumping. So, the heart is dependent on the soul, the power of God. If the soul does not pull the breath, you will get heart failure. So, to get spirituality, you should not keep your attention at the heart. It will give you *bhrāmayan sarva bhutāni yantrārūdhāni māyayā*. That is, the heart will place you on a treadmill of delusion, illusion, error, anger, pride, and cruelty. You are not to remain in the heart center. You should remain in the soul, which is the place to attain divinity.

Q: Swamiji, why do we remove our shoes when we come here for meditation?

A: The first reason is this: On the street there is so much filth and dirt. Even the dogs are passing their stool and their urine on the streets. Also, many contagious germs of diseases are remaining on the streets. The tuberculosis patients are spitting on the street and your shoe is carrying that germ. So, our shoe carries all types of infections. So no one should wear their shoes inside any room. These should keep the shoe outside the main living rooms of the house. Many keep them at the room near the entrance way. They should be kept in some separate place. Knowing this, should any person wear his shoes when he enters into the church, mosque, or synagogue? It is awfully bad.

Q: Swamiji, we heard that in India many practice panchamakara sadhana and that it is a very precious sadhana. Is this a good practice?

A: *Panchamakara sadhana* means five spiritual activities that begin with the letter *m.* The first *m* is *matsya sadhana,* which means eating fish. *Mamsa sadhana* (i.e., flesh eating) is the second *m* and the third *m* is *madya* means drinking wine. *Mithuna sadhana* is the fourth *m* and means to enjoy sexually. And the fifth *m* is *mudra sadhana,* which means to get money or to enjoy money. This is *panchamakara sadhana.* So in almost all the countries, many people are doing *panchamakara sadhana.* They are always busy eating fish and meat, enjoying sexually, drinking wine, and pursuing money. So they are all yogis. But are they truly yogis? No. This is not *panchamakara sadhana.*

Panchamakara sadhana is this: There are many who are killing fish and eating fish. But this is not the real meaning of *matsya sadhana*. The real meaning is this: Those who are controlling their senses — eating the fish — whose sense motivations are consumed by the power of meditation, get God-realization and remain in the superconscious state. *Manasā cendriya grāmaṃ samyam ātmani yojayet matsyasi sa bhaved devī itarā prāni hiṃsakāḥ*: means that the person who does not actually eat the fish is the divine fish eater. *Manasa cendriya samyam atmane yoyayet*: means that a yogi is one who controls his five sense organs by withdrawing his attention into the soul. By doing this, all our five sense transmitters will be completely consumed. You are a yogi if you have knowledge, consciousness, and superconsciousness and you know how to withdraw your attention into the soul. *Pareśyāt prāni hiṃsakaḥ*: means that they are not a yogi if they only kill the fish and eat it. That is not the real *matsya sadhana.*

Matsya means He is abiding in my whole system. *Mat* means from me. *Sya* means He, soul. *Mat* and *sya* together means He is remaining in me. He and I are one. He is giving God-realization to those who thoroughly control their senses — eat the fish. I am giving love to God, I am keeping my attention always on Him, I am worshipping Him and God is happy with me. Then He is giving me divine love and happiness and I have constant alertness in the inner Self. This is *matsya sadhana.* If you practice thorough control of the senses by withdrawing your attention to the soul, then you are practicing *matsya sadhana.*

Mamsa sadhana means that God is protecting me, by pulling the breath into me, and that is why I am alive. *Mam* means "to" or "into me." He is pulling breath into me. He is giving me all thoughts and He is nurturing me. He is always protecting me and conducting me. This is *mamsa. Mamsa* means flesh. *Mam* means to me. *Sa* means He, the soul that is within me. He is always pulling breath into me. By this, He is always protecting me and giving me life. If you withdraw yourself from the body senses, mind, thought, and ego (flesh), to the soul, then you will perceive that it is He who is activating and conducting your whole life and all mind, thought, finite intellect, and ego will be consumed. This is *mamsa sadhana.*

Mithuna means to enjoy sexually. But *mithuna sadhana* does not mean that you are to enjoy sexually. *Parā śakti ātma mithuna samyogānanda īśvara*: means the blissful sexual union of mother nature, the body and father nature, the soul. *Para shakti* is God, the Father, or father nature. *Atma mithuna* is the mother nature. The idea of sex enjoyment is that father nature, the soul, is causing the breath to go in and out of the mother nature, the body. The real *mithuna sadhana* is accomplished only when one perceives that it is only by the power of God, the soul, that this copulation is going on. *Pare layā nayet cittaṃ palāsi sa nigādyate*: means that we are to go beyond body sense and enter inside the pituitary and remain there. This brings divine bliss and joy.

The breath is going in and touching the soul and the soul is applying this to the father nature on the fontanel. This is *samyogananda ishvara ya aste mithunam tat.* They are in touch with the Almighty Father. *Mithuna* means sex enjoyment, divine sex joy. The breath is coming and going, coming and going. Just as one enjoys sexually. This is sexual enjoyment, the divine enjoyment, *mithunam tat. Paresastrinisevaka.* Those who are without divine perception and only enjoy sexually, in the name of God, they don't know the real *mithuna.* This is not spiritual *mithuna*, which is divine sex joy. This is not the attainment of spirituality.

Then there is *madya sadhana. Madya sadhana* means to drink wine. But this does not means you should drink wine.

somādhārā kṣaret yastu brahma randhrāt varānane
pittvā tam amṛtamayaṃ ya eva madya sādhakaḥ

If you fix your attention on the top of your head, in the fontanel, and watch Him calmly, then you will feel heaviness there on the top. At the same time, you are to keep your tongue rolled up and gradually, drops of nectar will come down from the fontanel and it will enter into your mouth. If the *sadhaka* drinks it, this is called *madya sadhana.* Drinking wine is not a spiritual attainment. The real *madya sadhana* is attained when one is drinking the divine nectar which is rolling down, slowly, slowly, and coming into the mouth. This is what is meant by the drinking of wine and this divine nectar is the spiritual wine.

Finally, there is *mudra sadhana*. This means *mahamudra*, the attainment of spiritual wealth. *Maha* means spiritual greatness and *mudra* means wealth. If you practice the Kriya Yoga technique, *mahamudra*, then your *ida* and *pingala* will become separated and the royal road to God, the *sushumna* canal will be open and you will attain the *samadhi* state. That is the real *mudra* and the attainment of true wealth.

This is the five *m*'s — *panchamakara sadhana*: *matsya*, *mamsa*, *madya*, *mithuna,* and *mudra*. So if those who are practicing it do not understand these things and meditate deeply, and keep their concentration in the soul and in the fontanel, which is the real *panchamakara sadhana*, then they are only doing so many worldly things.

In India, those who are eating fish and meat, enjoying sexually, drinking wine, pursuing money, and who are saying, "We are highly realized yogis." They are saying, "We are tantric." They are incorrect, as this is wrong. *Tantra* means *tan tatra* — "You are there." But you are there only when you are in the soul. This is *tantra. Sarva jñāna rājiṃ vistārena vistṛṇāti, yat śāstraṃ tat tantra śāstram. Tan tatra* means you are there, in the soul. When, in every action, you are doing it from the abode of the soul, this is *tantra*. If you constantly watch the indwelling Self, this is *tantra. Vistarena vistrinati yat shastram tat tantra shastram*: means that in your every action, *sarva jñanam rajim*, whatever you are doing, you are not the doer, God is the sole doer. When you get appetite, you think, "God has given me the appetite." You take food and you will say, "It is only by the power of God that I get food and that I am able to take the food." If God tells you that you should take food, you should take it. If He tells you that you should not take food, then you should not take food. In this way, constantly, in your money affairs, in sex, in eating, in the heart — thought, mood, word, and deed — and religion, you get direction from the soul. You get many types of knowledge, through consciousness, superconsciousness, and cosmic consciousness. If you watch Him and perceive that the power of God is the sole doer, this is called *tantra shastram* — *tam tantra*. Whatever is coming, the flow is coming from the top, from the soul.

Glossary

A

Abhishekotsava — the ceremony in which one takes the vows of monkhood; coronation, anointment

Acharya — spiritual guide or teacher; a person established in good conduct

Advaita-vedanta — state of unity and oneness; a branch of Indian philosophy

Ahamkara — ego, attitude of doership

Ajna chakra — the third eye, in the medulla oblongata; the place of concentration inside the pituitary at the base of the brain, i.e., the soul center

Anahata — non-stopping sound

Anahata chakra — the dorsal or heart center in the spinal column

Ananda — state of bliss

Antaryami — inner controller; God who is aware of a person's feelings

Antasthavarna — last six syllables (alphabet) in Sanskrit

Aparoksha — direct, intuitive perception

Arjuna — one of the five Pandava brothers in the Mahabharata

Asana — "seat," posture; a steady and comfortable meditative pose or posture for meditation and prayer;

	the third limb of Patañjali's Ashtanga Yoga
Ashrama, Ashram	"shelter," "refuge,"; monastic retreat for spiritual practice; a state of life
Ashtanga Yoga	"eight limbs of yoga": eightfold disciplines or aspects of the path of complete spiritual development of Patañjali's yoga system, i.e., *yama, niyama, asana, pranayama, pratyahara, dharana, dhyana*, and *samadhi*
Atma or Atman	soul, the indwelling spirit
Atmakridah	roaming only in one's own Self, and in nothing else
Atmavid	knower of the Self
Aum	see *Om*
Avadhuta	"shaken off, abandoned"; a naked renunciate monk
Avatara	an incarnation of the Supreme Lord in human form
Avidya	a term of Vedantic philosophy meaning want of spiritual knowledge, ignorance, nescience

B

Baba	father, affectionate term for guru
Bandha	a) lock, technique of controlling life force b) binding, bondage, one who is in bondage, obstacle

Bhakti	devotion, a path of experiencing pure divine love for God
Bhakti Yoga	the yoga of devotion
Bhramari	a black bee; sound of a bee
Bija mantra	"seed word": seed syllable; most basic mantra
Brahma	God in His aspect of the Cosmic Creator; the first Lord of the Hindu Trinity
Brahmachari	one who observes the vow of *brahmacharya*
Brahmacharya	abstinence or perpetual celibacy; sense control, to live in constant God consciousness
Brahmajñana	knowledge of God through realization, highest state of wisdom
Brahman	God, the Ultimate Absolute, Supreme Consciousness, the formless Spirit, all-pervading transcendental reality
Brahmin	referring to the *brahmin* caste in the Vedic social system of priests and teachers; metaphorically those who are on the spiritual path; to be established in God
Buddhi	the intellect; faculty of decision

C

Chaitanya Mahaprabhu	a realized master and God-intoxicated monk of fifteenth century India

Chakra wheel, disc; spiritual energy center plexus in the spinal column and brain; derived from the root verb *char,* "to move"

Chela disciple

Chit consciousness

Chitta memory, derived from the root verb *chit*, "to be conscious" its functions are memory, thinking, concentration, attention, and enquiry

D

Darshana philosophy, the path of direct experience and knowledge, (literally "seeing, experiencing, vision"); the blessing or purification felt in the presence of a holy place or person

Dharana concentration, attention, focusing, the sixth limb of Patañjali's Ashtanga Yoga

Dharma ordinarily translated as religion, righteousness, divine law, or discipline. *Dharma* comes from *dhri*, which means the power of receptivity, and *man*, which means life. Thus *dharma* means "that which upholds", i.e., the breath. Breath is the true religion.

Dhyana meditation, concentration, seventh limb of Patañjali's Ashtanga Yoga

Diksha spiritual initiation, instruction

Divine Mother — the ever-compassionate God, who teaches the supreme secret with extreme love to the able disciple and obedient child

F

Fire Ceremony — when one feels that every breath is an oblation to the fire in the fontanel for the love of God

Formless Stage — the state of vacuum and nothingness, where there is no feeling of body or worldly sense

G

Gairus — see salsai; an important pranic channel

Ghee — clarified butter

Gheranda Samhita — a classical treatise on yoga as taught by Sage Gheranda

Girish Ghose — a householder devotee of Shri Ramakrishna Paramahamsa, who was completely transformed from extreme negativity to deepest spirituality

Giri — the "mountain" line of the Indian Swami order

Gita — song, usually refers to the Bhagavad Gita, "The Song of the Lord," which comprises eighteen chapters and is a part of the Mahabharata. In the

	form of a dialogue between Shri Krishna, the divine incarnation, and his disciple, Arjuna, it teaches how to achieve union with the supreme Reality, i.e., liberation, through the path of knowledge, devotion, selfless work, and meditation.
God consciousness	every thought, word, and action are God-oriented; there are no other thoughts
God-realization	a state of constant peace, bliss, and joy
Granthi	knot, attachment
Gunas	the three qualities of nature known as *tamas* (idleness and sloth), *rajas* (extreme activity and restlessness), and *sattva* (purity and spirituality)
Guru / Gurudeva	spiritual preceptor

H

Ham	the gross body as the instrument of the soul. The soul is the doer and the gross body is the instrument. *Ham* also refers to the ego, the false identification of the soul with the gross body.
Hamsa	the material perishable body is *ham;* The power by which you inhale through your nose is *sa*, which means your own soul. In the *hamsa* stage you forget your existence and

	only feel that *sa*, inhalation, is the life of the gross body.

I

Ida	a pranic channel on the left side of the *sushumna* in which the vital air passes through; the *ida* corresponds with the tamasic quality of nature.
Ishta	personal deity; the aspect of God selected by a spiritual seeker, or by the guru; through meditation on the chosen deity, the seeker gradually attains concentration of mind, love for God, and ultimately illumination
Isha Upanishad	one of the principal Upanishads

J

Jagannatha	the Lord of the universe; the famous temple of Lord Jagannath is located in Puri, Odisha
Jai	hail, praise
Jiva	life or alive, the living self, individual life
Jivanmukta	living liberated; one who has attained final liberation while still abiding in the physical body
Jivanmukti	a state of consciousness achieved once final liberation has taken place and one continues to live in the world with the knowledge and wisdom of that experience

Jivatman — the living individual soul enshrined in the human body

Jñana — acquisition of spiritual knowledge; first step of *prajna*

Jñana Yoga — the path of reasoning and discrimination; yoga of knowledge

Jyoti Mudra — the process of regulating, controlling, and channeling the energy of the nine doors

K

Kaivalya — absolute state of aloneness, the highest state of God consciousness, eternal emancipation

Kali — one name of God as the Divine Mother, the destroyer of time, space and object, i.e., ignorance

Karma — a mental or physical act and their results, action, performance, duty; the law of cause and effect

Karma Yoga — the yoga of selfless action — to offer every action as worship to God; union with the supreme consciousness through action

Kena Upanishad — one of the principal Upanishads

Khechari — a special *mudra* practiced in yoga; the tongue is pointed towards the fontanel; the word is derived from *kha,* "space", and *char,* "to roam" — to roam in the inner space, vacuum of meditation

Kosha	sheath or covering
Kri	any work, activity, or action
Krishna	Lord Krishna, the divine incarnation, represents the indwelling, eternal Self of every living being, who is the conductor of the body
Kriya	any work, activity, or action done by the soul; the science of self-control and Self-realization through meditation
Kriya Yoga Ashram	ashram where the true Kriya Yoga techniques are practiced
Kriyavan	a practitioner of Kriya Yoga
Kundalini	latent spiritual energy in a person
Kutastha	changeless; metaphorically, *kutastha* designates the soul center, the unchanging anvil, on which the different life experiences are molded

L

Lam (*long*)	the seed sound in the first center (four-petalled lotus) which means earth
Lila	the divine play, in which the same actor — God — enacts all roles; the whole universe is said to be created by Him as His sport, for His pleasure
Loka	realm, plane of existence

M

Mahabharata	the great Indian epic scripture authored by Sage Vyasa which includes the Bhagavad Gita
Mahamudra	the yogic technique of physical, astral, and causal purification
Maharaja	"Great King," a title of respect
Mahasamadhi	a yogi's last willful exit from the body
Mahatma	a realized soul
Manas	mind
Manipura chakra	the lumbar or navel center
Mantra	a sacred word, syllable, or prayer
Maya	the basis of creation, sustenance, and dissolution; illusion; the cosmic delusive force, which veils one's vision of Brahman (God), the Absolute, as a result of which one perceives the relative, manifold universe instead of the one Reality
Moksha	liberation; the state of complete soul awareness, emancipation and *samadhi*; freedom from bondage and attachment that arise from delusion, ignorance
Mudra	position of body and hands
Muladhara chakra	the coccygeal or money center

N

Nadi	pranic channel in the spine; energy

	channel, through which the vital-force flows in the subtle body
Nirvana	liberation in Buddhism, state of complete extinction of the sense of individuality and immersion into the one supreme Reality
Nirvikalpa Samadhi	the state of no pulse and no breath; the state of cessation of all activities of the body, mind, thought, intellect, and ego — merged and absorbed in God
Niyama	principles of self-restraint, five ethical observances, second limb of Patañjali's Ashtanga Yoga: purity, contentment, austerity, self-study, and surrender to God

O

Om	also written *AUM*; *AUM* represents the three bodies of every human being and the three triple divine qualities: A represents the causal body (divine sound); U is the astral body (divine vibration), and M is the physical body (divine light)

P

Padma	lotus; chakra
Pandita	a learned man, scholar
Para	supreme
Para bhakti	intense love for God

Paramahamsa supreme swan: the swan is the only creature that is capable of separating milk from water once they have been mixed together. Similarly, a *paramahamsa* is a realized person who, having attained the supreme yogic state, or *nirvikalpa samadhi*, can always distinguish between the Real (*sa*) from the unreal (*ham*).

Paramatma the supreme Self (soul); universal or cosmic Self

Paramaguru the guru of one's guru; superior guru

Parameshti Guru the guru of the *parapara* guru; supreme guru

Paraparaguru the guru of the *paramaguru*

Paravastha superconscious stage beyond the perception of the perishable body; a state of extreme tranquility and inner peace

Patañjali the author of the Yoga Sutra, aphorisms on yoga, a classical text dealing with concentration and its methods leading to spiritual emancipation; Ashtanga Yoga

Pinda the gross, physical, fleshy body

Pingala pranic channel on the right side of *sushumna*, in which the vital air passes through; it corresponds to the rajasic quality of nature

Prajña wisdom

Prakriti creative force; the veil of nature, or

	the material substratum of creation, consisting of the three *gunas*
Prana	life force; vital breath; vital air; also name of one of the *pranas* (vital energy), responsible for the process of absorption; metaphorically *prana* refers to exhalation
Pranayama	control and regulation of the vital energy and the breath; special breathing techniques; fourth of the eight limbs of Patañjali's Ashtanga Yoga
Pratyahara	withdrawal of the senses into the mind; principles of self-control; fifth of the eight limbs of Patañjali's AshtangaYoga
Puja	ritualistic worship
Purusha	the indwelling Self; the Absolute Spirit, Brahman; the conductor of the life force of every human being
Purushayata	self-exertion

R

Rajasic	quality of restlessness and activities in human beings
Ram	the seed sound in the third center (ten-petalled lotus), which represents fire
Rama	an incarnation (*avatara*) of Lord Vishnu, like Shri Krishna

Rishi seer or sage; person of right vision and action

S

Sa the real doer, the soul

Sadguru the true preceptor, guide, guru who has attained God-realization; the inner guru

Sadhaka a spiritual aspirant who practices spiritual disciplines (*sadhana*)

Sadhana spiritual practice

Sadhu a saintly person; the real *sadhu* is one who keeps the attention on the breath, and through every breath loves God

Sahasrara chakra the chakra located at the top of the head in the fontanel, crown of the head

Salsai salsai and gairus are two important pranic channels

Sam (*song*) seed syllable in the money center

Samadhi state of communion with God; realization; superconscious state; complete freedom from nature's three *gunas*; the eighth limb of Patañjali's Ashtanga Yoga

Samsara unending cycle of birth and death

Samskara stored impressions of previous experiences, thoughts, and actions; latent tendencies

Sannyasi renunciate monk; one who is

	detached from all worldly affairs and devotes one's life for the experience of God-realization
Sanskrit	the language of the old Vedic and classical texts of India
Sarvodaya	all-round development
Sat-Chit-Ananda	a name of God; absolute existence — absolute consciousness — absolute bliss; the state of God-realization
Sattvic	a quality of calmness in human beings
Satya Yuga	the *yuga* or era where truthfulness (*satya*), honesty, and spirituality prevailed
Savikalpa Samadhi	a state of *samadhi* in which the sense of duality remains
Shakti	creative power of Brahman; divine energy; Divine Mother
Shambhavi mudra	open-eyed meditation technique to perceive the divine light, wisdom of Shiva
Shankaracharya	a great sixth century spiritual master, incarnation of Lord Shiva, who revived the monastic tradition in India
Shamkhya	one system of Indian yoga philosophy
Shanti	peace, serenity, balance, harmony
Shastras	ancient Indian sacred scriptures

Shiva — God in His aspect of the dissolver/destroyer; the third Lord of the Hindu Trinity. In relation to His power — the dynamic, creative Mother aspect of God (*shakti*), Shiva is the transcendent Absolute, or Father aspect. Shiva is also considered as the guru of all gurus — destroyer of worldliness, giver of wisdom and detachment, an embodiment of renunciation and compassion

Shri — a title of respect or praise

Shvetashvatara Upanishad — one of the principal Upanishads

Sushumna — the central pranic channel between *ida* and *pingala* which extends from the bottom of the spine up to the fontanel. (Diagram 2, page 59)

Svadhisthana chakra — the sacral or procreative center

T

Tamas — one of the three qualities of nature (*guna*), expressing sloth, inertia, idleness, and laziness

Tapas — purification, self-discipline, austerity, penance, self-mortification

The Holy Science — a book written by Shriyukteshwarji at the request of Babaji, which corrects the inaccuracy of Hindu almanacs and informs us that the world entered into the Dvapara Yuga in 1899. Mankind, in general, is thus ready to comprehend the fine matters

	of creation, as is evidenced by the current worldwide restlessness and search for Truth.

U

Upanishads	the conclusion portion of the Vedas, also known as Vedanta, which deal with the knowledge of the supreme Reality

V

Vam (*vong*)	the seed sound in the second center (six-petalled lotus), which means water
Vedanta	the end or knowledge portion of the Vedas, i.e., the Upanishads
Vedas	the most ancient scriptures of India, regarded as direct revelation and supreme authority in all religious matters. There are four Vedas — Rig, Sama, Yajur, and Atharva.
Vidya	knowledge leading to liberation
Vishnu	the preserving or sustaining aspect of God; the second Lord of the Hindu Trinity
Vishuddha chakra	the cervical center; center of religion or throat center

Y

Ya	the soul

Yam — the seed sound in the heart center (twelve-petalled lotus), which means air

Yama — restraint, self-discipline, self-control; the first limb of Patañjali's Ashtanga Yoga; five ethical disciplines of yoga: non-violence, truthfulness, non-misappropriation, celibacy, and non-possessiveness

Yoga — the act of "yoking" or "joining": to perceive the constant union, unity, or copulation of the individual self with the divine Self in every breath, in every moment, in every activity, and in every achievement and also the method by which such union is achieved. Yoga is the way one can perceive divinity manifested in the whole universe as well as in the entire body.

Yoga Nidra — yogic art of relaxation; a sleep-like state with consciousness

Yoga Sutra — aphorisms on yoga as described by Sage Patañjali; Ashtanga Yoga

Yogi — one who is constantly united with the supreme Self

Yuga — The ordinary meaning of this word is "age" or "era" and denotes one of the four ages into which the duration of the world is divided according to Hindu mythology. But the real meaning is "dual" or "two." Every breath consists of an inhalation and an exhalation; this is the dual state or *yuga.*

KRIYA YOGA NETWORK

As foretold by Lahiri Mahashaya, the time would come when people worldwide would accept Kriya Yoga because of its practical importance and universal attitude free from all limitations. Slowly the message of Kriya Yoga touched the heart of people through the writings of Paramahamsa Yoganandaji. He also requested Gurudev Baba Hariharanandaji to teach sincere people in the path of Kriya Yoga. Since 1950, accepting the role of an acharya, he traveled far and wide in India.

Later on by the subtle advice and instructions of his master Babaji and Shriyukteshwarji, Paramahamsa Hariharananda left India in 1974 to share his radiant love, blessings, and knowledge with the whole world. Baba Hariharananda first went to Switzerland in 1974. Before that thousands of Western seekers were initiated and guided by him from Karar Ashram, Puri. Subsequently he visited some South American and European countries and was recognized by people as a loving and compassionate teacher.

In 1975, he arrived in the United States to spread the message of the authentic Kriya Yoga as taught by Babaji, Lahiri Baba, and Shriyukteshwarji. Later on, he visited South America, different corners of the USA, France, Holland, Canada, and other countries extensively and worked endlessly.

From this time until 1998, in spite of his advanced age he traveled tirelessly far and wide around the globe to shower his divine love through the teaching of Kriya Yoga meditation technique. To accelerate the process of teaching and guiding people he not only trained many renunciate monks and householder yogis to assist him in his divine mission, but also established several ashrams in different parts of India and abroad. Apart from taking good care of Karar Ashram, which was founded by his beloved Swami Shriyukteshwarji, he started a beautiful ashram in a remote village in Bengal over 60 years ago and named it, Yuktashram. His main ashrams actively involved in spreading his divine teachings are: Kriya Yoga Ashram in Cuttack, Hariharananda Gurukulam in Balighai, Kriya Yoga Institute in the USA, and Kriya Yoga Centers in Austria and Holland. His life was not only for teaching Kriya Yoga, but also to serve the most vulnerable and weakest section of people wherever possible. With this end in view a lot of charitable activities are undertaken at various places to fulfill his mission. His trained and designated monks and teachers carry on this spiritual heritage in the following countries: India, USA, Colombia, Peru, Brazil, Costa Rica, Canada, Australia, Austria, Belgium, Croatia, Denmark, England, France, Germany, Greece, Hungary, Iceland, Luxemburg, The Netherlands, New Zealand, Poland, Spain, Sweden, and Switzerland. Lately, after his *mahasamadhi*, Paramahamsa Prajnanananda has taken on his mission as his designated successor.

The Kriya Yoga initiation programs, retreats, and training activities are regularly conducted in many cities throughout the world also by his loving designated acharyas. Although he is not physically present, his work continues in a galloping way touching the heart and lives of sincere seekers.

For more information any of his ashrams listed can be contacted.

KRIYA YOGA CONTACTS

USA
Kriya Yoga Institute
24757 SW 167th Avenue
P.O. Box 924615
Homestead, FL 33092-4615
Tel: +1 305 2471960
Fax: +1 305 2481951
E-mail: institute@kriya.org
www.kriya.org

INDIA
Hariharananda Gurukulam
PO Chhaitana, Balighai
Puri 750002
Odisha
Tel: +91 6752 246644
E-mail: missionprajnana@gmail.com
www.kriya.org
www.prajnanamission.org

EUROPE

Kriya Yoga Centre Vienna
Pottendorferstrasse 69
A-2523 Tattendorf, Austria
Tel: +1 43 2253 81491
Fax: +1 43 2253 80462
E-mail: kyc@kriya.eu
www.kriya.org
www.kriya.eu

Kriya Yoga Centrum
Heezerweg 7
NL-6029 PP, Sterksel
The Netherlands
Tel: +31 40 2265576
Fax: +31 40 2265612
E-mail: info@kriyayogameditatie.nl
www.kriya.org
www.kriyayogameditatie.nl